Corporate Leadership
A Competitive Advantage

Corporate Leadership
A Competitive Advantage

U.C. Mathur
Director MDP
Integrated Academy of Management and Technology
Ghaziabad, (U.P.)

I.K. International Publishing House Pvt. Ltd.

NEW DELHI • BANGALORE

Published by
I.K. International Publishing House Pvt. Ltd.
S-25, Green Park Extension
Uphaar Cinema Market
New Delhi–110 016 (India)
E-mail: info@ikinternational.com
Website: www.ikbooks.com

ISBN 978-93-81141-60-1

10 9 8 7 6 5 4 3 2 1

Published by Krishan Makhijani for I.K. International Publishing House Pvt. Ltd., S-25, Green Park Extension, Uphaar Cinema Market, New Delhi–110 016 and Printed by Rekha Printers Pvt. Ltd., Okhla Industrial Area, Phase II, New Delhi–110 020.

Inspiration for the book from
Prof. Pankaj Gupta
Executive Director, INMANTEC
Ghaziabad

Dedicated to the biggest influence in my life
Bina my best friend and wife

PREFACE

Most students, professors and civil society have seen the highs and lows of the corporate bandwagon. Companies come and go, leaving some disgruntled employees besides other stakeholders including the shareholders. There can be two basic reasons for corporate downfall, managerial failure or unethical practices adopted by the company. Similarly, there are two reasons that account for corporate success stories. Success, therefore, can be attributed to the leadership, that needs to be always on the alert, ready with proactive stances, doing right things rightly and being both effective and efficient.

The role of leaders in corporate has been either overrated or neglected. The necessity is of putting leadership in the right perspective, especially in the current context where the marketplace has become a fluid entity with numerous changes in business and competitive environment taking place with irreverent consistency. At best it is like tightrope walking and the leaders need to learn not just the tricks of the trade but also systematic methodology of stressless functioning when they start loving their work and remain unfazed with the constant changes occurring around them.

Leaders have a major task of getting things done with the help of their team. Team motivation, work allocation, training the team members and keeping the stakeholders happy needs special types of characteristics, character traits and knowledge, skills that focus on adapting to the day-to-day business circumstances. Gone are the days of hereditary managers. Today, even family businesses are either training their progeny in management skills or are hiring trained managers with proven track record of successfully running similar companies. That managers can be trained has become a fully accepted fact. The book attempts to train, retrain, and provide refresher learning for different levels of managers, CEOs and wannabe managers, business leaders.

Leaders need special characteristics, like quality of patience, the "soft skills," that form a major focus area for leaders and hence is covered in some depth.

It is well known that companies managed and led with ethics and moral values invariably outperform other companies. Unfortunately, in the past few decades, a lot of "fly by night" operators have been coming, making fast bucks and then vanishing from the scene. Code of conduct has become an important issue as corporate governance too has come into prominence. The book is the result of extensive research in the areas of interest to the leaders.

The author wishes to thank the publishers for the help provided during the time the book was under preparation.

U. C. Mathur

CONTENTS

1

CHAPTER

Corporate Leadership Challenge

Business leaders have to be continuously learning and discovering new things, ideas, processes and systems for doing better for the firm. For this purpose, they need both far sight and foresight. In 2012, they should be focusing on the firm's entity in 2022, ten years hence. The leaders can themselves become competitive factors for gaining advantage over competitors. The leaders must be in learning mode all the time and this way they can create a learning organization.

From 1950s to 1970s, business was planned in a rational planning manner, in a mechanical or machine-like manner and the firms succeeded due to very moderate changes in the business environment over several years. Today with day-to-day changes the strategy of organizational learning has become extremely important. It must adapt an organic structure like a living organism with sharp proactive stances.

Earlier as a boss it was enough to have the managerial skills to perform; today's in volatile business environment leadership is important.

Leadership for learning organization has become crucial to the success of the firm, because all the management tools may not be enough. Most firms need to continuously develop means and improve ways of doing things and this requires organizational learning.

The following are the three areas, which cover the organizational learning:

1. Need for leadership in organizational learning
2. Elements of organizational learning
3. Leadership activities required for building a learning organization

ORGANIZATIONAL LEARNING NEED

Leaders need special traits for being successful in today's business environment. Leaders should be INSTRUMENTAL in changing the firm for success else they would not succeed.

In the history there have been born leaders like Nehru, Napoleon. They carried the masses through their charisma. Now, it has changed to leaders becoming instrument of change for the firm's success.

Leaders must get into the double loop learning process as can be seen in Fig. 1(b) Single Loop:

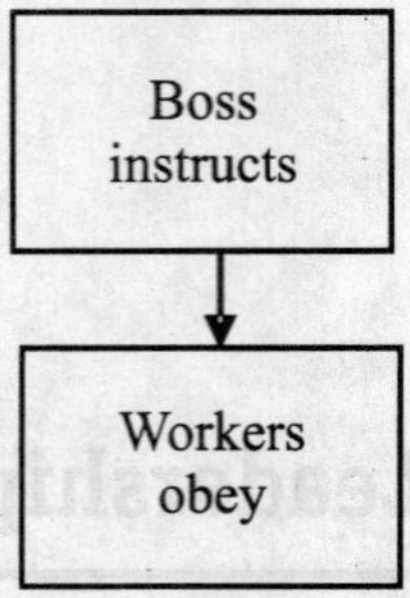

Fig. 1(a)

In double loop learning while the workers perform mechanical functions they also question the processes, methods and policies and adjust for the best fit for achieving the goals, objectives and the targets. The learning, therefore, becomes two ways, from the leader to the worker and from the worker to the leader.

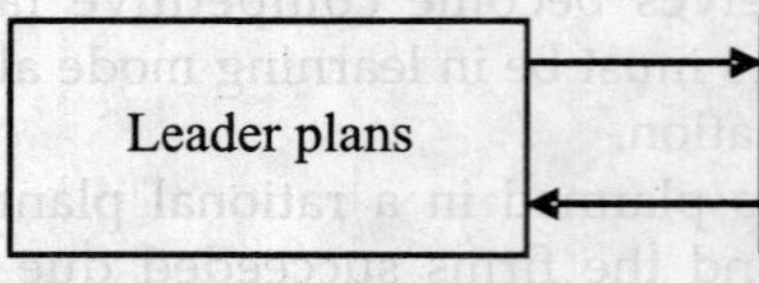

Fig. 1(b)

The definition of leadership, which is instrumental in the firm's success, is given below:

Firstly, the leaders develop and articulate exactly what the firm is trying to accomplish. Secondly, they create an environment in which the employees can figure out what needs to be done and then do it well.

Employees participate in creating the plans and processes of the firm.

In traditional management, the boss decided what is to be done and who would do it. In organizational learning, leaders with intellect, vision and wisdom show the ultimate goal and the followers find their own path towards success.

Leaders are, therefore, found at all the levels of the firm. A worker, through his TQM can change a process for the better, which gets known up the ladder and then it becomes the accepted norm. In this way the worker has contributed as a leader as others are following his process.

Leadership covers a wide range of actions that are instrumental in bringing about a change in the firm for success. Leaders should possess a high degree of creativity, should be strategists to create organizational synergy to increase the firm's output. The leadership mindset is defined below and illustrated in Fig. 1(c).

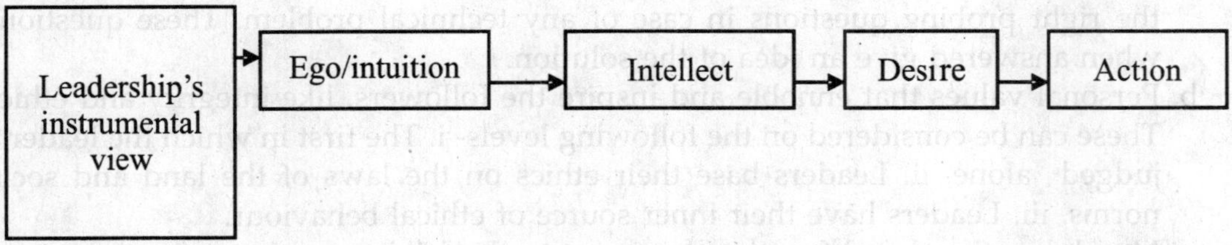

Fig. 1(c)

Leaders and the followers are supposed to achieve what is required but at times it does not happen. This gives the organizational learning a bad name. The cause is the basic distrust of the workers. Results can come when the workers are empowered to take decisions in their small areas to promote the firm wide synergy.

A leader can be described as follows:

- A leader is the innocent mirror of the collective consciousness of his followers.
- The only way towards success as a leader is to develop leadership qualities in his followers.
- If you are a follower you can lead and if you are a leader you can follow. Leadership must be supportive in nature, as leaders must support their followers. Leaders are found in the entire hierarchy of the learning organization. Followers (workers) should be encouraged to learn leadership qualities, as they have to lead as well.

ELEMENTS OF ORGANIZATIONAL LEARNING

In the organizational learning mode the firms use the scientific method of discovering new methods, processes by experimentation. The scientific method follows the steps given below:

- Start with a theory
- Convert it into a hypothesis
- Conduct experiments to confirm the hypothesis
- Compare the results of the experiments with the hypothesis
- Conclude or draw inferences (in science these become laws or principles)

Plan your action on successful experimentation and emphasize what the firm is doing differently because of the experiment and its result. Mostly firms do just lip service to the results of experiments, as people just do not want to change. This inertia deprives the firm of some good methods and processes and the time and money spent on experiment goes waste. Leaders who perform successful experiments at all levels connect the leadership with organizational learning.

SPECIFICS OF BUSINESS LEADERSHIP

Leadership for organizational learning constitute the following elements:

1. Develop a sound understanding of the following:
   a. Technical knowledge and skills. Technical knowledge enables the leader to ask the right probing questions in case of any technical problem. These questions, when answered give an idea of the solution.
   b. Personal values that ennoble and inspire the followers, like integrity and ethics. These can be considered on the following levels- i. The first in which the leader is judged alone. ii. Leaders base their ethics on the laws of the land and social norms. iii. Leaders have their inner source of ethical behaviour.
   c. Moral, emotional and functional support to the followers.
   d. Ability to get into the psyche of the followers, to inspire them.
   e. Have a personality of prime mover, of a man with a purpose and urgency for the right action.
   f. Have high values which motivate the followers.
   g. Have total social acceptance.

   Leaders must be able to arrange the following specific activities:

   h. Establish a shared vision with which the followers identify themselves totally.
   i. Instill a sense of urgency in the followers, as happy talk that **all is well** is just not right.
   j. Gain commitment of the followers about the shared vision, mission, goals and objectives of the firm.
   k. Identify the current mental model of the followers; understand if it explains the cause and effect of what is happening in the firm, right or wrong.
   l. Understand the interpersonal relationships between teams and within team members to abort conflicts before they appear. If conflicts do occur, the interpersonal knowledge would be useful in solving the same, which is one of the basic tasks of a leader.

ACTIVITIES OF LEADERS IN ORGANIZATIONAL LEARNING

The leaders have to approach their role in a practical manner, which they can arrange as follows:

- Leaders must encourage experimentation by the followers.
- Must develop tolerance for mistakes. The best way is to provide for small losses during experiments. With one successful experiment these losses would be amply covered; without experiments, however, no fresh idea can be generated. The successes must be rewarded and used in the firm's operations and failures must be just ignored. (It is not right to rub the mistake in as it would discourage further experimentation by the whole lot of workers).
- Leaders should have the guts to admit their own mistakes as well; it proves they are humans too and it would do a lot of good to the morale of workers who have erred.

- Apply the middle path method–if the middle management carries out the experiments, it would bring sufficiently valuable results, if successful, unlike the results of experiments by the low down workers, whose results would bring only small improvements, if successful and of course would not cause much damage if they fail. On the other hand, experiments at the top could be risky, as they would involve large sums of money at stake. It does not, however, preclude anyone from carrying out the experiments. The middle management success can then be spread horizontally as also vertically to cover the entire organization.
- Act on the results of successful experiments, as it would be the biggest motivation for others to do one better than the winner.
- Back winners–it could be rewards in cash or promotions, better salary or perks.
- Discuss failures, not to put people on the mat, but to ensure they do not occur again. In fact, a good leader would discuss his own failures too to generate warm fellow feeling among the followers. At this stage it is a good idea to set boundaries for future experimentation to avoid failures to the extent possible. Clear guidelines to avoid fruitless experiments, to reduce wastages in experimentation must be made.
- It must be understood that people learn from making mistakes only and if they do not experiment, make no mistakes, the firm does not gain any benefits of successful experiments either.

Leaders who encourage experimentation and act on the results influence learning organizations. Therefore, the leaders need to do the following:

- Encourage leadership among followers to motivate them.
- Leaders have a broad range of actions, which are instrumental in bringing about the needed change in the organization.

Learning organizations differ from the traditional rational planning organizations as shown in Fig. 1(d):

Issues	Rational Planning Organization	Learning Organization
Status on change	Do not change if you are successful	You fail if you do not change
Management worries	Mistakes	Rigidity
New ideas' acceptance	Do not include outside ideas	Pick up all from outside
Innovation plans	With engineers/managers	All the members
Experiments by	R&D engineers	All involved in the work
Major or minor changes	Only minor changes	Continuous changes with drastic changes in between
Competitive advantage from	Products and services	Knowledge, skills and expertise
Management control	Through budgets and daily reports	Empowering the workers
Level of assistance to workers	Minimal or none at all	Daily motivation through leadership counselling

Fig. 1(d).

Vision for future can be developed by getting out of the conventional mould, understanding the customer value, evaluating the core competencies required for the firm.

These visions, mission goals and objectives would be best accepted by the members of the firm, if instead of informing them about these, the leader sells the ideas, or tests them by discussing them with the members. Consulting the members or involving them in the decision-making process would surely get their total acceptance.

END NOTES

Firms must keep improving methods of doing things for which they need organizational learning. The best learning comes when it is a two-way communication, leader to worker and worker to the leader. Leadership can beat all the levels of the organization and it is the role of the leader to encourage others to take leadership positions. Leaders can become change triggers, or instrumental in making changes in the firm, through charisma plus their own efforts of understanding the firm and its workers. Empowering workers to conduct experiments and including the successful experiments in the firms schedule is a sure way of improving the system as also of motivating the workers. The leader must have sound technical knowledge, ethical and moral values and the latest on the firm's front. A shared vision developed in consultation with the members of the firm gets commitment of the workers.

2
CHAPTER

Strategic Action

The strategists of the firm have scanned the business environment; evaluated the strengths and weaknesses of the firm and planned their strategies. The next question that comes to the strategists' minds is, who is going to implement the plan, what has got to be done and how would the implementers do it? Besides, the issue of leadership in the implementation programme is of vital importance.

IMPLEMENTATION PROBLEMS

Learning from the past experiences, the following major problems are encountered by the firms during implementation phase:

- Unprecedented major problems crop up.
- Implementers work in isolation resulting in lopsided implementation.
- Delays are caused due to ineffective teamwork and at times by uncontrollable causes.
- Team members are not fully trained or qualified for their job.
- Vague instructions by the team leaders, insufficient resource mobilization, inadequate authority to the teams.
- Lack of awareness of the total change in picture with the changed teams.
- Poor control system for monitoring the activities.

If the implementation is inadequate it can derail the best of plans and well-implemented actions can upgrade even mediocre plans.

PRE-IMPLEMENTATION EXERCISE

Mostly, the planners and action people, the line managers, supervisors and the teams are kept away from the planning process and they are ignorant of the huge amount of data collected, theories used before the plan was finalized. This happens because the management does not want to disturb the line management from their daily operations. Or at times it could be because of their inadequate experience in the planning process. However, it must be understood by the entire management that no implementation can be successfully carried out unless its implementers are fully in the picture. The following is suggested as a tried and tested method:

"Changeover" action calls for a "changeover" conference involving the implementation team to the last person. The conference should preferably take place in a calm atmosphere away from the workplace. The conference should be fully attended by the top managers, the CEO, all of which shows solidarity towards the change plan, management's commitment in terms of time, money and resources. The management must initiate the conference in the following manner:

- Giving a review of the present situation in which the firm finds itself, while highlighting the opportunities coming its way.
- The strengths and weaknesses of the firm.
- Changing business environment, both general and competitive.
- New USPs of the firm, like new equipment bought, new personnel inducted.

At this stage the change plans should be introduced in the following manner:

- How the changes will benefit each employee of the firm.
- How the change will benefit the firm, in the short and in the long run.
- Broad out line of the change to showcase it in an ideal way, of course it should remain realistic and should sound workable. Too esoteric a plan using difficult words can frighten even the most optimistic person.
- The plan division based on functional or work areas can now be projected. The team members would start having numerous questions at this stage and it would be a good idea to pre-empt the questions and keep the replies ready by first testing the plans with a few chosen trustworthy employees, who would be able to voice their opinion freely.
- Employees should be encouraged to air their worst fears as this would provide the management an opportunity of giving a detailed expose of the plan, as they set the fears to rest.
- Once most persons have accepted the plan in principle, it is time to move on to detailing the plan. Some difficult ones will always be there to keep putting their spanners in the plan's smooth moving wheel of exposure. Such persons should be given some heavy calculations to keep them busy while the rest accept the plan. These people are present everywhere and they need careful handling if they cannot be totally dispensed with.
- Detailed plans should include the tasks and the teams responsible for executing the tasks, the authority to be given to the teams and the time frame for completing the tasks successfully.
- Next the teams or their leaders should be asked to come to the podium and confirm their acceptance of the plan, the task given to them and that they are proud to have

been entrusted with such important task. They should show their enthusiasm, commitment and devotion for the same. (This is an essential and important aspect of the conference as after the conference this would be the only reminder to the employees when they are back to their day-to-day mundane work and existence and spur them into action towards implementation of the plan, and that too in time.)

- The participants should be given a bound copy of the complete plan with step-by-step instructions regarding their tasks. Information regarding the persons to be contacted in case they get stuck at any point in the task should be provided in the Instruction Manual. The reason for giving them the complete plan and not just their activities is to keep them in the picture, keep their morale high as they would perceive themselves as important members of the firm.

The above would be amply clear with the example of a foreign oil company Esso, which was in India as a joint venture of Standard Oil Company of New Jersey and Mobil Oil Company in the name of Standard Vacuum Oil Company as given below in two boxes:

Standard Vacuum Oil Company (SVOC) was operating in India as a joint venture of Standard Oil Company of New Jersey, USA and the Mobil Oil Company also of the USA. In the year 1961, the two companies parted ways on a worldwide basis and in the division of assets Indian business came to the lot of Standard Oil (at that time it happened to be the largest company in oil business). The changeover with stock transfer was to take place in the following year effective midnight of the 31st December. The changeover exercise started in June of the same year and three changeover conferences were organized to make it a huge success.

The Ground Reality

SVOC was operating in the entire country, with 23% market share. Its assets included the refinery at Mumbai, large oil installations at major ports, depots at several towns in the entire country. Besides, it ran the business with a criss-cross of petrol pumps, service stations, kerosene and diesel dealers, and lube oil distributors. Besides the country office at Mumbai, the territory offices were located at the metro towns with district offices in major towns. The SVOC had a general manager to head the Indian operations, territory managers to head the territory offices and district managers for the district offices. Besides these, there were sales and service force, finance and accounts department, the HRD and depot and terminal management. The refinery was managed by a separate set of managers.

The SVOC team was proud of the company, its products and believed that in no time they would come close to the sales of the market leaders like the Burmah Shell. And then came the shocking news that as far as SVOC was concerned, it was pack up time and the same team would be saddled with new products, albeit unwillingly, with brands unfamiliar to them and naturally to the Indian customer. The other option could be to leave the company.

Pre-conference activities

The Esso management in the USA segregated the physical, emotional and financial aspects of the changeover. On the physical side the following needed to be done on the midnight of 31st December, not a day earlier or later, due to international legal bindings:

Change the offices, depots, terminals, petrol pumps, service stations, dealers' and distributors' offices, shops into the new colour scheme, design and pattern of ESSO.

Change the letterheads, stationery, visiting cards of the entire management.

Keep ready new technical literature of ESSO products to be given to the concerned salespersons after they have been trained into selling the products.

Ensure availability of ESSO products in the depots, dealer shops, and petrol outlets on the midnight of Dec 31st.

For the above tonnes of paint, local painters, printing presses, signboard makers were kept on hold to be activated at the shortest possible notice. Product stocks were earmarked for different locations and kept at the nearest storage point to be rushed to the location of sales.

The other two areas, financial and emotional were covered with great deal of empathy and detailing as given in the box two below:

ESSO had earmarked sufficient funds to make the changeover plan a success. Besides authority to prioritize activities was given to the local management. Massive changeover manuals were made well in advance, which were distributed to each team member before the conference.

The actual conference started with the managers airing their misgivings about the changeover. "We have been promoting the SVOC brands for so long that these have gone in our bloodstream. Our customers are also equally convinced about the utility and benefits they derive from our products." The planners did not give the reply by saying that it is imperative under the US law that we now sell the ESSO brand. They convinced the managers about the huge superiority of the ESSO brand over the SVOC as also over other competitive brands like SHELL and CALTEX. This was done through undisputable facts collected from all over the world. ESSO's success stories were the main themes of the discourses. At the end of several sessions covering a week, the team was fully in agreement that the changeover would be good for them. They, in their speeches, pledged their full wholehearted support and active participation in making ESSO the number one brand in India as it had been in the world for decades. After the initial shock, the managers wizened to the new reality in their company. As was proved by the ensuing events the new company, ESSO, really gained market share as was envisaged during the changeover conferences.

The matter of timing of the changeover was solved in an ingenuous manner. The team members were asked to start meeting the customers, including the dealer network at their own personal level, as Mr. Tandon, not as a representative of any company. In fact, they were given visiting cards which had their names and addresses, phone numbers and no company's name was printed. Similarly, the letterheads were also personalized, with the person's name only and no company's name. This lead to gradual erosion of the SVOC brand from the customer's mind and **this can also be considered the beginning of RELATIONSHIP MARKETING IN THE COUNTRY, because, the salespersons were meeting customers in their own personal capacity, building relationships with them, which could be transferred to ESSO at the appropriate time.**

The Result

When the time came to changeover to ESSO, the teams were so charged up, without any misgivings that they were able to convince the customers, the dealer network alike, about the great company they are dealing with and naturally not only the changeover went smoothly, the new company, ESSO gained market share over its predecessor SVOC.

The above stated changeover exercise has been given in some detail to enable the readers to understand the mechanism fully and when needed they can take ideas from it to make their strategic plan implementation a big success.

In the beginning of the chapter the question asked was, "who implements the strategy"? The answer lies in the nature of the firm's structure. However, as the rule for learning organizations, everyone should be involved in a positive manner in the implementation stage, as it would give them confidence in the plan, and they would ensure that the plan achieves its declared objectives.

During the implementation stage the following must work in greater coordination:

- Marketing team, the sales force, channel members, advertising and promotion people. New methods of working, new product lines do create their own problems; hence greater cooperation between the synergic groups would bring healthy results.
- Finance team, the asset creation team should ensure optimized functioning of different areas of the firm, especially during the implementation stage.
- Production team has to keep close coordination between bulk material purchase to get the best prices, low inventory levels, just in time purchases, large batch productions to avail of economies of scale.
- Management expertise is required to maximize the harnessing of resources, manpower deployment, problem solving and locating improvement opportunities in different work areas, making use of previous experiences in similar situations. The most important aspect of the top management's task is to keep the teams motivated, enthused through the example and monitors their tasks to ensure that the teams do not stray from the objectives by having a narrow outlook towards the task. While detailing in the work is better left to the experts in their fields, it is a good idea to cross-check a few of the vital points, which could alter the decisions and therefore the ultimate results. The management has to be proactively associated with the plan implementation and visibly show their interest in the same, else it would be put on the back-burner. This happens more often than not that in their presumably more important assignments like further development of the firm, the top management forgets to give the plan the stress it needs. This particular problem has affected the best of strategies, which have got a bad name, making other firms shirk from taking strategic steps in their operations.

The success of implementation comes from cohesive action, where all the members of the team, right from the CEO down to the worker are involved in thinking about the changes that are taking place, streamlining the processes, modifying through minor changes to suit the changed environment. The days of the boss ordering and the subordinates obeying are over; the need of the hour is that the CEO only creates an atmosphere for success, gives the objectives and lets the team members decide what is to be done, how it is to be done and who will do which part of the tasks. This calls for a learning organization as against the usual mechanistic organization in the order-obey syndrome, which is structured with well-defined roles for each member, authorities and responsibilities charted out to avoid any mistakes or misunderstandings between the team members.

Learning organization gives freedom to the teams to plan out their implementation schedule coinciding it with the schedule for the entire firm. With educated workmen, the more confidence the firm shows in them the better they perform. Team members are motivated in such a way that in case some member gets a little demotivated, others pull him up to ensure a well balanced and timely implementation of the plan.

FIRM'S SIZE AND PLAN IMPLEMENTATION

The firms can be categorized as small, medium and large; each one of these categories has a different set of problems at the implementation stage of the strategy as given below:

Small firms operate on short-term plans, decisions are personal of the owner, strategy is to make the best of the situation, evaluation is done by the owner and is subjective. The owner knows best, can take care of problems as they arise, can hire and fire, at his discretion, any employee as per his wish, or whim. (In a chapter on small sector firm's strategic management for these firms has been dealt with at length). It can be rewarding to the result oriented employee as the owner lets loose his inhibitions when he sees big success.

Medium size firms grow around their products and their strategies revolve on their products. They can invest in developing product sales, in solving product related problems. They operate on the basis of functional organization, with experts in each of the functional areas. They promote products, services associated with the products. Structural controls based on functional performance are put in place. Reward and punishments are also well defined.

Large size firms are based on divisional or Strategic Business Unit structures. Each SBU operates with functional freedom and yet reports to the head office, which helps them in making growth and diversification plans, in their investment decisions for gaining competitive advantage in their marketplace. Assessment of each unit and of the combined units is done on a complex programme based on weight given to areas in the SBUs. ROI, EVA and other financial ratios are used to evaluate their performance. Rewards and punishments are based on complex systems evolved over a period of time and generally accepted by most team members in each SBU.

DEVELOPMENT PROBLEMS

In small and medium size firms the situation regarding development are mostly the same. They both lack the will to change, believe that existing situations are sufficient for them. They do not have the required people who can effect the changes. They can plan their day-to-day operations and hence are not prepared for making strategic changes.

Professionals, who lack guts to take risks, manage the large size firms. This is despite the fact that the major decision may have been taken by the board of directors. During implementation stage a number of small decisions need to be taken, which these people shirk taking. The large monoliths get into the inertia and become rigid in their approach to change. The fact that several firms, who tried the strategic route, did not succeed gives teeth to their thinking process. It is not realized that the failed firms did not have the top management commitment to enforce change and they asked the juniors in a lackadaisical manner to implement change. The senior members on the board of directors believed that their age old methods of working, which incidentally brought the firm to such heights, are still good enough for a few decades, little realizing that the business environment is changing so fast that unless the firm keeps pace with it, it would lose its very existence.

Like products, markets, even firms have their life cycles. They are born and come into market, and then they grow, mature and finally start declining in terms of turnover and profits. In the maturity stage, the firm should start planning for strategic changes, which can culminate during or just before the decline stage, for the firm to keep its foothold in the market.

END NOTES

Firms are of three different sizes, the small, the medium and the large firm. Each of these has its own compulsions for not accepting strategic change. How these problems can be overcome and changes made successfully depends on how keen the top management is in implementing changes.

3
CHAPTER

Role of the Leader in Strategic Change

Every action taken by individuals affects the implementation process and as can be imagined the actions taken by the top person can affect the firm quite a lot. Leadership, as a consequence entails huge responsibility on the shoulders of the leaders, the CEOs of any firm. Position gives power to the concerned person and he can either use it to his firm's benefit or abuse it for his own. Firms have known to reach great heights just because of their CEOs, reverse is also true unfortunately.

Persons who do not wield the power but are in some manner connected to the government or firm; in political or business arena usually criticize power. In politics it can be seen at the election time that incumbency factor goes against the ruling party. In business once it is understood that CEOs, power has a great influence on the firm and its results, it becomes important and necessary to know about the power and how best it can be canalized for the maximum benefit of the firm.

CEOs power can be used to influence other employees for the benefit of the firm. Hence, the CEOs personal action can be a powerful instrument for influencing strategy and bringing about organizational change.

The CEO has roles to play in the following areas, where his actions can bring about the changes as dramatically as possible.

1. Power and influence through personal action
2. Organizational politics
3. Negotiator
4. Communicator
5. Role model

If we look at the history of the world, great men have always influenced the masses. Hitler the evil genius had the power to brainwash the entire German nation into believing that Jews as a race have no business to live on the planet. His megalomaniac vision for himself as the supreme lording over the entire Europe came close to success because of his personal influence. Likewise on a different mission Mahatma Gandhi could influence the Indian nation to have a non-violent revolt against the British rule in the country. Taking a parallel, the business CEO can influence his followers (employees) for achieving great and difficult objectives.

PERSONAL ACTION

The leader of a firm uses his influence in his personal capacity and also due to his position as the CEO of the firm. On the followers in the following manner:

- Ordering the employees
- Making subtle cultural changes
- Persuading the employees
- Inducing the employees

In the ordering level, the leader is using his authority as the CEO. He can direct the employees to perform certain tasks in a given time. Disobedience can cause a great deal of problems for the employee. The use of ordering about the employees is being rarely used these days as it brings about resentment in them. However, on a routine structured way the ordering is done for achieving the results.

When it comes to changing the work systems, making structural changes, the ordering method scores over others, as it saves time, is direct to the concerned employee, thereby avoiding ambiguities and misquoting. For example, if a firm decides to change to flatter structure, the CEO has just to give instructions in this regard. Systems regarding follow-up on orders received, replies to letters, attending complaints from the customers are of vital importance to the firm and in case the CEO finds a better system of managing these areas, he has to give orders in this regard and if necessary train his employees in operating the new system.

On the other hand, when the CEO wants to make cultural changes in the firm, giving orders cannot bring about these changes. Cultural ethos are deep-rooted in the employees' collective thinking, work triggers and mindsets, which have become part of the firm's environment. It is therefore, difficult to bring about changes in the firm's culture. Still, if the CEO uses the right approach it can be done. For making these changes, the CEO has to patiently act on revising the firm's agendas, and reworking the information networks. Through these agendas and networks he has to plant stories of success in the firm and gain employees' acceptance for the revised cultural streams in the firm. For example, a laid back firm can gradually become a live wire firm in this manner.

As would be noticed in the above methods the CEO is using his influence on the employees in his official capacity as the firm's CEO. Given below are the ways he uses his influence as an individual member of the firm:

The CEO uses his charm of persuasion when he is dealing with negotiations with the employees, either in the situation of employees versus the firm or between two employees or two sets of employees. He also uses persuasion in communicating with the employees.

The CEO has to use inducements in his personal capacity to set the firm's politics straight and try to have principled politics for the benefit of the firm. He has to use his charisma and as a role model he can induce the employees into changing their ways of work, their negative thinking towards the firm.

The CEO acquires his charisma by performing such acts, which appear to the employees as near miracles. (A new imported machine broke down and the complicated replacement part was to take six months' time to arrive in the country. Using his engineers network, he organized a meeting of the best brains in the field, got the design copied and the part made in India in just six weeks. In another case, when the research manager remained an academician and therefore perhaps adamant about having timebound product development, the CEO sidelined him, got the other engineers and motivated them into performing with timely results as per the market demands. The manager felt that he would be better off in a university research laboratory and quietly left the firm. When the employees start believing that their CEO can perform difficult tasks with relative ease then he can use his influence to induce the employees into accepting his decisions and ideas.

The following table describes the above process:

Various Capacities of the CEOs	Open use of CEOs authority	Disguised use of CEOs authority
In his official capacity as the CEO of the firm	Ordering about the employees	Making cultural changes
In his capacity of an individual member of the firm	Persuading the employees	Inducing the employees

POLITICS IN FIRMS

The CEOs must accept that politics is inevitable in every organization. Politics in the national perspective is the act of governing. In case of firms, politics is caused by clash of interests between employees and it can cause a lot of damage to the firm unless it is channelled properly into the creative side of the firm's activities. One-upmanship, putting others down to gain prominence in the eyes of the CEO, and competition between the employees gives rise to politics. The functional managers believe that their job is more important than that of the other functional manager. Finance manager considers the task of arranging funds as the most important as he convinces all those who listen to him that what would anyone do without money. Can the production manager make anything without buying the raw material for which he gets money from me? If there were no products to sell, the poor marketing manager would remain idle. And who pays the salaries to all the persons the human resource manager employs in the firm?

The production manager strongly believes that unless there are products to sell there would be no firm. Marketing manager says, have the best of finances, production, people, just close down the marketing department and you could just put a big lock on the firm. This competitive spirit is good to an extent, until it starts pulling down the firm by constant bickering and worse by non-cooperation between managers.

As a practical example, the R&D Manager wants Rs. 300,000 for a new test instrument, while the maintenance manager also wants Rs. 300,000 for changing the old pipeline. The CEO is in a dilemma that he has only Rs. 300,000 to give under these heads. If he gives fifty per cent of what they want both would remain dissatisfied and would blame the CEO for any problem, which may crop up in their area of operation. Under the circumstance, the CEO has the following three options:

1. With openness and transparency he can talk to both the managers and find out their real requirement. In most cases as managers believe they would get only about half of what they ask, they tend to inflate their demand. When the three meet and appreciate each other's viewpoint, the two demands would come to a realistic figure, which the CEO can meet with his available finance for these expenses.
2. In case the CEO finds that both the demands are genuine and urgent, he can try to increase the amount for these tasks by rescheduling some other tasks or by further borrowing the money required. Instead of dividing the cake it may be a better idea to increase the size of the cake.
3. If both the options given above are not possible, the concerned managers should be informed that to start with they have to use alternative methods and as soon as the finances are available they would be given to them.

Some forms of influence are so unobtrusive that they are not recognized as forms of power. These implicit forms of power are among the most effective ways for an individual leader to affect organizational results.

CEO–NEGOTIATOR

The CEO has to take up the personal role of a leader, in which he gets the organization's support. However, when he is in the role of a negotiator he has to perform as an individual member of the firm. The most important aspect of negotiations is that the problems for which they are required cannot be wished away under the carpet. As the time elapses they tend to become acuter, needing unnecessarily long drawn out negotiations and at times making compromises, which could have been avoided earlier. (In case the CEO is busy, it may be a good idea to let the general manager or the departmental head carry out the negotiations). Irrespective of the fact that who is doing the negotiations, the following needs to be kept in mind:

1. Do not negotiate on position. If the demand of two persons cannot be met, the one who shouts more should not get want he wants as it could lead to anarchy in the firm with everyone trying his hand at shouting all the time. Justice demands that both sides should be given patient hearing and their position, their demand weighed in the firm's scale of achieving its objectives and then again before announcing the decision the parties should be made to realize the reasons for the decision and made to agree to it wholeheartedly.

2. Create value rather than divide it by increasing the size of the cake. The demanding persons would realize that a small portion of large cake is better than large portion of a small cake. Use the negotiations for getting the persons to agree to increase productivity, reduce absenteeism in workers.
3. The CEO should negotiate on the problem and not involve the personalities of the people party to the negotiations. If the CEO has some grudge against any person, it should not influence his judgment while he is negotiating with the person. (As an extension to this, in most annual reports to be filled by the superiors, the instructions are clear about leaving the personal likes and dislikes out of the appraisals).

CEO–COMMUNICATOR

The CEO wields his personal power by communicating with the employees. The CEO has to communicate the firm's vision, mission, goals and objectives, besides its plans for coping with the business environmental changes using strategic management. The role of the CEO as a communicator exceeds the informative range; it goes on to listening to the employees' complaints, their problems, when it becomes a two-way communication.

In any communication people tend to forget the importance of listening. Most of us do listen, but only to give a prompt reply and not to really understand the problem. "Yes I know your problem; I do not want you to repeat it. Just give me time and wait, it would be sorted out" is the usual refrain in which the superiors talk to their juniors. Problems, as is well known, if not settled promptly, have a tendency of growing out of proportion. *A stitch in time saves nine* is a good maxim to remember. The CEO must listen to understand the problem first so that he can think it out and then respond in a positive manner to the satisfaction of the person facing the problem. Replies given without understanding the problem can prove to be erroneous, making the CEO bit of a laughing stock before his team.

For better communication, the CEO must relate to his listeners, must know what they want to hear, what is important for them for the moment, any advice given out of context would tend to fall on deaf ears. While the seasoned CEOs learn the trick, the new CEOs should prepare their speech in advance taking the audience into consideration, keeping the language simple, easily understood by those for whom it is meant. Gestures, body language are the real giveaway about the mindsets of the CEOs, therefore, they should be effectively used to convey the subtleties of his communication, avoiding any wrong signals from reaching the audience. Right communication given correctly at the desired time can motivate the employees; charge them into performing the most difficult tasks with ease. (A parallel can be drawn from the defence services, when the army is facing its enemy; it is the duty of the Commanding Officer to exhort his soldiers to march ahead, even in the face of coming bullets to safeguard their motherland. Such speeches have the ability to emotionally enthuse the soldiers into acts of unparallel bravery.)

Oration, speech making is an art, which can be cultivated with training and practice. All good CEOs have been known to be good orators. Writing speeches well in advance, practicing before a mirror first and then before an audience of a few close friends, would benefit the new speakers a lot. Oration has been considered the most effective way of influencing a large number of people. Politicians use their oratorical capabilities to get into the electors' psyche for getting their votes through emotional appeals.

The tonal quality, the timbre of the voice, the change in decibel levels (loudness) along with proper gestures help in conveying the message properly. The beginners in speech making are worried about their hands. "What to do with the hands," is a general question. The best thing to do in the beginning is to keep them upfront in a clasped position, to enable the speaker to unfold them to point out on something, stress on a point and indicate towards any direction. The rest of the time they can remain just folded in front of the speaker with practice, a seasoned orator can use his hands to literally dramatize the entire speech without looking like a circus clown.

CEO–A ROLE MODEL

Political leaders, sports stars, film stars become role models for the young generation. Similarly, the CEO in firms is looked upon as a role model whom the employees try to emulate; subconsciously attempting to get into his shoes. It is common knowledge that in firms where the CEO comes late to the office at 11 a.m., when the office opens at 10 a.m.; most employees would walk in about fifteen minutes before the CEOs arrival time. Conversely, if the CEO is always punctual, the entire office staff would be coming in time. Similarly, the employees are known to emulate other traits of the CEO, his method of working, and his conversation style, even his walk. The CEO, therefore, has a great deal of influence on the employees and hence must remain impeccable in his actions, demeanour and even character. His acts must always be above board; and they must also appear to be so to others. Be good and show every one that you are good!

As a role model the CEO has to act in different positions as given below:

1. Catalyst for transformation
2. Reaching out to the entire firm's administration
3. Planner of strategies
4. Problem solver

As the catalyst for transformation, it is his actions, which create the right ambience in the firm, leading to the desired changes, as the employees look up to him for not only guidance but also inspiration and direction.

While the administration of the firm is the job of the administration manager, the CEO has to assure the employees of fairness in dealings related to them.

The departmental heads are busy with the day-to-day matters, it is left to the CEO to plan the strategies and ensure that they are executed to perfection and in time.

The CEO is a problem solver and in this role he must become a good listener to understand the problem thoroughly before trying to solve them, as half baked solutions can lead to further disaster.

> *Above all the CEO must be farsighted, have a large heart and must be fair to all his employees and with these qualities he is sure to win the respect, admiration and total acceptance from his team.*

Being farsighted the CEO would be envisaging the firm's position five to ten years hence and planning his strategies for achieving that position.

Having a large heart the CEO would concentrate on the bigger picture and ignore minor pinpricks to keep him free from getting bogged down with these minor problems. He would assess the size of the problem before trying to solve it; delegating most problem solving to his team members.

When the CEO is fair in his dealings the employees know that any reprimand given by him is only for some shoddy work done by them or for some mistake committed and there is nothing personal against them in the CEO's mind. In such situations, the employees give their best to the firm and nothing less.

TIME MANAGEMENT

In the fast paced life of the CEO, time becomes a casualty, which renders the best of the CEOs ineffective. The simplest way of time management is also time tested as can be seen from the following method:

Every day in the morning make a list of all the pending tasks. Next, prioritize the tasks as per the ABC analysis as given below:

1. Tasks in A category, which are urgent and important needing the CEOs personal action.
2. Tasks in B category, which are not so important and can be handled by others too.
3. Tasks in C category, which are not important today, but they may come in A or B category at a later date.

The CEO should start by tearing off the C category paper as it would only keep him worrying at the moment when there is no need to be worried on the task. Next, he should delegate the B category tasks to the right person for the job. With only A category tasks left he can put his total concentration on the same, while keeping an eye on the B tasks with the person entrusted with the task as part of the control system of the firm, without of course breathing down his neck as he tries to perform the task.

The above stated method is time tested by several successful CEOs and it helps the CEOs in managing their time, to ensure they have enough time for their main tasks of planning, organizational leadership and people development.

Given below is the preferred time the CEOs want to spend in various tasks and the actual time they spend, which results in lopsided developmental approach of the firm.

Tasks	Preferred time in %	Actual time in %
Strategy Development	35	10
Monitoring Performance	15	45
Organizational Leadership	30	15
External Stakeholders	10	35
People Development	10	5

As can be seen, most of the time of the CEO is spent in monitoring performance and in meeting the external stakeholders, like the government officers, shareholders, financiers, which could be easily delegated to other persons in the firm; there are PROs and company secretaries for doing these tasks. There is no point in the CEO trying to usurp their prerogatives and in return rendering their positions unimportant in the firm.

Role models like the heroes are supposed to have extraordinary powers, stamina and insights. They are to be emulated by the employees for the benefit of the firm and therefore, it becomes essential for them not to put their defences down at any point, except only in certain circumstances as given below:

As a role model the CEO has to reflect the condition in the firm by his actions. If the firm is having financial troubles he can start by taking a cut in his salary (Lee Ioccoca did this when he joined Chrysler Corporation as its CEO and it was in dire straits.), he can travel economy class instead of first to which he is entitled due to his position as the CEO. These acts of symbolic synergy with the firm would pay dividends even in the short run; in fact, if the CEO is travelling economy class the general manager cannot even think of travelling in business class as per his entitlement.

The CEO is also a human being and can make mistakes. This show of being a vulnerable person by the CEO would go a long way in bringing the CEO and the employees together. It would also encourage the employees to experiment in their workplace and such experiments are a part of worker empowerment through TQM and are essential parts of business strategies for continuous process improvement today.

The CEO's major task is team building, making leaders from followers. This is possible through a. worker empowerment, b. delegation of authority, c. training and d. monitoring the workers' progress through controls and appraisals.

The CEO should prove the maxim that the "leader can be lead and the followers can lead." As a result of successful experimentation, the follower can redefine a process, and up the ladder even the CEO would accept the same. A good leader can build leaders from amongst his team members for performing more responsible tasks than what they were doing before.

Effective leadership depends on effective communication and effective communication begins with effective listening. To influence the employees the CEO must first try to understand them.

As the strategy deals with the firm's fundamental ends and its fundamental means it is often considered the prerogative and responsibility of only the persons on the top. There are certain areas of strategic management, which are confined to the top management; the practice of strategic management is not at all confined to any particular level.

CEOS, ACTION THROUGH MARKET LIFE CYCLE

Depending on the life cycle of the product the CEO has several options for taking appropriate actions. The options are given below:

1. Introduction stage
   a. If the product is new to the market and there are no competitors in the field, the CEO can go for skimming prices; get maximum market share before competition starts entering the field.
   b. If the product is new only to the firm and is available from competition, the CEO can plan for penetrating prices, better availability of the product through more acceptable channels, heavy promotion and advertising.
2. Growth stage
   a. As competition starts operations in a big way, the CEO has the option of remaining market leader by heavy promotion, or becoming a follower to reduce marketing expenses and yet making the same net profit as before.
   b. The CEO can change the marketing paradigm by product differentiation to continue enjoying the leadership position.
   c. The CEO can promote the brand and build its equity to the level that the product sells on its name.
3. Maturity stage
   a. In maturity stage there is no increase in the market, competition is severe and it is for the CEO to decide on the firm's product portfolio, pricing and going in for niche' market or for divesting from the market.
   b. The CEO should activate the firm's R&D to get differentiated product to increase the lifespan of the product.
4. Decline stage
   a. When the market reaches the decline stage the CEO of a single product firm must research the market for a suitable product, which can be made and marketed with the same infrastructure and the same team. Next, he must either get the new product developed within the firm or buy its technology before it is too late. Time, therefore, becomes the most important dimension in the decline stage of the market.
   b. Reposition the product, going in for niche' markets, going for larger geographic marketing including going overseas are the other options for the CEO.

END NOTES

Leaders in business, the CEOs, through their actions can influence the strategic implementation process. They can smoothen the problematic organizational changes with their motivation in getting their teams to work in a cohesive manner. Leaders can make changes with their official authority by ordering about, which is seldom enough. They have to resort to using their authority in their individual capacity for persuading and inducing the employees. This they achieve by becoming a role model for the employees. The best way to achieve success is to combine the two, personal charisma and official authority to influence the employees to bring about the desired change.

The CEOs must accept the firm's politics as a part of the system. Playing healthy politics, which is transparent and value based, can, in fact, go in favour of the firm. CEO has to negotiate on a number of issues, with the workers, in disputes between employees. Negotiations must bring the parties closer together to be of lasting value and this can be achieved by negotiating on the basis of set rules applicable to the entire workforce and in an unbiased manner, which would strengthen the relationship with the employees.

The CEO's effectiveness depends on how best he can communicate with his employees. The content and the method of communication, both are equally important. Effective communication depends on power of listening to understand their problems before the CEO attempts to solve them.

The CEO must project himself, through his actions, as a role model, worthy of emulation by others. The respect and faith he generates with his employees helps the firm to tide over difficult situations, helps it in affecting organizational changes and making it a fully learning organization.

4

CHAPTER

Inspirational Leadership

AIMS AND OUTCOMES

The chapter concentrates on the finer attributes required by the leader in business. The students will get to understand the virtues of honest hard work, transparency, commitment, dedication and truthfulness so essential in leaders.

Look around the world and its people and you will find that they all are reflections of yourself, like the mirror images. If you are good, doing good to others, you will find that they will do good to you. Everyone knows this universal truth and yet the tendency is not to put it in practice in life. If you consider the scientific laws, from the third law of motion, you know that every action has an equal and opposite reaction. Equal clearly suggests that the intensity level of your action towards others will be reciprocated with same intensity. Opposite only suggests, the equation would be "you to me" and "me to you".

The purpose of the organization is to achieve its vision, mission and goal, which is possible with good intentions and planning. Leader as a strategist must look at the means of achieving the ends, i.e., the goals. If the means are not fair, the achievements would be temporary and fragile. It is the natural law that as you sow so shall you reap. Karma is an individual act and there is neither undeserved pleasure nor unwarranted suffering in the world. Universal justice is the fundamental law of nature.

Great success can be achieved in the following manner:

1. Creating trust among the team members.
2. Unidirectional efforts.
3. Total coordination and cooperation within the teams.
4. Transparency in action.
5. Clearly defined and communicated goals.

6. Keeping self subservient to the organization
7. A sense of urgency

Perfection comes from knowledge, which is an external manifestation, which leaders have to internalize with practice. Leaders are able to unleash the powers within them, with consistency. With pure knowledge base internalized, leaders get dynamic intelligence, available to them for decisions and timely action. It would help the leader to perform at peak performance level, which would result in extraordinary success with genuine efforts. Leaders get organizing power beyond compare, ability to go for organizational diversification, mergers and acquisitions, in the chosen trade.

Leaders' creative genius can work on diverse projects and they can still remain connected with the basic organizational management.

IDEA MANAGEMENT

The Idea Management can be achieved through creativity, which results in diversity of ideas, views, and opinions and arranges these diverse thoughts in the best possible orderly manner. Thus, the leaders can conclude that perfect management is a phenomenon based on two diverse values, the single entity coming from combining of the multiple factors and the multiplicity coming from the myriads of ideas. In simple words, the organization has one vision and yet it may have several goals. These goals emerge out of the vision and hence while they are separate entities, they also merge into the vision statement. In such an event, leaders can rest assured that the organization can attain great heights with their efforts and their team's.

When leaders operate with such unified goals and one vision they get spontaneity in their decision-making and they remain ever fresh, clear-headed and highly creative, self-starting and self-sufficient for all their activities.

Success, however, should not bring pride and with it the downfall. The downfall is caused by the following reasons:

1. When you are proud of your achievements you lose focus on your job
2. You start living in the past glory, which can be short lived
3. Your sycophant friends push you up, which in fact pulls you down

WHERE THE GREED RESIDES

It the modern times greed is the omnipresent dweller in practically every person, every home. Organizations are no exception to the greed. Greed has devastated individuals, organizations, societies and even nations. In organizations, it could be greed of individuals or of the organization itself. Personal greed manifests itself when the individual cheats others including his organization for personal gains. Organizational greed emanates from the CEOs and takes the shape of profiteering. While profits are the legitimate need of any business organization as they are required for satisfying the stakeholders and growth, profiteering could become self-destructive in the long run. Profiteering invites competition as also the wrath of customers. It works well only in monopoly situation; but these never remain as monopoly for long and sooner than can be imagined the organization comes to grief.

Greed is unending as once you have gained the desired object of your greed, you start aspiring for something else. The strength of gratifying greed increases in arithmetic proportion, while the strength of greed increases with geometric proportion. When you become happy and satisfied with gratification of your greed, someone else is becoming unhappy. The happiness you gain by making others unhappy can never be long lasting.

TRANSPARENCY IN OPERATIONS

The propagation of information and knowledge in the team does the following for the team:

1. Makes them more committed to the organization.
2. Makes them loyal.
3. Makes them feel important enough to be told the vital information.
4. Motivates them for achieving the goals as nothing else can.
5. Builds the team, as all its members have the information and a common goal.
6. The team believes in fairness in the management's treatment towards them.
7. The information base makes the team members more analytical and sharp focused.

The difference between management and the employees diminishes with wider knowledge base, the working of the organization becomes smoother. Leaders also build leaders from among team members, who can be delegated important tasks and portfolios, leaving the leader free to do the task of planning for the organizational future. Ultimately, when the leaders retire or are ready to take up a higher position, someone will be there to takeover from him, and the organization work will go on smoothly even during the transition phase.

HELP FROM CORE ADVISORY GROUP

Good management ensures highest returns with lowest investments. For this purpose, the leaders need to have courageous, knowledgeable, strong-willed persons with high emotional quotient as their senior team members. Faced with complex problems, the decisions should not be taken unilaterally or in consultation with too many persons. That is why, the leaders need an efficient core group. It is better to have one wise man, sincere to the organization than even a hundred mediocre ones, as the wise will ensure prosperity even during recession periods. The leaders should have tested and trusted persons of integrity for strategic positions, who will be their secret weapons against the strongest of the competitors. The persons should be well paid to make sure that they stay with the organization and remain loyal. They should be allowed to work in a transparent atmosphere, where they can obtain any information they may need and their grievances must be settled promptly.

There are certain factors, which protect and nurture the organization. They are knowledge, skills, correct attitude, transparency within the organization, and generosity towards the weak. Organization should be considered sacred as it truly looks after the present and the future of its stakeholders. The organization consists of top brains, average persons and mediocre persons, and they are allotted the tasks accordingly. However, as each of these persons interacts with the others, these categories should be forgotten and they should live in friendship, unity and harmony. The organization provides the opportunity, a platform to use and enhance the talent of the employees, to enable them to achieve their goals, fame and money. Their intelligence blossoms in the organization.

The skilled and the learned persons do not while away their time, if they have to achieve the goals and that too with minimum efforts. Each one puts his best efforts and the result is that the organizational goal is achieved. Achievement of goals increases their energy level and strengthens the influence of the organization in the market-place.

As the leaders plan the business strategies, the environment affects them. In the same way, the strategies can affect the business environment. Business related issues, like demographic, social, cultural, political, legal, macroeconomics and global environment impact the business, as the CEOs/businessmen are aware of. However, good business strategies can have impact on governments' political will, which affects the environment. The government policies of opening up the telecom sector have been influenced by the business organizations. The good strategies affect the right way, and the reverse is also true.

The nature of good management is always progressive, always evolutionary and therefore leaders' vision, perception, activity, naturally needs to be on the top. Leaders keep going for more and more until in the relative they find the supreme value-based management for success. The other important aspect of management is the management of change as through change only, the leaders evolve and if they do not change they can forget about evolving into a successful leaders.

The leader operates through feelings, intuition and his ego and then his mind, intellect take over, he learns through his aspirations and desires what are his priorities and goals, which propel him to action. He is a discerning thinking person and as long as his ego does not interfere, he achieves his goals easily.

A leader is the mirror of the collective consciousness of the followers (employees). As the followers are trained to succeed, the success story gets reflected in the leader's mindset. No man is isolated and has to operate in teams. This is the quintessence, the summary of the laws of nature. Once understood, it imparts infinite creativity and organizing power to its practitioner. And this knowledge is the basis of right action.

MARKET AND ORGANIZATION

Market is the essential, basic necessity for the corporate organization. The organization, however, is attuned to its own creativity, and fails to appreciate its true nature. It is important for the leaders to understand the changing nature of the market, as it controls the organizational activity, its life and dwells in the core of the organization. The market has been in existence for centuries in different forms. The leaders should recognize that their organization is for the market and not the other way round, because there are several competitors to take away the market on the slightest mishandling by the organization and its leader, of the market constituents, the customers.

OVERDRIVE GEAR

Organizations need to develop a friendly relationship with the customers. While it is possible rather easily in the service industry and in industrial marketing, even FMCG firms have innovated their marketing efforts to build relationships with their customers to develop relationships leading to customer loyalty. Scratch cards; find gold earrings in the soap cake package are some of the methods employed in this direction. The entire business paradigm has shifted to the overdrive gear to make business transactions as friendly to the customers as possible. The box below gives an example of the shift in banking process:

If you want a bank draft made from your bank account you can get it in the following different ways:

1. Go to your bank, get the requisite form, and fill it with your cheque for the amount and bank commission. Wait for the bank to clear your cheque and prepare the bank draft before it is given to you.
2. Go to the bank where the concerned person completes the formalities, takes your signatures and hands over the draft to you.
3. Telephone the bank, declare your password, and inform your need and then the bank does the needful. In a short time you get the draft couriered to you.
4. Call the bank who sends a bank employee to you, who completes the formalities at your place and hands over the draft to you.
5. Visit the bank's website on the Internet give your password and the instructions regarding the draft you want. You can view the draft online and it is sent to you by courier.

The five methods given above are possible transaction modes. The actual method will depend on your needs and the facilities available with your bank. The ultimate aim in the grossly competitive market is to be friendly with your customer by building relationships with him.

INSURANCE POLICY FOR SUCCESS AND ITS PREMIUM

Can success be insured like the life insurance? If yes, then what is the rate of premium? With the CEO working in the right direction, fortified with the support of nature, he produces great influence on the other employees. With concentration, the mind gains the super achiever status, and can make value judgment of his actions, as also on the actions of other team members. The effort required for achieving such a state is minimal and yet it has profound effect on human mind. With concerted efforts, in unity, of consciousness, strength and balancing of tasks, one becomes part of the fundamental coordinated action, which would bring extraordinary success.

The balance you bring in the activities of different employees revolutionizes the success story of the organization. As CEO when you make the effort daily, you are paying the premium for the insurance policy for the success of your organization, besides the additional premium given in the next paragraph.

As the CEO, you form teams for specific goals, train the teams, enunciate the goals in clear terms and motivate the teams by a variety of incentives, and this is the next level of insurance premium. The teams, in their turn support you with their efforts. As the teams live in harmony, the organization becomes great. It attracts the best skilled and talented persons, who help you in combating competition. The organization keeps moving forward, enriched and prosperous.

THE BREACH OF TRUST

Organizations, which rise after trampling over other organizations, gaining success through non-ethical illegal means do not belong to the real civilized society. Search around you and you will find several organizations indulging in such acts. Bribing to gain favours, paying speed money to get their jobs done quickly, out of turn, has become a significant part of the business life in India and in most countries round the world. The businessman has made the bureaucrat and the politician corrupt. Politician, seeing the personal benefit makes such laws, which help them fleece the businessmen. Bureaucrats being the executive branch, who process the laws become conduits for siphoning money from the businessmen and (naturally) the conduits are not foolish enough to not take their share, before they pass on the rest to the politicians. This tripartite arrangement serves all the three parties, the politician, the bureaucrat and the businessman, to the total disregard of the interest of the common man, the customer. The deep-rooted malady has become part and parcel of the country's business paradigm. To add to its strength, the consumer movement in the country is weak. Therefore, it now appears that the bubble may be ready to burst and the public anger, through a new vigorous consumer movement may catch up with the culprits, sooner than anyone can imagine. The answer appears in a mass movement against the demon of corruption. It usually starts with one or a few individuals, who take up the cudgels of fighting corruption without fearing the politicians or bureaucrats' reprisal. The answer, therefore, is to start from oneself!

If all the CEOs just accept the principle of doing business as per the laws of the land, come what may, you will see increasing success coming your way in no small measure. This can be proven scientifically. As you walk on the right side of the law, you walk without fear and you do not seek favours from anyone. You get the right materials; have good marketing plans, products and profits. You share the profits with your stakeholders, the customers, the employees, the suppliers, the government (by paying the taxes), the trade bodies and the community in which the business operates. You have a good product. You get good market share, brand equity and naturally great growth prospects. As a good corporate citizen you earn goodwill, which helps you in the following ways:

1. Get better employees.
2. Larger market share.

3. Easier finance at lower cost.
4. Government support for infrastructure.
5. Goodwill of the community.

Leaders can bring about a sea change in their organization provided leaders are ready to be bold, radical and a stickler of ethical legal business. Leaders will be surprised to find that their actions and policies have a snow-balling effect with more and more organizations falling in line with the principles of honesty and ethical business behaviour. Leaders can start the desired revolution. This would in turn prepare a level playing field, where only merit will prevail, the hush money or speed money will not have any say in it. These words, hush money, speed money will become extinct from the dictionary of Indian business and hence from the Indian society and the nation. Tough tasks, yes, but leaders know great successes come out of such tough tasks and decisions. Moreover, leaders do not lose anything, and yet leaders gain the following:

1. Self-respect.
2. Confidence of the employees.
3. Loyalty of your customers.
4. Gratitude of the community.
5. Support of the government, with no strings attached.

The path of righteousness is filled with initial despair, loss of face, monetary losses and yet when you look closely, you find that all you are doing is following the tenets of your childhood, the training your parents gave you. The demonic vices have for long taken a stranglehold on the psyche of business, the bureaucrats and the politicians, which must be defeated, sooner the better.

One more major reason for leading an ethically correct life is the onslaught of international competition in India and opening up of the international markets for you. You can never prosper in the international arena with a tarnished image. The brand equity you must have in the international business will come only when your organization remains overboard all the time and is known for its straightforward business deals the worldover. Caesar's wife should always be above suspicion and business in India should be like that only, if it has to succeed in the international arena, especially to combat the competition looming large from the big international brands.

Just imagine how you would react; when you come to know of a foreign firm, which has been cheating the customers, the government and other stakeholders. You will run miles away from it. You can imagine the reaction of foreign firms on Indian organizations, which are having a bad name in their business dealings. Even a minor blemish is enough to have the Indian firm thrown out of the international market. Not only the reputation of the organization but also of the country, is at stake!

The only remedy, therefore, is to cure yourself of the major ills of corruption, malpractices, and get rich quick techniques. Otherwise, the firm is ready to sell India's reputation for a song through its nefarious activities. Is it too harsh to equate people indulging in such acts as international pirates?

Therefore, the training of the CEOs should include an integrated approach from the beginning; they must take the business as a single unit, a strategic entity and not as a collection of several functional areas joined at the top, with the CEO at the apex. Besides they must get to assimilate the vision, mission and goals of the organization to be effective CEOs, as without believing in them himself, the CEO cannot make others accept the vision, mission and goals in totality. The CEOs must learn to develop the star performers in the organization to ensure that they are operating to their full potential. In return, the star performers must remain transparent with no need to cover up any performance problems. They should, in fact, thank the problems, as without any problems they may not be even required in the organization. Transparency in interpersonal relations and skills in developing relationships must be part of the training programme.

Long-term success of an organization can be predicted by knowing the strengths, intensity and focus of its leaders, their understanding of the business, the reliability of their structures and the depth of their talent. The best training for the CEO is to be taught to develop the success mindset, which must be made to descend to the next generations of the leaders, when the transition time comes.

The CEO has to be creative, with a sense of urgency and fully alert to the changes in the business environment, to value the following resultant gains:

1. Better health.
2. Better planning process.
3. Increased profits and customer satisfaction and delight.
4. Competitive edge.
5. Ever increasing success with least efforts on his part.

THE MOST EFFECTIVE ACTION

Any action becomes effective if the performer is tuned entirely on the same. It has the concentration of Arjun, who had to pierce the eye of a speedily rotating fish, and that too while looking at the fish through its reflection in a trough of water. After hitting the fish's eye he was asked how he could perform the task of hitting the fish eye. He responded by saying, "which fish you are taking about? I only saw its eye".

The strangest quality of knowledge and skills is that as you use them for the right purpose, these will improve and increase in geometric progression. Theoretical knowledge can bring you kudos as you give speeches and may bring more such opportunities of making speeches. Other than that you will not become any wiser. If a person claims to be knowledgeable, of good character, he also wants to be well known in his circle. Such ignorance only brings ego, which is difficult to leave behind.

When any organization fails to achieve its goals, the blame is usually given to lack of resources needed for success. In most cases this would be only a lame excuse, as the problem lies in deployment of resources. Proper utilization of resources can be achieved in the following manner:

1. Human resource – Get the right people, train them and place them according to their suitability to the tasks and not as per some preconceived notions about demand and supply ratios. Human beings are not mere employee numbers; they have their individual needs, aspirations and skills and should be treated as such.

2. Financial resources – Usually you have enough. You should make proper use of it. There is ample time and opportunity. You must only make optimum use of all your resources and you will find no dearth of anything. The only criterion for having enough resources is that your requirement should be genuine and just enough. If you ask for more than what you require the chances are, you may not get even your just needs. It is like asking for an easy life, with all the comforts and achievement of goals, without any proper planning for the same.
3. Success and failure is in your hands – It is the ultimate reality of business today. The vicious mind, untrue thoughts and illegal actions bring failure and resultant sorrow.
4. Success results from pure mind, true thoughts and legally correct actions. You need only ordinary efforts in bringing great successes to your organization if you follow the laws of nature, and focus on controlling your mind through concentration. As the CEO if you can consider yourself as the chief liaison person, the chief service provider, chief spokesperson of the employees, you are assured of extraordinary success with minimal efforts.

If you waste your resources, your knowledge, your skills, how do you expect to achieve your goals?

WHAT ABOUT THE MISFITS AND THE CRIMINALS

In spite of the best effort and care of the CEO, at times, misfits and criminals join the organization. They may come with recommendations or fake certificates of good conduct and work. Initially, they will try and out perform other team members showing honesty, hard work and efficiency. It is only later, when they have gained your confidence that they start their nefarious acts of squeezing the organization at places where detection is not easy. They can adopt two different tactics for the purpose, one they can gradually milk the organization and secondly they can kill it in one stroke. Such persons are highly intelligent, smart, knowledgeable and yet evil-minded. They can do immense harm to the organization before they are caught. Without your knowing they start creating their own evil sphere of influence, with temptations to the gullible team member. They try to destroy the culture base of the organization with irretrievable tenacity. As CEO you have the following tasks to perform to rid the organization of such persons, as you learn to improve your selection process, which would preclude such persons from joining your organization.

1. Get the act of throwing out such persons, completed smoothly without any rancour with the outgoing employee.
2. Better screening of the employees entering the organization, cross-checking their antecedents, their references.
3. Have close control points for newcomers at all levels, especially the senior levels.
4. Train them in both hard skills like skills for the job, processes, and procedures, and soft numbers like the organizational culture, ethics, motivational skills and team spirit.

It is extremely important that such persons are apprehended quickly, allowed to change their ways, if you see signs of desire for change for the better or made to quit in good grace. However, very few persons change their characteristics for the better, if they are given a chance to do so. Some do play acting only to stay on in the organization, to do further damage, spoil the team by luring others into their trap. Once you decide to throw such persons out of your organization, it should be done with positive vibes only, so that they do not cause any harm from the outside, later on. For die-hard culprits, a public denouncement with or without legal action is required. The organization is not a correction house and as the saying goes, "tigers do not change their stripes."

If you want to succeed, give up the company of all those who distract you with temptations, idle talk, gossip and unworthy goals, even if they happen to be your close friends. Friends they may be, but they are not your well-wishers. You should keep such friends out of your ambit totally.

The only qualities required for gaining strength from nature is, purity of mind and commitment and eagerness to gain nature's support. You can gain eagerness, not just by being good; for that you have to be continuously interacting with good pious persons. Surround yourself with these people and you do not have to go to the temple or ashrams for this purpose. They are there all over, just look out for them. However, you must be aware of the fake champions of spirituality, who are out to grab your psyche first and then your organization. Beware of such charlatans.

One major ingredient of the success recipe for the CEO is catholicity or breadth of outlook. He should be above the close binding rituals of procedures, without in any way denigrating them. When the CEO's thinking is shackled with procedures, he tends to operate in a closed loop. He should be a thinking, living, vibrant entity, which fosters lateral thinking, thinking on absolute and on abstract, and then only he can be a good planner. Historical benchmark in process, strategic planning make no reference to the present. Only a broad all encompassing outlook of the CEO can keep analyzing the vagaries of today's market, which makes him a better planner. Distortions in thought process clouded by the lurking fear of the past lead to systematic dismantling of the CEO's confidence and the goals start receding into oblivion.

As CEO you should stop manufacturing your own insecurities, which take you far from the practical ways of success through nature's help. If you are primed to do your task in full radiance of natural laws, your duty, tasks are performed leaving your doubts far behind.

Keeping the balance in the world of nature definitely helps you in gaining maximum benefits.

Business and industry have been the worst offenders. They have taken the maximum toll on nature's resources and therefore, have also suffered the most. However, living with the laws of nature is so easy and simple that it is almost unimaginable how business and industry can destroy the nature's bounty for small organizational gains; the main problem is that most CEOs give only lip service to the environmental issues, keeping the short-term gains in the forefront.

If you tamper with nature you are bound to be punished, nature is a great guru and leveller. You learn from nature and become wise. It treats big and small business alike and does not discriminate one from the other. You just cannot bribe your way out of nature's wrath. You have to comply with its laws and you can draw great strength and get positive results from your modest actions.

As the CEO you have to keep your control points in place so that you are aware of the possible mishaps and can take timely corrective steps. As you keep your ideas and ideologies clear to your team, they will not only understand the same, but also subscribe to them. Your simple words and activities can bring about massive revolution in the organization.

THE MILLION-DOLLAR QUESTION

The sceptic CEOs ask the question, "in today's age where everyone is resorting to using minor aberrations and getting away with them besides getting better results, why should they keep spending extra money and time, energy to stick to the rules of the game, when even the major competitors are doing it?" You tend to be trapped into doing the same. However, you must realize that the most suitable path for success is through superior quality in products, services and ethical conduct.

There are classes of customers who are just cost conscious; they do not look for quality. They almost want to be cheated. The cheating organizations take advantage of these persons. They can at least make a first sale; repeat sale may not be possible. By the time they have gained enough volumes of the first sales, they are ready to move out to a different location, leaving their buyers stranded and feeling cheated. However, their ill deeds catch on them sooner than later.

The ultimate knowledge of product acceptance, quality of the product and service should be the fundamental right of all customers. Your success hangs on your acceptance of this right. You should be, in fact, directly informing the gullible customers of their rights.

GROOMING THE TALENT

While you must shed the unwanted obtuse characters from your organization, as they will never fit in its cultural ethos, and bring ruin to it; you must, on the other hand, nurture and groom the talent with you. You can spot the talent in the organization in the following manner:

1. He would be a team person.
2. He would happily take responsibility in the team.
3. He would be a keen learner.
4. He would exude confidence in himself, in his work and the organization.
5. He would go an extra mile to complete his task and do it with speed, quality and grace.
6. He would be humble and yet fixated to his tasks.
7. He would always be ready to impart knowledge, training and skills to others.
8. He would not be daunted by the difficulties he would face in his tasks.
9. He would always be pleasant, polite and disciplined.

You must believe that there are a lot of such persons in your organization. Persons with such virtues exist, although they may not be part of your elite group. They may be just doing their tasks with commitment, without even knowing that they have that magic touch, the will to succeed.

As CEO you should develop an eye for spotting such talent. The keen insight is possible through the practice of mind control through meditation. Once you have located the talent, you must do everything to groom it for higher echelons of the organization for shouldering greater responsibilities. Then only these persons can do real good to the organization, the community and finally the country. Following are some of the ways of bringing up talented persons:

1. Do it without offending others, may be less talented persons, their turn may come soon too.
2. Do a Strength Weakness Opportunity Threat (SWOT) analysis for him by listing down his strengths, weaknesses, opportunities and treats.
3. Build on his strengths, through training programme, job relocation or job rotation.
4. As his strengths grow, his weaknesses will start disappearing.
5. Provide him with opportunity to show his talent (an engineer trained in construction of bridges was made in charge of maintaining roads and the one who had only maintained roads was given the task of building bridges). Reward his good work, not as an eyesore for others, but as a spur for them to emulate the good work and receive similar awards.
6. If, however, he fails to click, recheck your assessment of the person, may be he is in the wrong slot, or may be not worthy of the selection.

The group of talented persons, properly nurtured are the strength of the organization and they hold the key to its future prosperity. With such a teamworking for you, you would enjoy great success with ease and minimal efforts.

The main concern about such talents is the following:

1. They become egoistic, want the best compensation, have only derision for lesser humans.
2. They move out easily given a minor temptation by your competitors.
3. They do not allow the upcoming junior to join their elitist club of super achiever.

OTHER SPECIES OF THE EMPLOYEES

There are always a variety of persons working as employees in every organization. Some of them are given below:

1. The shirkers – They prefer to avoid doing much work. They have plenty of time for gossip, have all possible answers, copied down from the elite group. Since they have time, they are ready with faultfinding from among the elitist group and if the CEO is willing to hear their stories they are more than willing to tell.
2. The clerks – They are totally engrossed in their work, not interested in taking any additional responsibility. They can hardly look beyond their immediate assignment, mostly are perfectionists in their own little way.

3. The work loaders – They work like mules; give them any task and they will complete the same in time and ask for more. They do not like shirkers at all. They make the best salespersons and accountants.
4. The avoiders – They tend to pass on their workload happily to whosoever is willing to take it. They are ready with several excuses for non-performance. These persons have no place in today's organization.

THE PEOPLE FIRST

In the last decade of the twentieth century the organizational theory was Customer First. In the first decade of the twenty-first century can organizations make a paradigm shift in the theory by making it as People First? Has the time come when you can tell your stakeholders that your team, the employees are as important, if not more than the customers. You can take an analogy from the medical profession, where, while patient is the most important person, the doctors, paramedics, the hospital employees are equally important in looking after the patient. As they cannot neglect the patient, can the patient afford not to obey instructions from the medical fraternity, the doctors and others? They will be doing so only at their own risk and peril. They can, of course go to another doctor, another hospital, but they may not find much difference in the treatment or behaviour anywhere.

In business, the marketing team is wooing the customers, unlike the hospital, where patients come because of the reputation of the doctor or the hospital. Your competitors are also pursuing the customer. The organization, which provides better service and product, will win the customer. And who provides the product and service to the customers, only your marketing team, your people. As sales is becoming increasingly service oriented with little difference in products, there is close interaction between the salesperson and the customer. Therefore, recruitment, training, motivation and control of your marketing employees should rank as your number one activity.

Most organizations have realized that even employees of other departments play a significant role in the business of the organization. With such importance of people, the HR Director is usually involved in all major decisions the organization takes.

In an ideal scenario, you have got the best team, energized and motivated, round the clock ready for action, performing and getting the desired results and you may find yourself with no perceptible work. Is it time for you to move on, leave the organization and join someplace else? No, definitely not and for the following reasons:

1. Your main task remains that of motivation and planning.
2. Even in good organizations 10-15% persons leave each year for better prospects and therefore, the cycle of recruitment, selection, training and motivation keep coming on to you. You will find that these 10-15% persons become smug, as they believe they have been good performers. They tend to take life easy and lose their grip on the job. They are eased out of the jobs.
3. As your organization becomes successful, it must venture into new projects, as growth is an essential part of organizational success. Either you grow or you shrink – there is no room for remaining steady at all.

4. As people keep performing good work, they can get into the materialistic mode. They start running after money faster than you can provide to them. Such people may be better off elsewhere and need to be sent out of the organization.
5. It is common human nature to fall prey to sycophancy. People who indulge in this art should be warned and if they do not mend their ways, should be asked to move out.

When the emphasis is on your people, it is best to have a lean organization. With less number of people, you can give them important assignments, better designations, good money and you can expect each one to be performing the task normally done by two to three persons. As they succeed, the organization succeeds. Hence, they can be looked after even in a better way. You do not need a whip in your hand, as a hard taskmaster; it is enough to recompense good efforts and result oriented timely actions. The employees need to show their total commitment towards their work and their organization.

CEO–DATABANK

In day-to-day workloads, the CEO can get bogged down with trivialities, which divert the CEO's mind. To remain focused on the vital issues concerning the organization, the CEO needs to have the following information on the fingertips or on the computer:

MARKET ORIENTED DATA

1. Product demand and supply position on monthly basis.
2. Competitive activities.
3. Opening of new markets.
4. New alternative product launch plans.
5. Market segments.
6. Consumer behaviour and brand preferences.

INTERNAL DATA

1. Product costs.
2. Availability of raw materials with different suppliers and prices.
3. Availability of finance, its utilization and its cost.
4. Recruitment, training and motivational programmes.
5. Effectiveness of the infrastructure.
6. Sales and service teams and their activities.

Since the information is fluid in nature, the CEO would have to keep updating it on a day-to-day basis. The feedback loop from his team; the marketing, finance, HR, purchasing, and production is essential for the CEO for remaining with the current data. These reports provide you with a control point as you look for deviations in the reports from the plans and you can take timely corrective action. LAN, WAN and Internet are the tools you require for continuous update of your databank. As you get on-line current information, your decision-making also improves, as you take more correct decisions than the decisions you would take with the old data.

EXPERTS AND PRETENDERS

Several self-proclaimed market savvy persons are just pretenders, trying to grind their own axe. They do not know the market and yet they cheat the management with impunity. Market knowledge is what drives an organization. You have to be right in the marketplace, not sitting in your ivory tower, the air-conditioned chamber. What you do not know you ask the research team to investigate. However, if you are in touch with the suppliers, customers, investors, banks and industry bodies, and you keep your eyes and ears open, you do get to know the market. As the market is ever changing you have to remain vigilant always. You can never become complacent. This is the gift of the twenty-first century business where the LPG the liberalization, privatization and globalization of the market has brought about great opportunities, threats, which you can decipher, once you get out of the chaos in the marketplace.

As the CEO, you may find that certain functional heads like the HR, finance may not be aware or even interested in market dynamics. They are either happy with what the marketing team tells them or just with their own half baked knowledge. It is the job of the CEO to keep updating their market knowledge to be perfect team members, as every organizational action must be market driven.

It must be understood that market dynamics and market knowledge are permanent, for any organization. They are always present, although they by themselves keep changing. Hence, as CEO you need to have a permanent organization which keeps updating the databank for this most important aspect of business. You must avoid totally the fake market gurus' geniuses. They will lead you on the wrong side of the planning process, be it production planning, advertising or purchasing. You can identify them from the following telltale signs:

1. They are always overconfident.
2. They are all-knowing.
3. They avoid your experts, even deride them.
4. They are suave, smooth talkers.
5. They gain your confidence by being right in some small areas.
6. They have some hidden agenda of personal gain.
7. They love to boast if you are ready to lend your ear.
8. They throw big names all the time to impress you.

Once you have isolated them, it is best to ease them out, before they can create problems for you.

Market knowledge and market dynamics are important inputs for knowledge bank for the success of the organization. The other area, which is very much part of the same, but deserves separate identity because of its special importance, is information on competition. The following information on competition obtained on weekly basis will make your task effortless:

1. New product, price, placement and promotion.
2. New distribution network.
3. Changes in their geographic coverage.
4. New staff in marketing and service.
5. New plans, policies, procedures.
6. New contracts, terms for channel members.

With a weekly dose of such information the CEO's task becomes easy.

THANKSGIVING CEO

With unwavering accuracy the predictions of extraordinary success from ordinary efforts can be made as you follow the simple rules of the game. Positive thought, word and action is bound to help you get positive results. And let us not even talk about the negatives.

As you achieve success extraordinaire, you must praise all that is sacred to you, thank the team members and the Almighty. This thanksgiving must be done with humility, fully realizing that without their support and that of the Almighty, you would never have been able to achieve it. You have your team members, who supported you throughout, deserve your thanks and a word of praise and appreciation. The thanksgiving and praise should not be a one time, end of the road activity. This should be given even when you reach a minor milestone on the road to success. A word of praise and thanksgiving purges you of any negative thought, reinforcing your faith in yourself. Self-assessment, leading to confidence in yourself, is a prerequisite of having faith in others. It is, therefore, important to thank yourself also for the achievement, without being smug about it. Thanking yourself will allow you to take yourself away from the achievement, as you are closing that chapter and would spur you towards your next goal.

There are a whole lot of people you have to offer appreciation, praise and thanks as given below:

1. Team members, but for their unwavering support you would never have been able to achieve the success. They are the people who actually perform the tasks leading to success.
2. Employees who support the team perform a valuable task, as without their catalysis, the team would suffer.
3. Suppliers, who provide cost-effective quality products on just in time basis, helping you to keep your inventory and current assets low, yet maintaining production in full steam with superior quality products.
4. Financers and banks, which give you loans at the appropriate time at low rates of interest, help you cover any short-term financial crisis.
5. Government, which assists you in smooth running of your operations with infrastructure support and law and order situation.

6. Industry associations, which take up your issues concerning the industry with the government and interacts on your behalf.
7. Community, which provides you with the workforce.

The CEO, who bows his head in humble tribute towards the contributions of his stakeholders, gains their confidence and they in turn give him full support.

CEO'S CONTROLS

It has been found that the CEO is either too strict with the employees or too lax. When you are strict, the employees react in teams. Such reactions are not conducive to achievement of goals and smooth working of the teams. If you are lax, the employees are sure to take advantage of your leniency thinking that either you do not know the rules of the game or you are yourself lax. The young employees would also get scared that if their minor misdemeanour is not even noticed leave alone punished, it may lead to bigger follies, unchecked. This could surely cause their ouster from the organization and it could make them less employable in other organizations too. The fear is of not being able to find a suitable alternative job in case they have to leave the present one. Therefore, CEOs must keep control points, as given below:

1. Budgetary control – The planned expenses are provided in the budget of each functional area. The budget plans can be then compared with the actual expenses on a weekly basis. Major deviations must be located for enquiry and setting house in order.
2. Reporting control – The functional heads must provide a clear picture of achievements and failures, with reasons for the same. Achievements should be discussed to understand the methods used for the same so that these could be emulated. Failures should be discussed as a learning experience, to find out where the team has gone wrong and why; where does the aberration comes from, is it from people, plans, policies, processes, plant and machinery or raw materials purchased by the organization.
3. Seeing the incoming and outgoing mail would tell the delays in replies to the letters received by the organization. Besides delays in replies, there can be incomplete replies, letters sent without the enclosures. Corrective action can be taken before it is too late, by sending the required extras. People seldom realize the importance attached to a mundane activity like receiving and sending letters. Each letter could mean a few million rupees gained or lost. Letters are the lifelines of the organization with outside world.

CEOs can device their own control systems, as per the organizational needs.

Employees develop a false sense of pride and importance due to their hierarchal position. This could lead to organizational disaster. Even the work of the lowly peon who receives and sends letters is extremely important. Therefore, you have to convince the employees that there is no sense in having false ego, which should be replaced by a sense of unity, camaraderie that everyone is working for the success of the organization.

According to Freud, ego tries to preserve the person by organizing and controlling the critical demands, which everyone has. Such demands can make a person go down to a lower level in asking for what he wants and it is only the ego, which prevents a person from lowering himself, when he has to make requests to his juniors. The super ego reinforces control and it can be a source of making the person disciplined and honest. Super ego may, however, take away some of gentleness and make the person hard hearted, almost cruel, besotted with self-righteousness as he is able to control his desires.

However, the ego, super ego are manifestations of physical desires. Once your team gets into thinking mould, the better senses take over and humility prevails. You have to lead them on the path of self-righteousness with humility, of progress and success without personal pride, of achievement but only as shared with the team. Introspection controls the mind, the intellect and the soul and the sense of false ego disappears. You would be taking the egotists out of their persons as you take them on the path of humility and of surrendering their own goals to the goals of the organization.

The ego is the counterpart of a person's anxiety towards the results of his work, the preservation of his job and welfare of his family. It is your primary task to keep the employees motivated on these issues, so that they can shed the false ego. The other reason for the false ego is the desire of material wealth, health, happiness, which controls people's minds and a show of superiority, is made to cover for any shortcomings. The desires keep changing, as when you get something you had desired, you ask for more and this can be frustrating. The CEO's task, therefore, is to assuage the anxiety and ensure that the employees' desires remain within the realm of reality. You give them what they want, once they stretch themselves to achieve the organizational goals. When the desire is not fulfilled, anxiety, frustration, anger, all emerge. Can the doctor allow a heart patient high cholesterol diet or sweets to a diabetic? Similarly, you have to counsel the employees about what is really good for them, for which they can aspire and what they can achieve with efforts.

TOP 7 CHALLENGES OF THE CEO

The top seven challenges of the CEO are given below:

1. Lack of knowledge
2. Lack of confidence
3. Lack of motivation
4. Lack of energy
5. Lack of authority
6. Lack of system
7. Lack of vision

Knowledge – The CEO needs to have a wide-ranging knowledge and information base in the following areas:

1. Worldwide business related to his products.
2. Country's business environment.

3. International business environment.
4. Competitors' strengths and weaknesses.
5. 4 Ps of the competition.
6. Market shares of competitors.

Business environment consists of demography, social and culture ethos, political and legal scenario, macroeconomics, technology and global environment. The CEO must have a clear idea of the business environment.

Confidence you gain by starting to do small tasks successfully, which would lead you to increasingly bigger tasks and responsibilities.

Motivation and energy comes from a positive attitude, good health and a bright outlook.

Authority you gain when you display confidence in your behaviour, work and interactions, without overselling yourself.

Systems need to be in place. Systems should be a help to the working of the organization and lead to achievement of goals.

Vision, with high motivation and energy levels, helps you to be ready for the future. You have to plan the organization's future with vision.

As the CEO you need to prepare yourself to face the challenges boldly, lead the team from the front and you can be assured of extraordinary success with ordinary efforts.

TOP 7 ASSETS OF THE CEO

The top 7 assets of the CEO are given below:

1. Brand equity.
2. Market share.
3. The CEOs charisma.
4. Tested and proven team.
5. Positive attitude.
6. Clear vision, mission and goals for the organization and total commitment of the team towards them.
7. Sensitivity to changes in the business environment and competition.

If you ask any CEO, he will tell you that his biggest assets are the brand equity and the market share. They go a long way to keep improving these for the organization. As the CEO if you have confidence in yourself and in your organization, attitude towards firm action and quick decisions, you develop a charisma for your team members.

You build your team with care, train the team, give each member the right slot, as per their skills, ability and inclinations, motivate them, you can trust them to produce positive results.

Your positive attitude, faith and confidence in yourself, in your team will help you operate with minimal efforts.

You must provide a clear vision, mission and goals to the team to galvanise it as a unified force.

As CEO you must be sensitive to the changes taking place round the world in business, which will help you in making the correct decisions.

CEO'S SCORECARD

As the CEO you must set up the motivation and energy level meter and keep placing your position on the graph at least once a month. The meter can be made as given below:

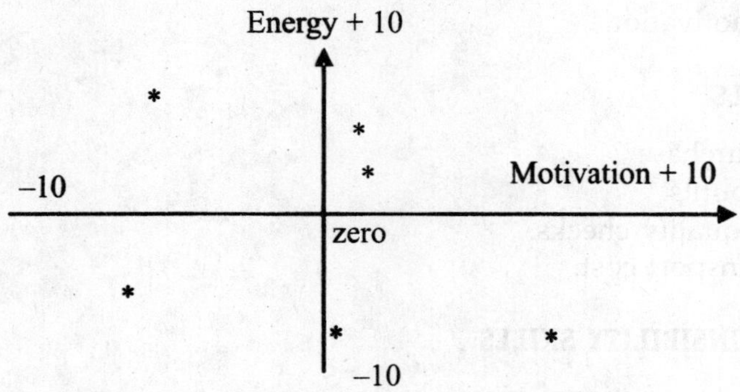

Besides having full force of energy and motivation as the CEO you must also use the following scorecard, on a quantum basis with the scale being 1 to 10.

FINANCE SKILLS

1. Ability to get finance at lowest interest rate.
2. Optimization of finance resources.
3. Low level of current assets.
4. Proper allocation of finances.
5. Financial risk management like credit to customers.
6. Budgeting.

MANAGEMENT SKILLS

1. Vision, mission and goals clearly defined and the entire team committed to them.
2. Creative organizational culture.
3. Importance and value of time management.
4. Control points in place.
5. Information system across the board.
6. Delegation of real authority.

MARKETING SKILLS

1. Increase in brand equity.

2. Increase in market share.
3. New product launches.
4. Speedy redressal of complaints.
5. Motivated team and channel members.
6. Transport and finished goods' store management.

MOTIVATIONAL SKILLS

1. Your team's motivation level.
2. Channel members' motivation.
3. Stakeholders motivation.
4. Community motivation.

PURCHASING SKILLS

1. Just-in-time purchase.
2. Quantity discounts.
3. Raw material quality checks.
4. Control on transport cost.

INTEGRATED RESPONSIBILITY SKILLS

1. Concentration on functional areas.
2. No area neglected.
3. A firm grip on control points.
4. A close understanding of goals and the distance between the actual ground reality and the goals; ways of bridging the same.

RATING SCALE FOR THE CEO

You should perform the rating task on the scorecard to know your real worth to the organization. Be honest while rating yourself, just do not fool yourself. Rating scale (10 of each area) is given below:

Top score	300
Excellent leadership	250-300
Impressive leadership	200-249
Above average	150-199
Average	100-149
There is a hope	50-99
Change your profession	Below 50

The CEO is the basis of the organizational success.

WAKE UP CALL FOR THE R&D

If you look at the R&D units in business organizations, you will find that they are basically places for people to sleep. Most R&D engineers are on a simple mission of sleeping through their working hours, as there is practically no accountability for them. They take advantage of their superior knowledge and expertise in the particular branch of technology. Because of this reason they keep asking for bigger budget allocations for their lab. The lab keeps the latest equipment in the field, but barring a few exceptions, most R&D engineers are not making full use of the opportunity. They are always ready with some excuse or the other. Some of the common excuses are given below:

1. Not enough time was given.
2. Purchaser does not know how to buy the right product for us.
3. The specialist engineer is on leave.
4. The equipment is not complete without the balancing instrument.
5. The product you require will never sell.
6. The product you want is impossible to design.
7. You always favour other managers in allocation of funds.
8. Now we have reached the final stage of development and the prototype will be ready in the next month. (Please be assured it will not be ready even in the next six months).
9. We do not want to give you half-baked product, which will fail (in fact, they will give only such a product).

As the CEO you need to assign time bound development projects to R&D engineering teams. A liaison team should be in place with purchase, and finance persons joining hands with one R&D engineer, to ensure timely purchase and availability of finance for the same. The R&D operations, like any other, should be transparent as, besides you, other teams like marketing, production, HR, finance should know the progress and the likely time of availability of commercially viable and marketable product. R&D engineers must also be in close coordination with the marketing research team, to understand the exact product specifications needed and also have an idea of its demand in the market and the likely selling price. The information will be the guiding factor for the engineers; they must be told that the industrial research is only designing and development and no basic research is expected of them. For this reason alone, there is need to bind them in a time frame, to help the organization reach the market at the appropriate time. Those engineers who do not subscribe to this philosophy have no place in the R&D. They should either be moved to other technical sea or just be shunted out. Harsh though it may seem, but ultimately it may be the best solution for the engineer concerned, as he may do well somewhere else.

R&D's importance has increased tremendóusly, as the PLC for virtually all products has shortened, with competition coming out with new products, ever so often. There are new manufacturing techniques and also new technology products. If your R&D is not fully capable of delivering the new products in time, you may think of buying the technology, if it is available. In the absence of any patent, you can go for reverse engineering for technology by cannibalizing the existing competitive products and reassembling them for your production use.

5
CHAPTER

Leadership Leverages

The actions individual leaders take can become the biggest levers in uplifting the organizations and with the help of these levers, the tasks become not only easy and pleasant but also time saving. As the CEO your actions influence your team, the market place and at times even the government decisions.

It is the power that the organization bestows on you as the leader, which, along with your personality, is responsible for making your actions become powerful influences on your team members. Power, it is said, corrupts and absolute power corrupts absolutely. How important is the role of power, which if misused can become catastrophic for the organization? There is a lot of societal criticism of power in this connection. People talk of democracy and of taking management decision on the basis of democratic principles, by consensus. However, as in the government there is a hierarchy of authority and power so it is in the business world. Therefore, while the power is your right as a leader, it devolves great responsibility on you for making legitimate use of the power. It is assumed that only in rare cases will the CEO need to use his power, which can be termed, as its good use. The legitimate use can become the success catalyst in the organization.

Great men have influenced nations by their action, the example in living history. can be that of Mahatma Gandhi, Martin Luther King, Nelson Mandela, who moved vast number of citizens through their thoughts and action. Gandhi is, perhaps the only leader, who practiced what he preached, like living in the slums and cleaning himself the dry latrines in the slums where the schedule caste were living. He could, therefore, move the entire nation, which stood behind him in non-violent Satyagrah or protest, to force the British to leave India..

The business leaders should take a lesson from these leaders and learn to perform the meanest of the tasks, to let the employees know the value of each task.

The leaders in the organization use power for two purposes as given below:

1. For influencing others
2. As a lever for performing difficult tasks easily

CEOs personal actions can be a powerful lever for influencing strategy or for brining about organizational changes.

The management of the power takes its course in the following manner:

1. Power to influence through personal action
2. Organizational politics
3. Leader as a negotiator
4. As a communicator
5. As a role model

It is the power of leaders' charisma, which lets them lead even more intelligent and skilled persons than the leader himself at times.

SOURCE AND USE OF POWER AND INFLUENCE

The leaders powers basically emerges from the following areas:

1. Institutional power, which the leaders use for a. Commanding b. Shaping others whom they lead.
2. Individual power, which the leaders use for a. Persuading b. Inducing others whom they leads.

The manner of use of power is given below:

Source of power	Explicit use of power	Implicit use of power
Institutional	Commanding – giving orders, making structural changes, system changes	Shaping-making cultural changes through revised agendas and rewired networks
Individual	Persuasion by expert negotiations and good communication	By the use of charisma, playing good politics and being a role model

The leader uses institutional authority openly, by Commanding – giving orders, making structural changes, system changes. The leader has to ensure organizational discipline for which he needs to see the employees operate within the framework for which he has to give his directives to them. If he finds the organizational structure out of tune for the present operations he can make changes in the same. For instance, when the organization gets into multi-unit, multi office mode he can plan the SBU structure, (the Strategic Business Unit Structure) in place of functional structure. If he finds some function proving to be not cost-effective he can plan the virtual structure by out that function. Similarly, if there is a flaw in the human resource system, he can ask an outside recruiting agency to help out in that activity.

The leader uses the institutional authority covertly by making cultural changes through revised agendas and rewired networks. Cultural changes, if required need a lot of effort as given below:

- Understand the existing culture of the organization, is it a laidback culture, or is it too brash?
- Plan for the new look culture.
- You may need to change some senior people, who are totally against any change.
- You should avoid any confrontation with team members as the changes need to be made in a subtle evolutionary manner.
- You may consider changing the organization's vision statement, if it does not fulfil the cultural aspirations of the organization.
- Create stories of success and circulate them through all possible media among the employees like the newletters, notice boards, staff meetings and even grapevine. Such stories help in reinforcing the image employees have of the inner working of the organization. New symbols can help create a new ambience of culture and should be tried.
- Most of all, you must persevere and not give in easily as changing organizational culture is a time-consuming and arduous task.

Leader uses his personal authority and power openly by using persuasion while having expert negotiations and good communication with the employees. He should ensure that the communication channels between him and the employees are always open and remain in good condition, without any rancour or illwill. He can use his negotiating skills for making the employees believe in the validity of organizational goals, and their time based activities.

Leaders use their personal authority covertly by the use of charisma, playing good politics and being a role model for the employees, in the following manner:

1. Do not negotiate on your high position. If there are two employees asking for the same thing you must understand the real problem first. Suppose you have 5 crore rupees and both advertising manager and R&D manager are asking for Rs. 5 crore. Most of the time people ask for more than what they actually need in the hope of getting what they really need after negotiations. If both have taken this view both could be unreasonable, while each tries to prove that the other is unreasonable. The person who gives in loses both money and face. Both are unhappy if you divide the money between them. You should get into the details of the needs to uncover the bloating of the budget and when you have found the culprit, you would be in a better position to negotiate. If possible, instead of dividing, increase the size of the cake and give each what he wants.
2. You should negotiate on the problem and not against persons. The personalities should be kept out of the negotiations.
3. You can use your personal power through communication skills. During any communication, you must listen to understand and not just to reply. You need to

listen to understand before you can make a value judgment on any issue. It is a good idea to practice the art of speaking in public.

4. You can learn the art of public speaking from professional coaching. The following tips will certainly help in this regard:
   - Prepare your speech; initially write it down and then instead of remembering it by heart, note down and remember the salient points in the right order.
   - Understand clearly what you want to say and why.
   - Your speech should be tailor-made for your audience and they should relate to it. If your speech is going beyond the range of your audience, it will never have any effect on them.
   - The speech should be in the language your audience understands well and therefore, use simple language.
   - Use of audio-visual aid makes a powerful impact. Get your slides, films ready and tested before the start of the speech.
   - Use the tone and pitch of the voice effectively by changing them to suit the words for creating the right impact. Sometimes even a pause at the right time can be effective.
   - At times you can speed up your speech and then you can slow down for the effect.
   - You must prepare the punch lines well and remember to give them at the appropriate time.
   - Here should be a central focus of your speech and you must keep your mind on it always.
   - You must make all your points for which you are giving the speech.
   - You should look at the person sitting in the middle seat in the third row in the auditorium while speaking and each person in the auditorium will think you are looking at him.

LEADER AS A ROLE MODEL

As the CEO or the leader of the team, you would be performing a number of tasks, and in each of your roles, you remain in the eyes of your employees. They watch your every step and get influenced by your actions. (If the CEO comes at 11 a.m. in the office most other employees would come just about fifteen minutes earlier than him. If the CEO comes punctually, the employees would do the same).

The different roles the CEO plays are given below:

- Change agent
- Administrator
- Strategist
- Planner
- Problem solver
- Negotiator

As the change agent the CEO is engaged in the following actions:

- Analysis of general business environment.
- Understanding the competitive forces.
- Internal analysis of the firm, to understand its strengths and weaknesses.
- Locating various factors, which can contribute to the organizational competitive advantage.
- Planning strategic changes in the 4Ps of the organization.
- Better utilization of human, financial, technological and information resources by the organization.

As an administrator, the CEO has to ensure that the employees maintain discipline in the organization. As a strategist he has to be vigilant with respect to the changes taking place in the business environment as well as the changes in competitive strategies and their strengths. As a planner the CEO has to get both the financial and non-financial budgets readied for keeping a track of the path the organization is taking in pursuit of its goals. Problem solving calls for skills in negotiations and straight thinking through a maze of incongruous information that the CEO has. And it is his primary duty to ensure proper resource allocation in terms of organizational goals. If the organization had missed out on the goals earlier, the redeployment of resources becomes extremely important.

These tasks become easy and routine with the help of meditation, as it teaches, among other things self-discipline, which leads to self-confidence, so essential for the CEO.

TIME MANAGEMENT

The story of today's CEOs is simply covered with extra working hours, rushing around from one meeting to the other all the time. The office hours are meant for attending both external and internal meetings. The CEO is, therefore, obliged to stay late to finish his own work. He is missing on family life, being with his children, parents. Today's CEO is a jet setter, a globetrotter, who finds himself more outside his office in the aircraft. In such conditions, the CEO has to estimate what tasks were completed and what remained undone, despite the hectic schedule.

An ABC analysis of the tasks would help, where other than the A type tasks he can leave for another day, and delegate the B category tasks to others. In this way, when the CEO is not trying to perform all the tasks by himself, most of the tasks will be completed in time.

The following table shows the average amount of time spent by the CEOs in performing various tasks as against the preferred amount of time they would rather spend performing there task.

Task	Preferred time	Actual time
Strategic planning	30	10
Monitoring performance	20	40
Organizational leadership	30	15
External stakeholders	10	30
People development	10	5

From the above table (it is not an absolute table, but only an eye opener for most of the CEOs), one can see that a lot of time is spent on monitoring performance. The reason, it appears, is the lack of confidence the CEOs have on their employees. It could also mean interference in their tasks and could lead to gossiping elsewhere in the office. Strategic planning and leadership issues take a back seat in the CEOs' time management, which causes derangement of organizational activities.

CEO'S ROLES

The CEO has to be a role model in different ways, as given below:

1. Symbolic Acts – When the organization is facing financial problems, the CEO should show the way of cost reduction by spending less than even his allotted funds. If he is allowed first class air travel, he can travel either business class or even economy. A classical example is of Lee Ioccoca. When Lee joined the Chrysler Corporation as its CEO, it was in real bad shape, with most shareholders wanting it to declare bankruptcy. However, Lee, as a symbolic gesture, reduced his own salary to only dollar one per annum, till the situation improved. He could then persuade his team members for a fifty per cent salary cut, which was accepted by each one of them.
2. The CEO should display signs of his vulnerability, that he is also human, and can make mistakes. He should discuss the mistakes made in the organization, including his own, in a bid to find out the real cause of the mistakes to avoid their recurrence. When the employees find the CEO too can err, they will not hesitate in experimenting, which is a good way of finding better ways of doing things. Process innovation comes only through experimentation. It also helps in the TQM, as it empowers the employees to experiment and take spot decisions leading to process improvement.
3. The CEO should encourage leadership among his teammates by letting them do the experiments. Successful experiments must be respected, and acclaimed with rewards and results of such experiments should be used in the organization. He will develop leadership qualities in his team members, which would be good for the organization's future.

Effective leadership depends on effective communication. Effective communication begins with effective listening. To influence others, one should first strive to understand them.

MANAGEMENT FOCUS

As the strategy of the organization deals with the fundamental goals and resources (ends and means), it is often regarded as being the exclusive responsibility of the CEO and the top management.

While the strategic decisions are taken at the top levels, strategic management is not limited to any level.

ORGANIZATIONAL POLITICS

As the CEO one must accept that politics is inevitable in any organization, be it big or small.

Politics, basically, is the act of governance. It is the government's political will, which frames new laws, changes tariff rules and gives the perimeters within which the business has to operate.

Organizational politics stems from the different requirements of senior people from different functional areas, which clash with one another. As the CEO one should practice principled politics only. This is possible if he uses openness and honesty to undermine unprincipled politics. The confidentiality breeds conspiracy, which goes against the organizational interests.

Some forms of influences are so unobtrusive that they are not recognized as forms of power. These implicit forms of power are among the most effective ways for individual leaders to affect organizational outcome.

CEO AS A NEGOTIATOR

As a negotiator the CEO has to use his personal influence as he cannot throw his weight around as the leader. In other roles he gets organizational support but not as a negotiator, where he is alone. He gets confronted with only those problems, which could not be solved by the lower levels. Hence, they are usually serious in nature. The best way would be to negotiate on issues and not on people standing tall as the CEO. Between two persons claiming for the same slice of cake the need may have been inflated to get the actual requirement after negotiations. Usually, one person could be unreasonable; while at times, both could be the same. The situation arises when both could lose, become unhappy.

The best solution, of course, is if you can increase the value or size of the cake, rather than divide it. Small share of a big cake could be bigger than large piece of a small cake.

The best way, rather the only way is to negotiate on the problem and not on the persons. The CEO must keep the personalities out of the negotiations totally; otherwise he would succumb to becoming prejudiced.

LEADERSHIP LEARNING

It is often said that leaders are born and cannot be trained. However, a person with determination and desire to succeed can learn the methods to become a leader. In today's business world there are a lot of leaders who were not born as leaders. They acquired leadership traits through the following practices, which have been detailed hereunder.

Leaders need to have confidence and strength of character, broad thinking process and these can be developed by a few simple techniques:

1. When a child ties his shoelaces for the first time, it comes as a great confidence booster. As a leader, you should plan small tasks and perform them well, like making job profiles for your team. As you succeed, you gain in confidence. At times, small experiments in organizational structure, like rotating people and jobs can help.

2. Confidence is also built by public or team's acclaim of a job done well. When you are grooming a leader, find out reasons for praising him even for small jobs done well. Small successes will surely lead to bigger successes.
3. Keep no doubts about failure mindset, because nothing fails more than the worry of failure. Think positive, think success and the chances are that you will never fail. Small setbacks are only like spurs to goad you on towards your goals.
4. Have the courage of conviction. As you think big, a lot of detractors will try to pull you down by predicting loss and rejection. Do not listen to them; be sure of your goals and plans of achieving them. Dream big and big you achieve.
5. Keep experimenting, honing your skills through practice, as only practice makes you perfect. Be with the tasks; do not get disheartened even if you do not succeed at first. Be vocal about the support you receive from others, give them their due.

Learn to be resourceful, keep a number of friends in different areas of human activity who will come to your assistance when you need them. Be ready to take full responsibility for your actions when they go wrong, as it will show your character. Do never pass the blame onto your team. Be respectful to your team; they may be reporting to you, but they are respectable people and need to be recognized as such. They will not only give you respect in return, but will go all out of their way to achieve the goals of the organization.

It is your inner strengths and values, which lead you to being a confident person, a true leader.

Besides, the leader must learn to be an effective communicator. The employees get huge amount of information, data from various sources, through media and grapevine within the organization. The leader must be able to clearly and forcefully inform the employees, what they should know for remaining loyal to the organization, the distilled truth. It also implies that the leader must be able to say no politely and yet strongly, when he finds the employees' demands unreasonable. He should have a clear mind, uncluttered of unnecessary data, which is available, as it would only confuse him. With confidence he should be able to spot talent, nurture it for the benefit of the organization. He should be ethically sound and, morally correct, otherwise he cannot expect his team members to be like that. With these qualities, the leader acquires charisma, which transforms the employees into his followers.

Those who want to attain leadership position must give respect to the knowledgeable people.

You must respect the scholars, as when you come in their contact, you obtain their wisdom and you are prompted to do only good tasks and deeds. You should plan for seminars, workshops or any other kind of interaction with such persons with your team, to enable them to learn from their wisdom too.

Like humans, organizations also have a life cycle; they get conceived, are born, grow, reach their maturity stage and then they decline. Unlike humans, the organizational decline can be arrested. It is said that if a person exercises, his faculties will remain active even in old age. If he does not, then naturally they will cease to function properly. Imagine, at 70 a person has hopefully learnt a lot from life, is mature and can be highly productive mentally, while his physical body would not let him operate as per his physical health. It is also true that physical health affects mental state. Let us take a healthy and mature organization. It has remained healthy because it has, from inception, cared for its stakeholders and competitive environment and has taken mostly right business decisions. In spite of such care the organizations start declining because of external reasons, internal strife and human errors, caused by insufficient knowledge, lack of initiative and drive. There are ways and means available to cure the organizations and put them back on the success path. Let us see how the cure works.

The organization operates through its people or men, with the help of money, material, and machinery–the 4 Ms along with the 5th M, motivation. Let us look at the first M, the men who man the organization, because it is the men who operate the other Ms to make a success of the organization. The men can be divided into the hierarchy, the top management, the white collared, and the blue collared people. The top managers have the maximum impact on the working of the organization, while others have less. Nonetheless each one has his importance and without the entire team the firm's working would come to a standstill.

To understand the top management, you have to take them individually from their position of power and analyze them in the following manner:

1. How good they are as managers? Are they knowledgeable, skilful and proactive? Do they respect time and take prompt and timely actions and decisions?
2. How do they rate on physical appearance, do they create a positive impression, even on first meetings? Are they neat and tidy, full of glowing and visible confidence?
3. Are they fully articulate, forceful in their views and do they express their opinion without ambiguity and bias?
4. Are they full of enthusiasm, energy? Are they ready to take challenging tasks in their stride? Can they give directions about organizational goals and objectives forcefully and with serenity? Do they remain unperturbed even in crises situations?

The understanding of top managers' ability, especially in a declining organization would throw light on and provide insight on the causes of the decline. Once the analysis is completed, organizations can take corrective steps of weeding out the wrong decisions and managers, who had taken the decisions. With a clean slate new decisions can be taken with new managers, new vision, mission and new vigour.

At this point new leadership can be introduced in the organization. You have to ensure that the new entrants are endowed with certain traits of character, to be of use to the organization. These traits of character are discussed below.

The leaders need to have charisma, defined as a combination of personality, confidence, knowledge, skills, positive thinking, power, and a caring attitude. You have to look for the following:

1. Impression created in the first meeting, the handshake, its gentle firmness, a genuine smile, comfort and ease.
2. Posture of confidence, mixed with humility (not arrogance), the way a person walks in, sits, and his body language; does he emanate positive vibrations towards you or not?

3. As you ask him one uncomfortable question, which causes stress, you watch his reactions and response. Does he become aggressive or is he open to new ideas?
4. As you criticize any of his views, notice how he takes criticism? Can he lead a team of efficient employees through difficult times (ask him about adventure sports)?
5. Can he be trusted as honest? Is he flexible in his outlook?
6. Can he merge in the organizational culture and if you are planning to change the culture can he be the one to facilitate the change?
7. As a team leader where does he rate? Can he inspire confidence in the team, and can he motivate it?
8. Is he emotionally stable, can he be trusted with responsibility and authority?
9. Is he educated in the right discipline for your work?

Once the person joins you have to watch his steps, as now he is no more his bio-data. See if he really possesses the professional knowledge and the required skills in his job as follows:

1. Does he enjoy his work or does he find it a burden?
2. Are his skills current or are they outdated?
3. His record as an achiever.
4. His learning ability.
5. Does he apply to his job what he has learnt?

The person you are looking for must be prepared to excel in his job. Besides, he should have lucid oral and written communication skills. The next step is to find out his beliefs, is he a religious person, and comes from a well knit family? He must lead from the front and must have the ability to initiate change movement especially in the following areas:

- Vision and values
- Mission
- Innovation and creativity

At times companies go into a certain downhill path like a rudderless boat. As its leaders you need to start its revitalization process before it gets to be too late. A few methods for doing it are given below:

Before you try to correct what is wrong in the organization and what is sapping its energy, you must know what is wrong with the organization, is it the people, policies, procedures, practices, planning process, or plan execution. The best way to do so is given below:

1. List down the possible causes from among the 4 Ms, men machine, material and motivation.
2. Prioritize the list with the worst offenders leading the way.
3. Pick up each area, check it with the objectives and the benchmarks for understanding the level of deviation.
4. What needs to be done to correct the situation, by whom and when.

5. Plan control points for the planned action, provide coordination between the persons involved in various correctional activities.

Next, pick up other areas of negative influence, which can be as follows:

- Historical success
- Organizational policy
- Resource crunch
- Ulterior motives
- The basic plan itself

You have to decide, which areas you need to change in context of today's business environment and for that purpose do the following:

- List down the improvements needed
- Policy change or structural change is needed
- Discuss with the team who will do it and how would he organize it
- Plan the resources required for the change; money, men and material
- Build a time table on Bar Chart or PERT Chart
- Build teams to execute the changes

The teams ready for making the changes should define their tasks, innovate the optimum use of resources, make their own sub time tables with built-in monitoring systems and act with speed, dexterity and commitment.

Each team member should come up with his suggestions in the brainstorming sessions, where the team should arrive at a consensus about how the task will be done. Look at the technology, marketing, purchasing, manufacturing, communications and new product planning with a review of the entire product portfolio and see which areas, which team members can perform the best and which can be done collectively as a team.

The team can work for Core Process Reengineering and each area bench marked for optimum results. Cross-functional and coordination teams would ensure that the changes are completed in the given time frame and with innovative ideas even before that and with quality.

The teams must develop their action plan with a time frame and assign responsibility to each member according to his ability and inclination. The reporting system and controls are put in position with benchmarks to highlight the best way of doing the tasks in the given time.

In the meanwhile as the CEO you must keep analyzing your own role as follows:

- Are you underemployed and underpaid - if yes, you must understand the reasons for it and try to correct your own working to improve your lot.
- Are you up to multitasking, prioritization of your tasks and then standing by your decisions?
- Have you set high personal, moral, ethical standards and working goals for yourself?
- What irritates you at your office and at home?
- Are you satisfied with your health condition?

> There were two competing CEOs; both faced three major problems at the same time. They both started praying to the Almighty for help. God heard their plea and came to help them, separately. He gave each three boons and asked them to tell him what they wanted. The first CEO said, "Dear Lord, please solve my three major problems" the God bestowed his kindness on him by granting him his wish.
>
> The other CEO was also given three boons. He prayed to the Lord, asking for a. his good health, b. clear mind and c. skills for solving his problems. Needless to add his wishes were granted too.

As a CEO you have to remain creative in your work to be effective in your operations. As you try to rejuvenate your organization you need to look at your own creativity as also of your team, which can be done as follows:

- Have a vivid imagination, a way of telling stories to the team to excite their thinking process.
- Think of all possible solutions and by the process of elimination get to the correct one; make comparison through charts, tables and diagrams. The charts etc. can help you in arriving at a possible solution. Can you merge two or more solutions for better impact? Use sensitivity analysis if the number of variables is more than two. The analysis would help in selecting the best alternative. Two top alternatives can be tried in small areas and the results from them can be seen for taking a final decision. Eliminating unnecessary areas and modifying parts of the solution for streamlining the same can refine it. The above is shown in the following diagram:

Organization needing revitalization
Tonics like new vision, mission, goals, high motivation energy levels
Reengineer the processes and consolidate them
Innovate for success
Build innovative teams
Purposive approach and attitude
Result orientation
Larger than life image of the organization and CEO's personal charisma
Place the organization back on its feet, revitalized
Arrange for continuous improvement with positive energy and spiritual help

The problem faced by the organization can be divided into small units and as you search with lateral thinking process, solutions for each small problem can be found. Even the most deviant or bizarre solutions should be analyzed. These solutions can be put through the brainstorming process and juggled by mixing them to find the right solution for the main problem. Break the problem and then combine to get the final answer. If necessary, redefine the problem to get new approach for the solutions, without leaving out the basic thought process involving organizational core competencies and resources available to you. Use innovative approach, intuitive thinking, try uncharted route to success. Be unconventional, play the devil's advocate if required, get the best and worst case scenarios in perspective, before you take the decision. Ask the following questions:

- What is good about it?
- What will be achieved by the approach?
- Is it even practical?
- Does it go with the other processes and solutions of the organization?
- How positive you are with the idea, is it too wild?

With non-stereotyped thinking and innovative approach solutions can be found for dramatically successful positive results.

Generate ideas by thinking big and then expand them. Get small ideas and make them smaller. Rearrange the design, pattern of ideas and look at the solutions emerging from them from different angles.

The next method could be to locate two near opposite ideas. This way you can obtain new and unconventional solutions. You coordinate the ideas, which may be common, but the coordination is from different angles. A new computer and a new order-processing machine, both help in improving the organizational efficiency, and you can buy only one of them. Understanding of these two unlikely competitors can give a vivid insight into the real problem. Such relationships are not easy to comprehend, but with experience you would know their relative importance and hence urgency.

Next, can you make the problem work for you? With the negatives, which cause the worry, there are positives, which can be considered opportunities. It is the old story of the glass being half empty or half full. Suppose you miss out on an appointment and you lament on the missed opportunity, if you think positive, may be you call the person, and take another appointment and in the meanwhile do something constructive, like finalizing the next marketing strategy, or complete the tender document due soon. A positive frame of mind helps you in getting most of the bad situation. It has been found that in several cases you can get even into better results from what one could call a mixed opportunity.

Converting raw ideas from your brainstorming sessions can be rewarding experience as you can take the ideas apart, leave the irrelevant areas and add the needed inputs to make complete solutions.

Solutions and their outcomes – A good imagination and innovative thinking can make you realize the outcome of different solutions. You look for what should be the end result and not what exists today. You have to find out who or which areas of operation will improve or benefit and who or which areas will be the loser, what resources are needed and who will provide the same, who will give the expertise, motivation and in what time frame. What will be the best parts of the outcome from different solutions?

At times you not only question the status quo; you go much beyond with unthinkable, immeasurable and unprecedented thought process. Stretch your mind to the vast possible alternatives, when you can have unplanned and unique solutions.

With value based focus you enlarge your problem-solving abilities, as you concretize your goals for the entire area of problems needed to be solved. You start looking for hidden alternatives and opportunities, from where you can laterally think towards the problem and its solution. The most suited alternative would be with your value system and competence. This lateral generation of solution is an important tool for decision-making.

The CEO needs to maintain his diary of daily achievements; these may be basic and important or even trivial. They describe the way you have managed your time on that particular day – the amount of time you have spent on fruitless pursuits and the success percentage you have achieved that day in your decision-making and judgment. How has been your communication with your team members, peers and seniors? It also tells you if you had any idle time. It moves you on the path of success in your chosen profession. You get to know your weak points.

MANAGING WEAK POINTS

As you become aware of your weak points, it is half the battle won. Next, you need to physically remove the weaknesses from your mind, body and soul like sweeping them clean with a broom. If a weakness remains over which you have no control, like a physical disability, raise the bar of your good points, which will overshadow your weak points. As you remove your weaknesses, and those of your teammates, you would next remove the organizational weaknesses and revitalize it in the process.

Getting down to business, as CEO you have to get your own and the team's act together, with new ideas, new vigour. The teams you lead must participate in the organizational decision-making process. They should together look for the plan, which will succeed. The large number of ideas generated through a brainstorming session, needs to be sifted through, bisected, combined to select the right idea, which will work. You can go through the structured brainstorming, where the problem is told beforehand and the participants come prepared with their ideas and solutions. The only danger is that in this case the spontaneity goes away from the ideas.

The team can also be asked to talk about what is wrong with the organization so that later on it can be corrected. Delphi and step ladder techniques can be used to get the right decisions once a number of alternatives have been found and you have a number of experts whom you can use for the purpose.

DELPHI TECHNIQUE

You send the alternative suggestions to say 10 experts individually. They are asked to rate them according to their order of merit. As the replies are received the common views are sent in 2 by 10 suggestions and sent again to the experts. When the experts do not agree with the rating, they give their reasons. These reasons are sent to experts. The last list is sent to experts and then they meet to thrash out the differences to come to a consensus.

STEP LADDER TECHNIQUE

The number of suggestions is sent to, say 8 experts. They are divided into two groups of 4 each. The views of one group are sent to the other and vice versa. Next, these groups are further divided into groups of 2, making 4 groups and the opinions are exchanged among the groups. Finally, all the 8 groups meet to come to a common conclusion.

ATTRIBUTE LISTING

The management lists the attributes of the product or the problem and then the experts are asked to give their views, which are computed to resolve the degree of divergence and come to a conclusion.

Can you imagine yourself as part of the solution, can you use metaphors from nature to define the problem (like it comes as a tornado), and symbolize it with an item away from the business world. You can then go into the reality of the problem and solve it in an objective way. (For facing the tornado, you need to build dams and stay indoors as it passes).

A leader should be ready with HANDS ON work for setting examples; he should have respect for all kinds of work, including the menial work. He must know how to delegate authority and responsibility, prioritization of his work and time management. Most leaders are engaged in firefighting operations, correcting the wrongs of the organization. Once the wrongs are known the correction job should also be delegated as the leader learns to become proactive, when he can institute preventive measures, before wrongs start appearing. There is no room for negative thoughts, and the leader must plan for super success. He should inspire his team with the imaging of super success and what it will do to the organization and the employees, the changes in their lifestyle, as these are also motivating factors, along with the praise of a job done well.

A leader need not just be a goody-goody guy, he must be able to correct deviations in actions and behaviour in his team. Team members perform better when there are deadlines; they work faster and better under stress. The leader has to create a sense of urgency in the team. The leader should know exactly how much stress is positive and beyond which point it becomes counterproductive as the team starts failing all the time and gets demotivated.

The leader should never decry his organization, his team and other stakeholders even in private; as such messages have a habit of reaching the concerned person. If you want the best talent, be the best leader as the best people seek the best to work for.

A leader should also be the most consummate and articulate public relations person for the organization. Each employee should be a good PR person in his own right and in his area of influence. People who want to buy products and services generally interact with organizations whose employees speak highly of the organization. The leader has to inculcate the PR spirit in his team for the purpose. The most important aspect of leadership is setting pace for team members, make them all PR people by being the best yourself.

As a leader you should never drum beat your own achievements as you brush your mistakes under the carpet. Give your team the credit they deserve. Reprimand them for bad work in private only and praise in full public view. The team will go a long way to your toughest asks and tasks happily as they would know you are not against them but only the wrong you had done.

As a leader you must ensure that the job of the team is a challenging one. People love challenges, because of the rewards, which they bring upon successful completion of the task. Please check out if the team has enough authority to enable them to perform their tasks. See that none of the team members has reached a plateau in his career, as he would become an unwilling member, who would create disturbance in the work of other members of the team.

Please ensure your team members have been selected with the following in mind:

- Qualification, experience, skills and job knowledge
- Keenness to learn new skills
- Readiness to train the next level of workers
- That they can delegate authority and keep control points
- Can motivate, be a role model and give counselling to the next level
- Can do career planning and place the right person for the job
- Should absorb organizational culture quickly

Leader's time management is a crucial asset for the organization and it must be carefully studied and planned. The level of concentration span of a leader shows the degree to which he has acquired the leadership qualities. He should be adept at multitasking, a perfectionist, and quick in taking correct decisions. His table should be uncluttered always.

Leaders find it extremely difficult to delegate authority, while responsibility they always do. (In most cases the leader never accepts the fact that the authority he has is never delegated, if it is delegated, mostly it is in name only.) One of the main reasons for organizational downfall is the lack of authority with the person who needs it for his day-to-day work. As a leader you must delegate authority and you will never go wrong if your employee selection has been correct. You must keep control, points to ensure that the employee does not go astray. You should finish your tasks in time before it finishes you.

It is important that you handle stress positively, without getting bogged down by it. The problems you face at the top level are mostly of serious nature. The ways to handle stress with ease are given below:

- Define the size of the problem, is it in pennies or is it in pounds. Delegate the pennies' problems to your team member who is capable of handling it.
- You should sleep over major problems if the time allows you to do that.
- Morning is the best time to handle problems when your mind is fresh and free.
- Dissect the problem in small parts, which are of managable proportions.
- Handle the easy part first and then go on to the more difficult parts of the problem. Get experts to give their opinion after you have explained the problem to them and they have understood the same.

- Never run away from a problem or wish that it will disappear on its own. Learn to control your emotions, keep your cool, plan and act to solve the problem.
- Stress, which is related to your job security, should be handled by clearing the air in cool comforts with your leader.

Stress can come from anxiety that you are underpaid, your promotion is due and some body else may get it, you are unable to cope up with your daily tasks and are accumulating a lot of pending work. You could be having a persecution complex where you feel that some persons in the organization are against you.

Do not fight ghosts; confront those involved politely to know the truth.

It is believed by many that the juniors work better under stress. If you subscribe to this theory, remember the time when you were in that position. If you apply the stress formula on them, you must know the exact elastic limits, beyond which, the employee will just bust his guts and fall mentally and physically sick.

If you are organized in a way that you work by the organizational rules and regulations, work for the organizational goals, remain honest to the core, consider your organization amongst the best and you will be less stressful.

While you should never live in the past, remembering your major achievements would help you in regaining faith in yourself and removing stress from your mind. You should have an ideal person in your life; you can look up to his life and achievements. Aim high with your feet firmly on the ground.

Stress also comes when someone senior to you is critical of your actions. You must look at the criticism objectively and correct the areas in which you have gone wrong. Take criticism in a positive manner and thank him for his views, which help you in making amends. Take is as a method of improving yourself.

Once you know yourself and like yourself, you start liking others too, trusting them, caring for them. You start getting the same liking, trust and care in return. You become committed to the growth of the organization and achieving its goals; besides you achieve your personal, physical, mental and spiritual goals. Your behaviour pattern in the organization, with your team and other stakeholders improvers, generating goodwill so important for you and your organization's good.

GOLDEN RULES FOR THE ORGANIZATION

You decide the plans, policies and strategies for achieving the goals and then something happens and you have no option but to alter the policies and plans. How often you have to change your action path depends on the following areas:

- Internal problems with men, machines and materials
- External business environment
- Competitive environment

This can be represented in the following manner:

A–is the difference between goals and actual achievements after the plans are revised and new action is taken.

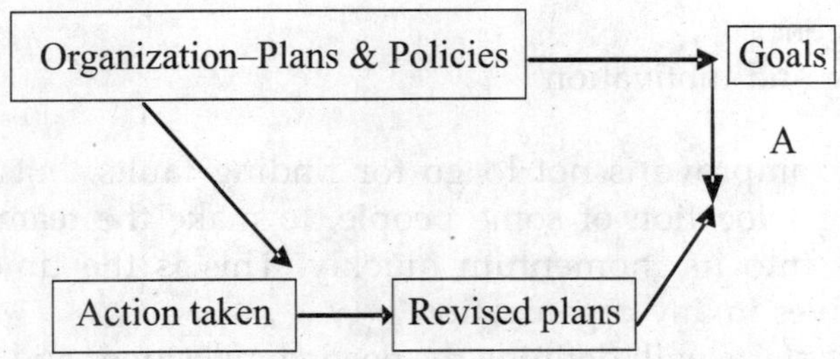

Control points, which tell you in time when the team starts going astray, is a practical solution to the problem. You have to decide whether your intervention with the erring team should be unobtrusive or obtrusive. Once you are ready for this challenge you are on the right road to success with least efforts.

What is the point of closing the gate after the horses have bolted?

The other saying goes like, "If everything is lost, including machinery, money, material, nothing is lost, as long as your team is with you. With the right set of people you can rebuild the entire organization in no time."

When you feel everything is lost you can get the organization back on its feet as follows:

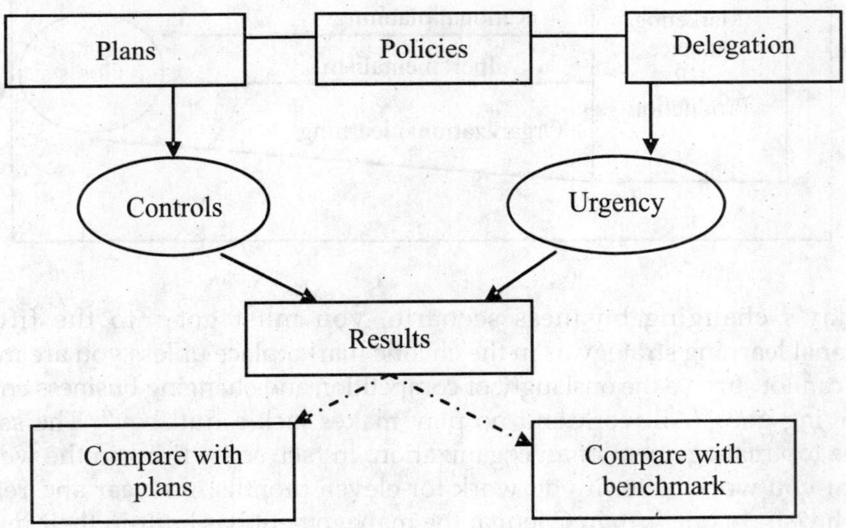

REDEFINE THE PLANS AND POLICIES

The CEO has to investigate into the causes of discrepancies between the goals and achievements, which can be done as follows:

- Shortage of resources
- Wrong allocation of resources
- Wrong selection of manpower
- No understanding of the goals by the teams

- No sense of urgency
- Lack of training and motivation

The best way to improve is not to go for finding faults, but changing the work paradigm, including relocation of some people, to make the team a solid monolithic wagon, which gets into its momentum quickly. This is the time-tested method of reversing the negatives in any organization.

Planning process starts with defining the needed milestones and the time the journey will take and can be represented on a bar chart or a PERT chart using the critical path method from where you can monitor the progress of the plan through deviations. As delays are part of the game, recovery from the time loss to catch up are the major parts of planning action.

An organization does not operate in vacuum as can be seen from the chart given below:

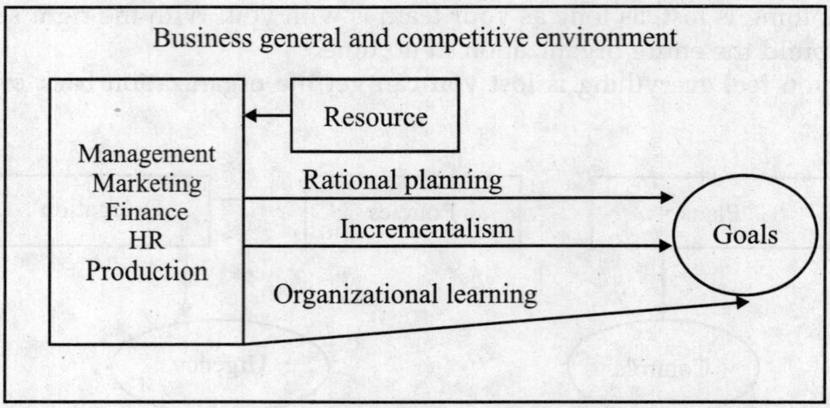

In today's changing business scenario, you must get into the fifth gear of organizational learning strategy as in the chaotic marketplace unless you are in a learning mode you cannot survive the onslaught of competition and changing business environment.

The saying goes "All work and no play makes Jack a dull boy". The same stands true for the top management of an organization. In fact, some firms in the west strongly believe that you work better if you work for eleven months in a year and relax for one month each year. In one firm in Chennai the management has built-in their multi-storied office building a club on the ground floor with a spa, a small swimming pool, and TV room. Any employee feeling tired can go there at any time, have a swim, get a massage, a sauna bath for fifteen minutes, with only two persons going at a time. The management found the efficiency level going up by 60 per cent in most employees since the club was started. In the evening and on holidays the employees use the club with their families to use the facilities for free. This has added another dimension to the club, as now the employees are not seeking jobs outside. Even if somebody thinks about a change the family vetoes it as it does not want to miss the facilities of the club, where they have kitty parties, games, cultural evenings and celebrate festivals together.

Success depends on the commitment to envision, mission, goals and belief in the usefulness of your action and the trust you have that the action will bring the desired results.

As you improve your power of concentration, your negative thoughts will leave you, any lacunae in action plan will be corrected immediately. When the haze of doubt clears, the vision brings the goals near, makes the path easy, reduces the time taken to complete a task and make the task enjoyable.

Effective action comes from effective planning, which depends on clarity of thoughts and the ability to decipher the right from wrong. Mental faculty at its peak helps in correcting any aberrations in action plans instantly.

Superior quality of action, timing of action can be affected by the changing environment of business. However, a positive mind will be conducive to positive action and results even in adverse environmental conditions. When the environment becomes friendly, actions bring results faster for you.

The next golden rule is to keep your personal goals in line with the organizational goals.

You must avoid all unproductive work. The following will help you in this task:

- Cleanse your mind, almost as if by using a broom on all thoughts.
- Place only positive thoughts in your mind, banning the entry of negative thoughts completely.

You can control your mind in the following manner:

- Do not live in your ivory tower away from your people and the scene of action (an army general never deserts his troops in the battlefield).
- Do not live in a fool's paradise by hallucinating yourself in to future successes.
- Instil positive thoughts in all those around you and in your team.
- Build effective team through training, motivation.
- Keep reminding everyone including yourself about the organization's vision, mission and goals.
- Prioritize your work.
- Bring a sense of urgency in your team.
- Tackle each issue with single-minded devotion.
- Keep measuring efforts and results against the goals.
- Bring harmony to the organization through you behaviour and action.

If you want your organization to grow, you have to be totally committed to your organizational vision, mission and goals and devoted to your work. You must develop good communication skills. Your team members want flexible working hours, friendly work ambience, supportive leader and career plan for them. See for yourself what are justifiable expectations and fulfil them.

When your and the team's action becomes interesting, the mind achieves satisfaction and the state of bliss and then can easily master the skills for positive result-oriented action.

PURPOSE OF THE ORGANIZATION

Purpose of the organization is to create economic value, which results from creating customer value. Planning of resource allocation should therefore be directed towards creating or adding customer value. Planning process should be carried out with total concentration, free mind and should be attempted when you are free of worries and problems. Matching resources with actions, arranging additional resources, if required, would become easy with an uncluttered mind. Right gut feelings, thoughts come naturally to you as routine and your plans are right for optimum results.

POSITIVE RESULTS PLAN

The planning process needs a strong commitment in the setting of organizational goals when you become unidirectional in your approach towards success. The commitment is passed onto your team members as it spreads through your high energy level. With the right plan and your goals in mind and keeping in view the business and competitive environment, you have a positive impact on the environment also. Your high level of confidence rubs onto your team members. With your power of concentration you achieve results with least action.

SKILLS OF COMMUNICATION

You should speak only when necessary. The golden rule is to listen to understand and not just to reply to be a good conversationalist. Listen with care, empathy and a helpful attitude. Your speech should be clear without any ambiguity, in simple words, pleasant, forceful and appropriate. You should say the things, which interest your listener and not just on an impulse.

TACKLING ORGANIZATIONAL PROBLEMS

Following are the normal technical problems faced by the organizations:

- Low productivity
- High wastage
- High capital cost
- Poor product quality
- Low level of technology

Besides, there are the following human problems:

- Union activities
- Poor training programmes
- Absenteeism
- Poor discipline
- Theft and sabotage

Following are the ways of handling technical problems:

Low productivity – For improving productivity, coordination and cooperation between workers, supervisors and managers is required. The best way is to have an open candid session with the concerned persons when the real problems will be unveiled. Is it poor machine alignment, backtracking of semi-finished goods where time is lost, lack of knowledge of running the equipment, or poor quality of the RM?

Placement of machinery on the shop floor should allow easy access to workers and the maintenance persons. The machinery may need fine-tuning to optimize productivity.

High wastage comes from lack of discipline. Knowledge of machine operations, workers' experience on the machines and quality of RM helps in lowering the wastage rate. Motivation, incentives for improved productivity and low wastage would help in achieving the desired levels of productivity and wastage.

High capital cost – Most people think you have to live with this problem. However, an imaginative management can find proper usage of unused machinery, i.e., the purpose for which they were bought in the first place. If that is not possible the machinery can be sold out, reducing your capital costs.

Quality problems can be best sorted out through the Quality Circle Programmes and TQM. The quality culture in an organization starts from the top and percolates down to the workers. If you do not show top quality in your own work, in the office and even socially, then be sure your employees will follow your example. Discipline, easy happy work ambience, praises when due and training will surely help in improving quality of work and resultantly the product quality.

Low level of technology could result in huge losses due to wastage, long production time and low quality. It is best to go for the latest proven technology.

HANDLING HUMAN PROBLEMS

In India, unions were very active in the 1960-1980 period. Since then unions have realized that today's enlightened management keeps the interest of worker's on top of the planning process. Unions are meant for collective bargaining with the management. They also take up the individual worker's grievances against the management. As CEO you have to realize that the workers are your assets. Today's terminology for workers is "human resource", which sums up the theory of their being the assets. (There is another school of thought that each worker is a living entity, with different emotions, likes and dislikes, needs and hence is it right to club them just under the term, resource or asset?). As CEO you should treat the unions as part of the business and give workers justice through the unions.

Lack of training programmes has been the bane of Indian business. It is time that enough importance is given to training and retraining for all levels of the organizational hierarchy. It would improve the workers efforts, coordination between workers and management and workers' motivation levels.

Absenteeism has been a crucial factor in low productivity. Usually, these are the reasons for high absenteeism:

- Lack of discipline
- Low ambition of workers

- No career plan for them
- Bad habits, drinking, gambling and drugs

Each worker is an individual and must be handled with care. Starting from the selection of workers, care should be taken to get the workers with the required skills, education and proper background research should be done. The workers should fit in the cultural ethos of the organization.

Discipline of the workers comes from the following areas:

- Right positioning of workers according to their suitability
- Training
- Motivation
- Team spirit

The CEO must ensure congenial working atmosphere even in testing times, as you cannot solve problems under tension. The workers will put their best efforts as per their capabilities in a positive manner. If the CEO pats the back of a worker in appreciation of his work, it should not mean that the worker could pat the CEO's back in return.

If you discover some worker indulging in theft or sabotage, you could lay, a trap if there is a doubt, and if found guilty, they should be thrown out of the organization and the police should be called to ensure that such things do not recur and the honest workers do not have to mingle with the dishonest ones. Bad company can spoil the best of workers in no time.

On a positive note the CEO's planning should include the following:

- Product and services needed by the customers
- New plant and machinery
- New infrastructure
- Manpower with various skills
- Additional resources as required

MOTIVATION FOR MANAGING CHANGE FOR THE EMPLOYEES

Employees need to be motivated to not only accept the changes being planned, but also actively participate in the change process. The employee should be praised and rewarded for his contribution in the Change Management. Increments, promotions, bigger responsibilities, authority are highly motivating factors. Employee's creativity and intellect should be harnessed for the organizational change.

It is a good idea to train the workers for the task (required to be done) during the change needed for the revitalization process. The training should be an interactive communication and not like a lecture. Practical exercises help them in understanding and assimilating the new methods and systems better. A feedback system would help you in knowing the levels of skills the workers have learnt, collectively as well as individually. No compromise should be made in the quality of training being imparted using training materials for reading, audiovisuals, case studies and group presentations. Feedback helps in improving the training programme further. The training needs are greatest when you are planning changes in machinery, methods, processes and systems in the organization.

The only way to revitalize your organization is to develop faith in yourself and in your team that you can achieve your goals. You want the organization to have the following:

- Become the best in its class
- Have best possible execution of the plans you make for the change
- Place your people first, and not just as a slogan
- Have top quality product and service
- The entire organization, everyone is geared for top level operations
- Have speedy informal communications
- Believe in organization's growth and profitability

The organization must believe that they have the best manpower, which works with excellence and is committed to its goals. It works well as a team with trust and cooperation. Such an organization will surely be revitalized in lesser time than you can ever imagine.

REMOVING ROAD BLOCKS

As the organizations need revitalization, you find they have over time downgraded their cultural ethos. Employees are interested only in their pay packets, holidays and perks and nothing else. To wake them up from their slumber, you need to give them a Culture Shock. This can be done by the following methods:

- Make changes in the organization's vision, mission and goals. This has to be done with great care, and with full confidence that the changes will help revitalize the organization.
- Change the working hours.
- Change or rotate the departmental heads.
- Create success stories and talk about the success stories of the past, of sister concerns, through formal and informal channels, including the grapevine. Encourage innovation through example, failure in innovation and experimentation should not be considered suicidal for the employee. However, failures, including your own should be discussed to avoid their recurrence. Discuss success also at length with the team to find out its causes so that it can be repeated.
- Put high energy levels and higher order values in your work so that others can get the right inspiration.
- Communicate with employees through newsletters in large organizations. Try to communicate through formal and informal meetings.
- Provide the required resources, reward good work and behaviour (even a pat on the back for good work can suffice most of the time)
- Arrange supportive infrastructure and back-up team
- Be a Change Leader, a Change Catalyst
- Train the team for the skills needed during and after the change has been accomplished.

You need the following to be creative:

- C-Competitive, communication skills, commitment to vision, mission and goals.
- R-Resolve to succeed, being a role model.
- E-Energy levels on the high and environment scanning.
- A-Accountability and administrative ability.
- T-Training plan for self and the employees.
- I-Innovative, initiative and intuition.
- V-Vision, visibility and accessibility.
- E-Enterprise for excellence, evaluation techniques.

In the era of 1970s and 80s, the product obsolescence was delayed in India as people did not want to throw out their old radio valve sets for transistors sets, cars, cameras, etc. and the only exceptions were the fashion garments and electronic products where new products were coming fast. Today, the rate of obsolescence in practically every product is fast and the PLC has reduced drastically. Therefore, creativity and innovation are a must for the organizations. This has brought out the R&D engineers, labs, researchers in the market, systems engineers, designers and innovators right in the front. Even the products, packages must look aesthetically appealing.

Organizations have to remain ahead of the competition, proactive in the market for which the following is required:

- Marketing research for understanding the consumer mindset from your designated market segment.
- The MR result should be discussed with the R&D team, production team, and design team to give them the full impact of what the customer wants.
- R&D and design engineers should speedily develop such a product, which can be commercially produced and should not remain a prototype model only.
- Once the product is ready it should be test marketed to get the feedback from the customers.
- The feedback should help in redesigning or modifying the product if required.
- Distribution channels, advertising, promotion and publicity should be launched along with sufficient availability of the product at the outlets.
- You should be able to optimize results even with possible resource crunches through innovations and cost management (read-cost cutting).

The CEOs will benefit from the following:

- Large operations decentralization.
- Culture of innovation and experimentation.
- Fast communication of the success stories in the firm.
- Failure in experimentation not suicidal.
- Create leaders from the employees through training and example.
- Encourage new ideas, have brainstorming sessions.
- Cut down delays, especially on resource allocations.
- Avoid interfering in the team's work unless someone is going astray.
- Reward success financially and even praise the deserving employees.

- Besides, plan for Just-in-Time (NO STOCK) zero-defect production (build quality and do not just test the product for quality). Let the suppliers become your long-term partners or associates, as you always keep a standby supplier from whom you may buy only 10 percent of your needs (this will help in case your main supplier has some problem like strikes).
- Introduce Quality Circle Movement; keep cross-functional multi-tasking teams for overlap in work in absence of any employee.
- Get the latest technology.

Problem Base A

For solving problems you must get to the actual size of the problems. Minor problems can be delegated to others and then you would be free to tackle the major ones. Next, take the problem apart into small pieces, look at these separately. Get the answers for each piece and then put them together as a complete answer for the entire problem. If you still get some alternatives, get to the best with the help of experts.

Problem Base B

Get the problem down to subtasks performed by the equipment under review. Look at the methods, procedures and see if they match with your objectives for the equipment. The close view like that of a scanner, would offer the relevant answers to the problem.

Experimentation for getting better methods and procedures would help in understanding the technology better. Even in the latest technology there may be areas, which you do not know and these could become problem areas. Experiments would make you fully conversant with the technology; they should however, be unobtrusive experiments, which do not harm the equipment.

If you analyze the work process, structure of the team and their skill, understand the subsystems, software and the equipment; you can achieve workable different solutions. Select the best and take immediate remedial action.

PLANNING FOR SOLUTION TO THE PROBLEM

Following is the route you can take for problem solving:

1. Look at the solutions found in similar situations before (if possible).
2. Plan to provide additional safeguards in sensitive areas.
3. Look for the result patterns of the machine in the past and see the deviations today. Is it a question of negligence only?
4. Look for a single idea as part of the solution and then offer the idea in a meeting of experts. Let the idea have a snowballing effect as you get a chain of ideas, for getting the total solution.
5. Matching subsystem solutions in different proportions and configurations could give the right solution.
6. Look for the most extraordinary, almost bizarre answer and work backwards changing it as you come close to the problem. For this kind of lateral thinking, you need to divest your mind from the entire usual, normal thought process.

If time permits, try and get different opinions on the problem; let the problem become isolated as stand-alone problem. Look at the known ideas and strange ideas and see if they could complement each other in formulating the answers. Think of the problems as an insider and also from a detached viewpoint.

The problem should be defined as precisely as possible, looking from all the eight dimensions (an eight sided solid figure type of problem), get viewpoints for each side and also for the total problem and then select the best option taking the help of experts.

IDEATION PROCESS

In order to get new ideas, plan a brainstorming session and list down all the ideas, imaginations, and hypotheses, both possible and even impossible ones. You should try to mix and match different ideas and get the best possible combination.

The interrelationships between ideas should be understood and debated with experts. The new ideas should be compared with the main problem statement and the possible relationship known as also the differences and the distinctive features of each relationship. Next, you firm up the final relationship and communicate the same to the team. The team should discuss the idea in light of their work and the team should have the final say, as it best knows the workable relative ideas.

The CEO has to demarcate responsibility in the following manner:

- Primary responsibility with the most critical issues.
- Secondary responsibility for critical issues.
- Tertiary responsibility for less critical issues.

TECHNOLOGY UPDATE

Technology Update is the buzzword in business today. You must understand why you need to update your technology. What are your objectives of getting the new technology and then work the sequence of getting the technology and timing of its assimilation in the organization. You should plan for the new infrastructure and trained manpower for the new technology. Your R&D engineers should be involved in the new technology assimilation process as it will help in faster understanding of the technology and further advancement on it as required.

At times, alternate technologies are available and you should select the one best suited to the organization. Experts should study each system and subsystem for the "State-of-the-Art" technology and its relevance to the organization and its products. Will it reduce manufacturing costs, time to make, ease of product usage, maintenance, packaging and transportation. Comparative statement on these lines will help you in getting the optimal technology.

ISOLATING VIRUS

Organizations need revitalization as over time they get debilitating factors, the VIRUSES, which sap the energy of the organization. The following two ways can be used to get rid the viruses.

1. Build strong walls of plans processes, procedures and the most important, the personnel, which overshadow the virus and define the virus infected part of the organization, which can then be cured.
2. Isolate the virus and then kill it.

The organization can be revitalized by one or both of these methods. Virus isolation is possible through intensive and extensive diagnostic programmes. Scan the Ps, Policy, Plans, Procedures, Processes and People minutely to locate the mischief-making virus. There are two types of errors made by people, errors of commission and errors of omission. Are the errors being committed on purpose, if yes to whose gain? Is someone trying to build his persona; fortune by cheating the firm? (Sales manager of one firm left it and when his CEO went to drop him to his house and invited himself in, the CEO found several tender documents lying on the dining table, as the manager used to bargain with competitive firms to disclose his quotations at a personal benefit. This is not an isolated case; there are plenty of such cases in several firms covering practically all the functional areas of firms). If there is no one with a personal motive then who is the laggard or, which of the Ps, Policy, Plans, Procedures, Processes and People are affecting the working of the organization? Place the Ps under scanner and look with patience before acknowledging the virus.

Please check if your vision, mission and goals are still valid and your Ps match with them. Are the employees motivated with the vision, mission and goals or do they suffer from a mental block, which acts as a virus in some of them? If there is one, isolate it, remove the people, before it spreads in the entire organization. The virus could be resource allocation plan, which could cause lopsided attention to some areas, resulting in frustration in the other areas, which could become the crucial virus for the organization.

If you find that the virus is deep-rooted and has infected the entire organization, go for Business Process Reengineering–the BPR. You need to throw the old process entirely, with the virus (even people infected by it). It will be a good time to get rid of the dead wood, the inveterate die-hard believers in the old system, as also the people on the edge – the corrupt but not proven as such.

Once you have debugged the organization it becomes sensitive to new viruses as it is in a state of change. You need to take extra precaution, reliable people to manage the changes you are planning for the organization. You must build extra support systems, cross-check timetables to ensure the organization remains virus free.

At times the virus is weak and operates only in some small area. It may be best to kill it then, making the required changes in that area only to improve the situation and to ensure that the virus is not in any position to spread its wings in the other parts of the organization. Instances have been found in some cases where the competitors have planted the virus, like a mole, or their agent in your organization. They have purchased your man, who tries to sabotage your organization and works as a spy for them. It is essential to get the antecedents of the people you hire checked thoroughly before you appoint them. (A liaison officer was caught changing the food sample of the firm with a bad one at the food laboratory of the government on the behest of a competitive firm.)

COST OF INEFFICIENCY

In several organizations, especially in the Public Sector Units, there has been a lack of accountability. Some such firms keep afloat by making marginal profits as they have low or no competition and can fix product prices as they deem fit, mostly high skimming prices. Others claim they spend a lot of money on being a good corporate citizen, by helping the society, by setting up schools, hospitals, and parks for the society's welfare. This may be true to an extent. Even in the private sector, TISCO and TELCO among others do a lot for the society. And yet, most PSUs have been showing losses. There can be a lot of excuses, justifications for the losses. However, a close look will reveal the following causes for the poor performance:

1. The result of Peter's Principle–far too many persons hired in the organization. When one person can do the job, three are hired. This adds to the expense as it adds to more idle gossip time for the employees resulting in less work totally.
2. Result of inefficiency–a number of persons recruited because of nepotism or political pressure. There are two types of employees, one who work hard and honestly and therefore are prone to make genuine errors. The others hardly work, have enough time for backbiting, highlighting the errors made by their working colleagues and reporting them to the leaders. They are perfect sycophants.
3. Result of some self-centred persons who are mired in greed. These people are smart, know their jobs well and they eagerly look for opportunities of making money on the side, at the organization's expense. As they are clever, they cover their footprints well and it is not easy to catch them.

CORRECTION STEPS

When you know the problem, it becomes easy to correct the situation. If you find extra persons, use voluntary resignation scheme or golden handshake. With one time extra expense you get rid of a lot of fat. With leaner organization, the other two problems would diminish to an extent. You have also to be vigilant to screen out the unwanted people from the organization. However, as several firms have gone beyond the redemption state, they would need to be either scrapped or you will have to use BPR-Business Process Reengineering, and TQM-Total Quality Management, together.

THE SUPER EMPLOYEE

In every organization there are some employees who have superior IQ and they get motivated quickly. They display leadership quality, are ready to take up challenging tasks, put extra effort for achievement of the organizational goals.

Many organizations now believe they can find the superior employee by a clandestine operation of closing on to these employees and honing their talents for higher-level responsibilities. The underhand process works well, because it does not disturb the other employees by hurting their egos. This becomes only a limited exercise of segregating the better ones from the rest.

The ever-increasing competition makes it imperative that organizations have the right persons in each slot. It is also important, because this way you can keep the talented employees in the organization. They will become loyal and committed to the organization. The chaotic competitive conditions prevailing the world over have created the new phenomenon of fast changing of jobs by the talented employees. The lure of money makes for the job-hopping employees. They want to know what the organization can give them extra to merit their retention in the organization.

The MBAs from IIMs look out for their batchmates to find out their levels and status and then only they evaluate their own position.

Employees, who are known with employee number tags, are like other equipment in the organization. The term "Human Resource", becomes a misnomer to an extent, each employee is an individual in his own right, with different aspirations and aims in life. The old loyalty factor has disappeared from both sides; the organizations do not think twice in sacking an employee and the employee is too ready to move on with even slight bit of inducement.

As CEO you have to decide if you want to focus on only a minor talented group or you want to develop others so far unsighted talents too. The best way is to organize training programmes as an ongoing process, which would help you in retaining the talent and build leaders within. For this purpose, the HR department must be given encouragement and support, so that the programme is successful. The programme in larger organizations must be flexible to cover employees from different disciplines. Career planning for the talented employees' besides spotting the talent, becomes the CEO's most important task. The employees must know the levels they can reach and in what approximate time frame, and only this factor can make them remain loyal to the organization.

KEY SUCCESS FACTORS

The following are the key success factors for the CEO in any organization:

1. You must be able to locate opportunity.
2. You must operate with a sense of urgency.
3. You must have detailed knowledge of what needs to be done.
4. You must seek outside assistance as required.

THE RISK FACTORS

The organization has limited liability, which creates a vicious sort of licence to take risks at the expense of their shareholders, this risk is an important part of the entrepreneurial function and his behaviour is reflected in it. It also provides opportunities for perpetration of fraud and abuse of power. As the CEO you must foster accountability at all levels.

Organizations, the world over are looking for becoming market leaders in their own fields. The new world message is for Free Trade and Competition. Market leadership comes from, besides other ways, through mergers and acquisitions. As the big become bigger, they are trying to attain the monopoly position, where they can rule the market, charge any price they like and hold the market at ransom by effectively shuttling competition and then use the feast and starvation policy of product placement in the market.

Some large corporations, conglomerates, who create wealth and do well for the planet, are influencing the world economy. They also have the financial muscle to cause problems for the smaller and less powered firms. They influence even small weak nations in this way. In the middle of last century foreign giants were exploiting India by passing on old technology and substandard products to Indian business. The main reason for this exploitation is the total vacuum of any policy in this regard. The famous WTO has failed to resolve the crisis situation as it has stayed firmly in the hands of the rich. And despite the great wealth they have created, few of them think of accepting even non-financial responsibility of the society in which they operate. The time has come when they will have to take care of the values and aspirations of the peoples of the world, otherwise even their financial muscle will disappear.

CORE COMPETENCIES

Collective and integrated learning can provide a competitive advantage. Coordination of different technologies, value additions from new technology, communication skills and information system are some of the core competencies of an organization. Besides management commitment covering internal and external customers are the important ingredients for the same. Organization's interactions and contact levels with the customers and suppliers form the core competencies.

Resource generation from core competencies can be used to develop new products.

As an example, Canon's core competency can be seen as given below:

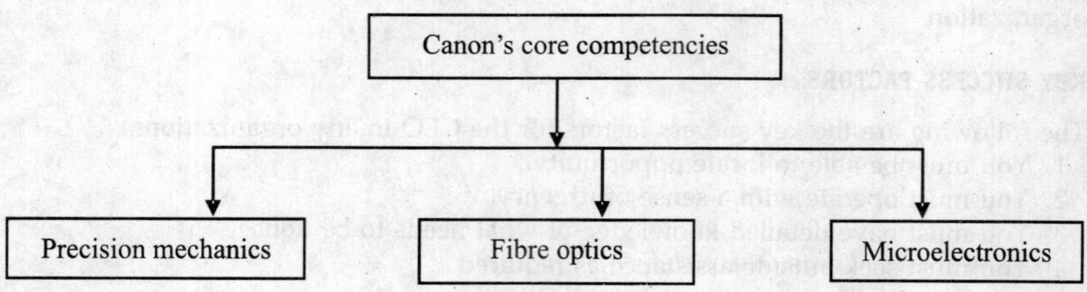

These core competencies have lead to a large number of products coming from the organization like, cameras, video cameras, bubble jet printer, fax, copiers, laser imagers and cell analyzers.

6

CHAPTER

CEO-Integrated Responsibility

AIMS AND OUTCOMES

The chapter deals with the most effective way of running a business house for its CEO who needs to have a holistic programme that is transparent and is motivating enough for the retail team. The students will learn the methods of planning for success, coping with stress and ensuring that the team members enjoy their tasks as they achieve the organizational goals.

The tasks before the retail CEO are multifarious, needing enormous amount of talent, patience and leadership qualities.

The buck stops with the CEO and unless you are ready to take all the blame for the failures you are not CEO material at all. The delegation of authority does not absolve you of the responsibility and blame. Therefore, it is essential to have a built-in system of controls as can be seen from the following example:

> One CEO got an outside auditor to go into the causes of huge production loss in his firm. A look at the inventory levels of raw materials confirmed that while some materials were in stock for six years' production, others were not enough even for two days. This lopsided inventory was caused by the purchase department's personal vested interest with some vendors. The CEO went round looking for new vendors and streamlined the purchase process. He now found that the raw material transportation was a problem. He purchased a few trucks to overcome this problem. The trucks needed maintenance and servicing for which the CEO started the firm's own workshop. The result was loss in profits. He had forgotten his main task, as the CEO was planning and motivating the team. If, however, the CEO had kept the control points in place he would not have faced the problem in the first instance.

Integrated responsibility does not mean the CEO doing everything. It means getting things done and keeping control points to ensure that nothing goes amiss.

The CEO usually worries if his teammates can perform the task given to them. This worry should not make him take up the task himself. The better way would be to equip the team with authority, information and tools for performing the task.

The CEO's job is to provide an ambience in the workplace conducive to achieving the goals and then let the team take action as they deem fit towards the achievement of the goal.

When the information is available to the members of the team, they gain the knowledge, and power to make the best use of the opportunity given to them. If the teams know the goals of the firm and they are committed to these goals they will definitely make a positive contribution to the firm's efforts in achieving its goals. Hence, the MIS should be changed to IS. The idea of Management Information System precludes some members of the team from getting the information and effectively takes away the tremendous enthusiasm it can generate in the team.

A TRULY PROFESSIONAL MANAGER/LEADER

Professional management has often been equated with non-family based management. However, it today's context, when you hear of so many scams in practically all types of organizations, private sector, public sector and the banking sector, the new definition of truly professional person should read as given below:

> **Truly Professional Manager**
>
> The person who keeps his personal interest subservient to the interest of the firm, his own goals in line with the firm's goals, would do everything possible to achieve the firm's goals without ever worrying about his personal goal. Once the firm's goals are achieved his own goals would automatically be achieved.

And this is the important task of the CEO to ensure that the team gets what is due in shortest possible time. The CEO can thus expect total loyalty from his team; this however requires integrated responsibility to be assumed by the CEO.

ONLY WAY TO SUCCESS

If you look at the history of the big firms of today, one thing common would be found and that is the founding fathers of these firms dreamt and thought BIG. Small minds can achieve small successes, never the big ones. For the CEO the success mantra goes as given below:

- Dream big
- Take integrated responsibility
- Give the credit of the success to the team
- Take the blame for any failure

In this manner, you will certainly gain the full confidence of your team, which would never disappoint you.

The best motivation comes when for mistakes the person is counselled with no third person present and for jobs done well, he is acclaimed in presence of the entire team and possibly the top management/the leaders. This looks like a common enough theory but in practice it is seldom found to be true. The CEOs are exhorted to try it out and they can see the positive results coming their way. Their entire team will willingly sacrifice a lot to meet the planned goals for their activities.

Organizational goals must enter and virtually live within the CEO, in their bones, brain cells and chambers of your heart. They thus become part of the organization like no one can. And then if they can enthuse their entire team to become like them, with their inspiration as a role model, the organization ceases to be mechanistic in its approach to changing business environment and becomes organic, which can mould and fine-tune itself to meet possible market eventualities and dynamics.

Organic organizations are always in the learning mode and can be called "Learning Organizations". They are forever scanning the business environment.

CEOs need to check out if theirs is a mechanistic organization or organic, a learning one.

Organizational goals should become the only truth and imbibing these will elevate the CEO as a speedy achiever, fearless in the corporate world.

Imagine if your entire team becomes like this (having imbibed the organizational goals fully) then it surely comes out as an invincible team. And this leads the CEO into other problem areas as given below:

1. Smugness for becoming an achiever individually and as a team.
2. Target of competitive reaction.

Successful persons and successful teams never look back on their achievements and the accolades received by them. Success is transient and to retain it you have to remain actively focused on achieving repeated success.

CEO needs to cultivate the culture of focusing on the organizational goal and the best way to do it is through becoming the role model for the team members. This way he can motivate them for achieving the goals and will still have time for his primary task as the CEO, that of planning the future course of the firm. CEOs need to keep their own tasks always on the front of their work agenda.

The Beaten Track of Plans, Policies and Procedures

Most of the business leaders tend to consider the firm's plans, policies and procedures as sacrosanct, like religious rituals. Organic organization members plan their strategies, taking the present and future situations and the business environment in view. The following affect the business results and should be constantly monitored:

- Business areas' demography
- Sociocultural environment
- Political environment

- Legal environment
- Technology trends
- Global business environment as it affects the business with numerous international players making inroads into the country.

In India, there is continuous migration of people from rural to urban areas, changing the demographic pattern. Do the retail CEOs see business opportunity in such migrations?

Social changes like increase in women workforce, festivals, political and religious environment have major impact on business. Political will is required for unshackling the business from governmental control. There are legal issues of patents, environment, piracy and intellectual property rights, technology updates, impact of information superhighways resulting in a large mass of available information changing the business scene for most businesses. Globalized markets too give opportunities to several firms.

TEAM BUILDING

Team members must be judged with a transparent yardstick. This would create the right atmosphere for team building, removing distractions, jealousy and ego hassles. Thus, the CEO would be able to build team cohesion. The problem comes in the form yardsticks for various disciplines like marketing, purchasing, human resource management, finance and merchandising areas. Suppose the sales manager gets five points for exceeding the sales target by one per cent, how much cost reduction the purchase manager needs to show to get the same five points. In the same manner how much efficiency the finance manager needs to achieve for the same points. It is possible to do multi-scaling in such circumstances and yet unless the employees of each discipline agree to the assessment plan, there would be heart burns not conducive to the achievement of goals. The CEO should ask the computer programmer to develop software taking the various parameters of each area for measuring the results of a variety of disciplines, which should satisfy the concerned persons.

The question arises, "Is there a respite for the CEO in the present scenario of business? The answer, which emerges today, is a big NO. And yet, the hysteria generated by the seers predicting doom is not justified at all. After all the entrepreneur starts business with an eye on the possible risks, which can be not only minimized but removed by taking proper care and timely proactive actions.

Today's successful CEO should not be wrapped up in the organizational or competitive mire. Remaining a little aloof they can perform their tasks on a positive note and successfully.

Long-term Planning with Short-term Goals

The CEO should draw up the list of available resources, the physical, mental or intellectual and spiritual. There is NO TIME to lose!

"I will do it now, today only"

Most persons tend to procrastinate, "I will do it tomorrow", but that tomorrow never comes.

The qualities needed for a CEO are given below:

1. Austerity – to show the value of money to the team.
2. Assimilation of organizational vision, mission, goals and objectives.
3. Ability for self-analysis.
4. Achievement orientation as a self-starter needing no coaxing to perform.

These qualities will help the CEO in generating extra energy required for the main task as CEO - that of planning.

Combining austerity with selfless service makes you the role model for your team. Assimilation of vision, mission, and goals will keep the organization on the right track. The goals may change according to the changing business environment and yet steering the organization with the vision and mission of the firm.

The quality of high self-esteem spurs you to reach higher levels of success and it should never be used for putting down others.

EGO HURTS

- Ego makes you believe that CEOs know everything needed to perform their job, blocking any further knowledge.
- Ego makes CEOs smug and satisfied and they can get distracted from their goals.

The CEOs need to try to avoid the uncharted route as they fear the extra toil, the pain may not be of any use. They may be going away from the new realities, the new horizons.

Ego is also a manifestation of low self-esteem, a brave front the CEOs try to put, as they fear losing all they possess and this could be the biggest road block in the path to progress.

What the CEO had sown yesterday they reap today and what they sow today they will reap tomorrow. The CEOs should never cloud the mind with past success stories as the euphoria they generate restricts the good they can do today for success of tomorrow.

The CEO's need to treat the team members without any discrimination, as it would cause fear among the team members, loss due to conflicts among the members. They should learn from the mistakes others make as also from their own mistakes.

PERSONAL BEHAVIOUR

The CEO's behaviour needs to be exemplary, a role model, goal driven and time prone. The importance of time as an asset is seldom realized in most firms.

The CEOs should maintain self-restrain and the best behaviour patterns. They should have clarity of mind, physical fitness, proper time management and should remove their weaknesses as given below:

1. Weaknesses of mind, body and senses

2. Tensions
3. Cluttered thoughts
4. Lacking the Extra Sensory Perception- the ESP.

IMPROVING ESP

We all have felt the availability of the sixth sense with which we get to know future events as they unfold themselves before us. This intuition is god given. You can develop your sixth sense or ESP in the following manner:

- You need ESP in crises times when you have to make split second decisions.
- Your past experiences form part of your ESP faculty.
- The present situation adds to your insight as you try to locate a similar experience of the past, match it with the present situation and then use the success formula of the past experience.
- Have belief in yourself that you can and will solve the problem.
- You should have faith in the Almighty who will surely help you in taking correct decision. Even for a non-believer, if he can do tight rope walking of being good and doing good to others he will get help from some superior source, like his guru.
- Think positive.
- If you remain alert even in unfavourable environment, uncongenial atmosphere, hostile competition can be overcome and these would not lead you to defeat. Efforts would, in fact take you to progress. For remaining on the cutting edge of activity, you should avoid undesirable company, people with negative ideas, indulging in idle gossip, people full of greed, backbiters, hypocrites, flatterers, liars, double-dealers and selfish. These are not your friends but your enemies.

Several persons remain on faultfinding mission. They either justify their acts or shift blame from themselves and if probed, plan for retaliation. The retail CEO needs to be on guard against such people.

Emotions are inevitable for human beings and the CEO must have a control on them as anger, hatred, sorrow and even happiness sap the energy. Even when they discourage team members and other stakeholders, they are wasting their energy.

Ideally, the CEO should remain modest, down-to-earth, never bragging as PRIDE always has a fall! Take success and failure in their stride; analyze to repeat success formula and drop the failed ones. This way they can acquire only a good healthy self-image.

Remain creative by doing something new and creative. Creativity has the power to keep the CEO organized in the face of environmental changes as they remain with their values and orderliness.

Unfolding Success through Environment Scan

The CEOs need to expand their horizon through the practice of analysis of business environment, the demographic, social, cultural, technological, political, legal, economic and global and competitive environment. You as the CEO should focus on broad issues, leaving aside trivial problems; this is possible through continuous search for the truth, the truth as it affects your organization, the truth of business environment.

You should develop flexibility in your mindset to enable you to take different approaches at the same time using your multi-tasking skills.

Can a MBBS Doctor refuse to treat a patient with pain in the abdomen, "Oh? I left the chapter on abdomen as I could pass the examination without studying it as well."

Can a CEO take this Approach?

CEO needs to be creative and dynamic with ever expanding vision and horizon.

> Suppose you plan a trip from Delhi to Lucknow by car. You will perhaps get your car serviced, fill the petrol tank, pack your bags and set the alarm for an early morning departure. As you move towards Moradabad everything goes on well. Reaching Moradabad you find that instead of the usual road, which you had traversed several times earlier, there is a sea, with no bridge.
>
> As CEO, you will encounter many such situations in real life and it would take a lot of ingenuity on your part to come out of the situation with flying colours.
>
> You could possibly take a detour via Kanpur or come back to Delhi and take a flight from there. Many options and many hurdles like loss of time & money would face you. You need to learn the art of taking spot decisions in such eventualities.

For getting your organization in the right mindset you have to make it a Learning Organization, which is always in a learning mode.

Learning Organizations alter themselves to suit the environment, while the mechanistic ones surrender to the vagaries of environment. (Your car, which works well in plains, would need special tyres, lubricants, which do not solidify, if you want to use it in snow territory).

FILTER PROCESS

ESP, the extra sensory perception, which you can develop and it is also based on your experiences and study of changing environment, helps you in filtering the unnecessary, the trifling from the important, which would otherwise occupy your time.

Filter can be built with the ABC Analysis of all the problems and related tasks as follows:

- Most important-take care of these immediately.
- Less important-delegate to the appropriate person.
- Least important-put in on the backburner-these could come back later, in one of the other categories.

Without the filters, the information, the data problems and related tasks create chaos, the white noise, which has become the waterloo of many CEOs.

The CEO surrounds himself with sycophants; false pride, ego, and self-righteousness, ignorance about environment and this clutter crushes him. They create a mirage in the path of progress, giving false hopes of success when none exist. You believe, with a sense of past success, that your ideas and attitudes towards business environment are correct. Past success can kill today's progress.

Why several prize winning managers fail as CEOs?

They fail because they live in the past successes. You must come out of the inhibiting "success syndrome" totally.

You should instead, prepare for broadening your vision with continuous environment scan–including your business opportunities. You must become proactive to the needs of your customers.

For this purpose, you need support of your team and therefore come out of "I and me" concept and converge into "we and our" thinking. Success always comes in teamwork.

With me and mine the citadel we built around us stops the positive waves from emanating from us. The team starts lacking information and the responsibility of even minor tasks shifts from the team to the CEO, in slow yet sure manner. With low level of positive drive and high level of responsibility the team is bound to fail.

A big office chamber, sleek speed limos, penthouses, the status symbols are enough to bloat the head with ego and this ego could be instrumental in bringing the downfall of the person wearing it and it may become instrumental in lowering the status taking the status symbols away in the process.

As CEO you should use the status and its symbols with a sense of detachment as these perks you get with heavy onerous responsibilities. More you cost to the company, more vulnerable you become – more expendable.

Outward success, top positions and perks should not become barriers to further progress. Therefore, right ideas and an attitude of detachment would help in maintaining a balance so important in life. The real development of a person comes from mentally relinquishing typical concepts of lifestyles (while you keep using the same) and not becoming their slave.

The top position of the CEO is a lonely place, full of anxiety and fear of loss of the position. One simple way to get out of the fear is to have as attitude change by becoming "others inclusive" – the WE and not ME.

POSITIVE ATTITUDE

If you change the way you do things, look at situations which lead to retrograde steps, bring you back to lower rungs of the organizations, maybe even ousts you out of it. Hit and miss attempts do not result in positivism. Fragmentation of ideas, stands take you farther from purposive process of broad, all encompassing personality, leaving confusion and ego only.

You can develop new broad identity, which would surmount all possible hurdles coming your way like the distractions, ego biases and narrow mindsets. Your expanded personality becomes larger than life covering the entire organization, touching your stakeholders as well. You start caring for the stakeholders, animate and inanimate, as you look after your own body. Then only you emerge as a true corporate successful CEO.

As the CEO, you cannot just say that any harm to one of your stakeholders does not affect you and that you can get away from your responsibility. The concept of self has to become all pervading to include both internal and external customers and environments. As your awareness increases you are ready to take on larger concerns and the responsibilities of the stakeholders. Your discernment of the stakeholders becomes acute and you realize that each one is equally important for the survival of your organization, which includes you as well. The importance of each must be felt deeply. The river carrying pollutants from your factory is killing the fish and other river creatures, besides it ceases to be a pleasant sight for your picnics. The nearby park, the beach needs to be clean for you and your family, besides other citizens of the world–your foreign guests. You need to come close to the reality and become part of the larger organism functioning in totality to keep the planet in the same shape as you got it for the next generation. Considering the importance of stakeholder value, a separate chapter has been dedicated in the book. In conclusion, the CEO must plan for common good for the entire range of stakeholders as WE and not ME and MINE for perfect harmony and balance in the organizational life. At that point the insecurities of ME and MINE will disappear.

CEO'S RESPONSIBILITIES

CEO needs to accept integrated responsibility of the organization. Yet you have to sub-delegate authority and responsibility to your team members for achieving the goals. You should dissociate yourself from the day-to-day working of the team and avoid having fixed images as how your team members should be operating. Watch only their results; motivate them to achieve the goals in the given time frame.

The CEO needs to locate the wise persons as you look for multiple opinions. Opinions or suggestions can be both positive and negative.

Negative suggestions dishearten and the learning process stops, while positive suggestions encourage and add to your wisdom. You should use your wisdom and the right suggestions and then priorities them for action. You must listen to the negatives also, the devil's advocate, which give the worst-case scenarios. These will help you in avoiding the pitfalls on your way to success.

With practice your inner sense and strengths increase and you can decipher the good from the bad, right from wrong and you can place these in your experience data bank. These experiences go into your subconscious as well, which help you in developing ESP.

IT IS IMPORTANT TO HAVE THE RIGHT KIND OF ADVISORS SO THAT YOU GET POSITIVE CHOICES FOR DECISION-MAKING.

It is hopeless to find answers from people who are either confused, opinionated or have ulterior motives. On the other hand, you must listen to the people with contrary views to get the best option in your decision-making process.

The most important thing is that the CEO must have firm belief and faith in the organizational goals and can pick up the right suggestions with greater accuracy.

The CEO's own vision, mission and goals for the organization must be made on a long-term basis as they provide the driving force to the members of the organization. If any change is considered necessary, it must be undertaken with a great deal of enquiry, expertise and care. These are the bedrock on which the organization's foundation is built. To make the vision, mission and goal really work for the organization these must be totally assimilated by the CEO as well as by his entire team. The CEO cannot forget the basic purpose for which the organization was built in the first instance.

When a CEO joins a new organization these commitments of the new firm's vision, mission and goals would tend to occupy his psyche in an evolutionary manner. Yet the CEO must make the transition into his new job and assimilation of its ideals of vision, mission and goals in a revolutionary manner by having the right mindset.

The CEO needs to cover the entire new organization quickly and then expand his horizon by looking at what is happening in the world as related to the new organization, in other organizations, different disciplines as these will complete his mind's canvas with the right tools for success.

CEO'S AUTOSUGGESTIONS

CEO keeps getting ideas of his own. These can be divided into two parts as given below:

1. Own thoughts
2. Subliminal state

Negative autosuggestions, like, am I good enough? should be removed from the mind immediately. Positive autosuggestions like, yes I can do it, should be nurtured and kept in the subconscious mind. In the cruel and harsh world, even temporary negative thoughts can derail the entire planning process.

Positive thoughts should be made part of self-analysis, attitude and mindset. Personal goals, which are not in line with organizational goals, should be eschewed. You become a truly professional manager when you submerge your goals with the organizational goals.

When the CEO focuses his mind on the organizational goals without wavering and with full concentration, the CEO gets the power to achieve the goals.

The CEO should know what should be the level of his involvement in the operations and when he should detach himself to concentrate on his basic tasks of planning and motivation.

Changing Roles – The CEO needs to have control points built in the process, to enable him to redefine team members' roles and the emphasis and priority on the assigned tasks in case he finds that things are going astray.

New Organization – Suppose you leave your organization and join a new one, you must find out the following about the new organization:

- Its vision, mission and goals
- Its promoters
- Its business environment

After that you get to know your team and their motivations and you would have made a good beginning.

If you find that you are not satisfied with your role then you are in the wrong organization. However, minor frustrations, ego hassles, interpersonal differences are present in all organizations and must be cleverly tackled. Being a team member, before becoming the team leader helps, as one person cannot produce results or run the organization by himself.

You should keep looking for signs of discontent among your team and if any of your decisions or actions is causing the same and becoming obstacles in progress. However, unpleasant decisions and changes you make, should not let you forget about them. You cannot be escaping from realities of business.

A good CEO can transform a badly run organization into a successful one and a bad CEO can spoil a good one.

TEAM PERFORMANCE

While building teams if you find that the members of the team are not combining well, be transparent, get to know the real problem, help the odd man to change or move him to a different location, unless he is a misfit in the organization. In that case he must be eased out of it immediately; may be he can make his career some place else.

The atmosphere at work should be easy and light even while trying to meet deadlines. You will find it easy to do so. Relationships with team members should be based on mutual trust, without ego hassles with impeccable behaviour from your side. You should concentrate on performing your duties well as a role model; at times even what others, your team members want you to do to prove a point, do not hesitate and do not feel exploited as well.

Authority as the CEO is important, but you should never become confused about it. Authority is full of responsibility for guiding the organization on the right path of continued success. You may have to face unhappiness, sufferings as you perform your duties due to your own or your teammates wrong deeds.

Authority and responsibility are intertwined. You must use the same yardstick for giving rewards and punishments to maintain perfect interpersonal relationships. You should learn the value of forgiving and forgetting.

WALKING THE CRITICAL PATH OF EXCELLENCE

There is no short cut to success in life!

The CEO faces many challenges, a few of them are given below:

- Profit squeeze due to competitive price cuts.
- New brands in the market with better brand equity.
- Competitive innovations, differentiations.
- Lower competitive cost due to larger scale in production.

You should start looking at the following areas in your organization:

- Team utilization–do you have too little or far too many persons?
- Over investment in production equipment for meeting the demand coming every ten years only for fifteen days or so.
- Over investment in finished goods inventory, raw material inventory to meet the seasonal demands.
- Low level of technology as compared to competition; are you a victim of technology ego?
- Are your safety norms correct and your factory obeys the pollution control norms?
- Is your team motivated enough?

TEAM MANAGEMENT

How do you view your team members, some are doing just enough to keep them in their jobs, others are going the extra mile to prove a point as they are motivated and do not take the easy way out, some need constant supervision, are kick start persons as others are self-starters!

The organization has a vision given by its promoters. Vision is an all-encompassing view, the higher order goal of doing good to the society or at least a section of the society. It does not speak of factories, pricing or profits. From the vision the organization derives its mission statement, which is vision in operation. Goals are more concrete than mission and they fix the perimeter in which the organization would operate. These three strategic intents vision, mission and goals prepare the organization for its role in the marketplace and hence, they must be understood and assimilated by all the members of the organization. To be of effect, the vision should be clearly stated in unambiguous language and the team members must become committed to the vision.

Vision can be defined as a unidirectional power arrow thrown by the leaders to provide the organization its proper direction. Vision provides inspiration to people to perform to the best of their ability. It starts by inspiring the leader in the first instance.

If the vision of yesterday is not inspiring any more, the leader should plan to change it. At times when the old leader goes and a new one joins, such changes become necessary. Vision should be team driver and not just for the CEO. The new vision statement should not just be a mix and match of various organizations' advertising slogans, if they do not provide the organization inspiration and direction of doing good to the society. A good think tank is essential for this purpose, which takes into account the very basis for which the organization stands for in the society and in the market.

Once the new vision is adopted it must be communicated actively through meetings and seminars throughout the organization to become the foundation of teams' activities. The team must be totally committed to the vision statement.

Vision statements consist of the following:

- Core values of the organization.
- Direction of efforts for the society's good.
- Plans for value additions for the stakeholder.

Mission statement should provide the organization the following:
- Organizational culture, what it will do and what it will not do.
- Individual behaviour pattern for the team members.
- Strategic outlines on achieving success in the desired areas.
- Plan and shape of the organizational future.

Goals are mission statement operationalized as given below:
- It talks of contrary things and tries to balance them like quality and price.
- It talks of financial and non-financial areas of business.
- It plans coordinated approach for different functional areas.
- It talks of human resources needed for the organization.

You are investing in finance, HR, technology and time, which must reflect in your goals as how you are going to optimize their usage.

Vision, mission and goals must be compatible with each other and must create enthusiasm and zeal among the team members and logically provide a healthy future for the organization.

The CEO's authority should be used only to motivate as a role model, communicate and mediate in areas of dispute among members.

Dispute resolution - The dispute may arise when two members are asking for the same resource. For example, if there are rupees ten crore for advertising and R&D and both the advertising manager and R&D manager asks for seven crore each. You as CEO cannot please either one of them. What should be your decision? Following are suggested for dealing with the situation:
- Increase the cake to fourteen crore and give each what he wants.
- Look into details of the demand. Mostly people tend to inflate their demand in the hope of getting what they really want. Be transparent in your negotiations with both the managers in this problem and you can still give what they actually want from your ten crores.

TECHNOLOGY MISSION

Technology mission gives the organization state-of-the-art technology of manufacturing, state-of-the-art products, and defines reduced production time, lower wastage, lower production costs bringing cost advantage to the organization. Technology mission, at times, asks you of letting go of obsolete products. These products could have been time tested golden eggs for the organization in the past and letting them go is a tough task as at times managerial ego is involved with such products. However, with the right mission statement the CEO can drop, modify or differentiate such products for the organizational good.

ORGANIZATIONAL IMAGE-BRAND EQUITY

Organizational image comes from consistent quality, innovative products, high standard of service and organizational communication skills of advertising, sales promotion and public relations. This image reaches the organization's stakeholders, which includes suppliers, customers and financiers.

In the past few decades several firms have come in existence with a bang and sooner than can be imagined, have gone without even a whimper. Therefore, the organizational power must be part of its impact in the marketplace and it would depend on the commitment of the entire range of its stakeholders to the organization's vision, mission and goals, their belief in its future.

Goals – In the middle of the twentieth century some firms had their goals and plans for up to seven years. Today, with hyper changing markets, maximum plans can be made for a year–a rolling plan, which is reviewed quarterly and altered as per the new realities of the market. The goals in the past were organization oriented–what should be the production plan, product mix, today they should be customer segment and service oriented.

The organizations must adapt to the new market realities and while focusing on customer segment and services, become proactive with organizational structure. (look outside first, then look inwards and correct your structure to suit the outside world). Besides the functional, divisional or SBU structures, new structures like matrix, networking, delaminated matrix and virtual structures have been evolved to fulfil specific needs of organizations and the CEO can pick the best option for his organization.

ORGANIZATIONAL AND PERSONAL GOALS

Each individual member of the organization would have his personal goals as they have different needs. Can the organization meet their needs? If not, it is the CEO's task of saying no politely. CEO should be people's manager to activate and motivate the team to get committed to organizational goals. He should not breathe down their necks. Most CEOs will deny doing it and are still guilty of doing just that.

THE REAL WORLD

In the corporate real world, problems are daily occurrences and as CEO you have cope up with them. You may need to change the structure or some process or a policy in the organization. There is always an inertia or reluctance to change in most teammates because of the following reasons:

- Satisfaction with existing state.
- Fear of the unknown.
- Extra work required to be done.
- Several changes to be done at once.
- Reduction in status may occur.

It is better to pre-empt the opposition to the change and prepare for countering the same. The following steps may be taken in this connection:

- Discuss the plan in detail with the concerned persons.
- Be ready with answers to their queries.

- Make the team realize that the change would not only be good for the organization but for them also.
- Place the benefits they will derive from the change.
- Give the benefits the organization will derive, which in turn would become benefits for them.
- Give specific tasks with time schedules and result expected to each member separately.
- Believe in transparency in change, planning and execution.

Wide dissemination of information would make the opinion of the majority of team members favourable to change. The execution of change should become manageable with a stretch. Any positive dissent should be looked into, as it helps in problem identification and its resolution. Wide ranging results and benefits of the change should be discussed and the best decisions taken.

However, putting the organization in a learning mode can make major change in the mindsets. The members of the organization have to continuously keep learning the changes taking place in the business environment and the strengths and weaknesses of the organization and its competitors. Once the learning process perpetuates the inertia to change it can be altered to become change catalyst. The energy to change comes from the common vision, mission and goals and the dreams of the future, which brook no interference.

VALUE SYSTEM DEFINES THE ORGANIZATION

It has been proven beyond even an iota of doubt that only organizations with high value system survive in the long run. You have to look at the Harshad Mehtas and Desais to get the full impact of the value system. Yes, any fly by night operator can just force his way in the marketplace and make his packet before either being caught or running away from the scene. The number of persons being prosecuted in scams leaves little to think about the graciousness of the value-based business. It comes from the following areas:

- Consistent vision, mission and goals intrinsically and with each other.
- Coordinated efforts using brain trust of the team members.
- Simple unambiguous statements as to why you do and what you do.
- As values are a reflection of the entire organization, they should be positive and inspiring.
- Use of clichés should be totally avoided in value statements.
- Value statement should be broad enough to cover the entire gamut of firm's activities.
- Employee's contribution and acceptance will help in getting their commitment to the vision and values of the firm.

Vision and value statements can be translated into making of the public image of the organization, if these are advertised properly, in the right media.

ORGANIZATIONAL LIFE CYCLE

Organizations, like people are born, they grow, mature and then they decline. The following gives an idea of how it happens:

- Start up – promoters have a vision and the will to fulfil their vision and arrange resources for the same. Thus, the organization comes to being.
- Early growth – is when competition is low, low level of product acceptance, power is with the channel members, profit starts to grow.
- Late growth – there is an increase in competition, power with the channel reduces as product acceptance increases, increase in profitability because of increase in sales.
- Maturity – heavy competition, price cutting, cost cutting and downsizing of operation takes place.
- Decline – the competition is severe, price wars start, some players including the lead players quit the field. Those who carefully analyze their product portfolio can manage to come on top at this stage also.

You should be watchful for the sudden spurt in competitive activities, new competition with big brands, increase in product flow, lowering of prices, new channels, and heavy advertisements. E-commerce, telemarketing, internet marketing is low cost channels and can provide penetration into certain market segments, which is into computers. You should proactively pursue these at appropriate times.

A major factor of the well-being of an organization are its people. The Defence Services know how to keep its people motivated and alert all the time through continuous training programmes. This way, the servicemen keep their skills honed and they learn new skills as well. Defence Services always have contingency plans, which take care of even the most unexpected events.

Firms in for quick money come and go. The moment they find the going getting tough they quit.

As the salary and wage bill keeps on increasing, the only way to reduce cost is to remove certain activities, which does not bring you near to your goal. These can be either totally discarded or farmed out. The American shoemakers have become only brand sellers as they get all their shoes made in the Far East, with low cost labour. Jobs, tasks need to be pruned.

Cut costs till it hurts but not hinders your activities is a good motto to follow!

DOWNSIZING OPERATIONS

While downsizing the organization take care of the following:

- Cut down people and activities which are unfructuous across the functional areas.
- Give the golden handshake to departing employees to keep their goodwill.
- Try giving some outsourced work to the outgoing employees.
- Retrain the balance employees with you, give them better job profiles, money, authority and responsibility.

- Outsource tasks, which can be given away without jeopardizing the organization in any way. The firm you use for outsourcing should preferably have similar cultural values as yours.

You must understand that in organizations there can be power groupings, control and authority of individuals, may be like the departmental heads, who believe they are autonomous in their area of operations. Such power brokers can take the organization almost on ransom. While you are pruning the organization, it may be the best time to give these people a golden handshake. Just because these people are specialists in their area they consider themselves as indispensable to the organization.

The specialists are giving way to generalists, as multitasking is becoming the way of life in most firms. The way to success is getting the best available brains, train them, delegate authority and responsibility, keep control points and see that they are committed to the organization's vision, mission and goals.

7

CHAPTER

The Leadership Qualities

The leaders must be confident, self-starting, no-nonsense accepting individuals with the following traits of character:

- Far-sightedness towards organization's future
- Sense of justice and fair play
- Large heart

In 2004, the leader should be planning for the organization, as it would exist in 2014. He should use the same yardstick for his entire team, while giving rewards and punishments. He should not be bothered about minor problems, which can be taken care of by any of his teammates to whom the task has been delegated.

TASKS FOR THE LEADER

- Following are the basic tasks of the leaders:
    - Finalize the organizational vision, mission and goals through participatory process and get the team's commitment for the same.
    - Build the team by promoting, hiring and motivating them through being a role model and adopting a reward system. Even a kind word can be highly motivating.
    - Build the infrastructure, ambience and organizational culture using the values you hold sacred.

"Leaders Ask" from the teams is given below:

- Timely execution of plans resulting in achievement of goals.

- Keeping organization's image high.
- Enjoying the work while remaining disciplined.

- Team Task is given below:
- Implement the plan in the best possible way that they can imagine.
- Keep the vision, mission and goals in mind and remain committed to them.
- Keep the firm's image high as its PR person.
- Stay within the organizational culture ambit.

- "Team Ask" is given below:
- Recognition of the teams and individual effort.
- Money benefits and extra perks.
- Non-monetary benefits like change in position or praise.
- Career planning.

Physical and mental work is divided as follows:

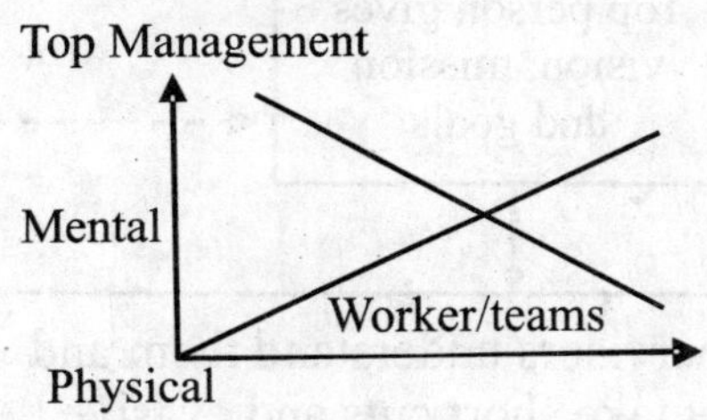

The top management builds the vision and mission statements in conjunction with the teams and with efforts the teams produce result.

Progress and results have to be measured in terms of speed. Therefore, the team must work with speed but not with haste.

Two important ingredients needed for success are motivation and energy. You can put these on a chart or a two-dimensional meter and keep modifying the chart as you reach upper echelons of energy and motivation levels. You can do it for your team members and ask them to do so themselves as self-analysis. The meter is given below:

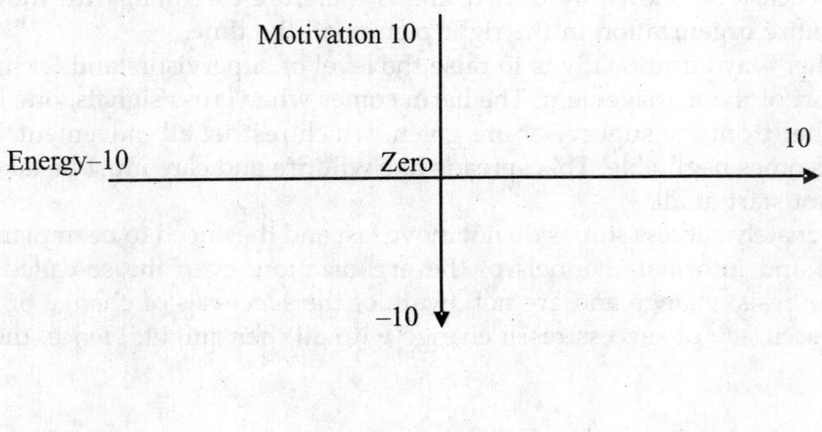

Place yourself on the meter and you will judge where you are going wrong. You have to be truthful to yourself to get the full value of the meter. You can feel happy as you move in the top right quadrant. With high level of motivation and energy you can produce quality work, which in turn will give you quality products and services, as these things, motivation and energy will certainly rub on to your team members as they look at you for inspiration. Pick up the person least energized and motivated as the worst-case scenario and see him pick up his life and with it his work when he starts taking pride in his work and converts the worst case in to the best performer. By effort you too can make your weakest point your strongest!

This way you will be performing the important task of building leaders in the organization. The fear that the next good person could take your position is totally unfounded became if you can produce leaders, you are almost indispensable to the organization. You are then on your way up.

The plan in actual situation works as follows:

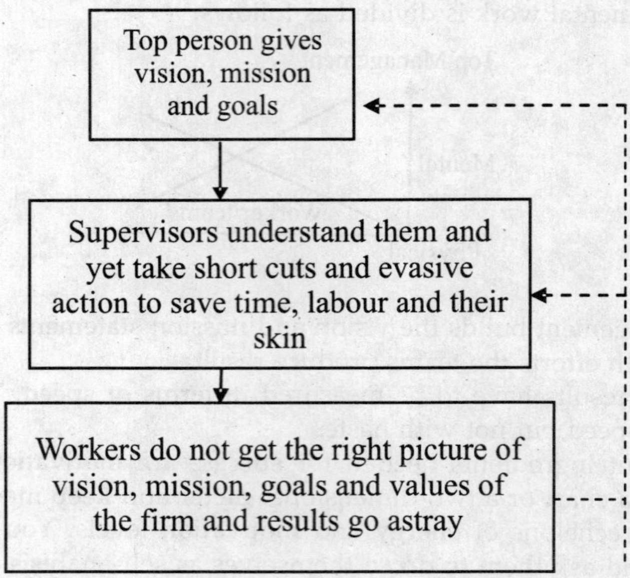

A feedback loop shown by dotted line is therefore essential, with transparency to keep the entire organization in the right picture all the time.

The other way additionally is to raise the level of supervisors and let them feel like they are part of the management. The harm comes when cross signals, one from the top and the other from the supervisor are given, which restrict all movement. Work either stops or becomes negligible. This spreads like wildfire and care must be taken that such fire does not start at all.

Unfortunately success stories do not move fast and they need to be implanted through the formal and informal channels of the organization, even the so-called grapewine. People who resist change and are not aware of the successes of change or who do not believe in accuracy of success resist change with all their might. Hence, the CEO must not lose any opportunity of putting across the success stories. The organization's coffee sessions, lunch meetings are also appropriate media for dissemination of the stories.

Suppose you find it difficult to repeat the success of the last five years, you must start by scanning the business and competitive environment and see the reasons for yourself. It means you have not been proactive in your planning process and may be the execution of the plans is not satisfactory.

Systems Perform, Not People?

It is said that once a system is in place, it will give you the result, even when the people manning the system move out of the system and new people take over. At times the system itself becomes obsolete with new technology entering the field, and new and faster information inputs. At this point, the CEO must plan to change the system. The new system must take the following into account:

- New business environment
- New technology available to you
- New competition

You cannot send the right signal to your team using the old system unless you train them about the use and the benefits of the new system. The team members will otherwise retain their view that the new system is difficult to use and is time-consuming.

> In a firm the statistical clerk was maintaining five different types of records in five registers, which were always incomplete. In consideration of the data needed for taking management decisions, the CEO pruned the registers of unnecessary data and placed the important data in just one register. Even then the result was the same, as the one register remained incomplete. On being asked the reason, the reply was that now there are six registers to maintain instead of five. Habits do not die easily, unless you remove the first five registers by sending them to the shredder.

With new systems and methods of working the systems, the CEO must define the new basis of team members' work norms, assessment yardsticks, as with new tools, speed and accuracy levels must change. If they do not, then it is time to review the new systems.

The CEO must encourage the employees to question the status quo in the firm and let them experiment with new ideas and systems; that is the essence of TQM.

TQM must lead to TCM–the Total Customer Management.

TOTAL CUSTOMER MANAGEMENT

The following steps will help you in TCM:

- Building relationships with the customers.
- Letting the customer decide the type of product he wants.
- Letting the R&D hone the product nearest to what the customer wants, if the requirement cannot be met in full due to technical reasons.

- Letting the customer know the reasons in detail in a language understood by him, why there is a gap between what he wants and what is available. However, make sure your competitor is not ready with the exact product required.
- Letting the customer decide the type of service he wants, where and when.
- Letting your employees know the products and service needs of the customers and providing training to them if they are not yet equipped with the training.
- Involving the customers in the firm through newsletters, upgrading options (airlines, hotels and now even maruti cars are offering this option by giving incentives to the buyers of their products the second time around.)

ORGANIZATIONAL HIERARCHY PROBLEMS

As you motivate your team, there is danger when you find some supervisors getting too big for their boots, with the newfound authority. The smugness or rebellion could be caused by any of the following causes:

- Feeling of being overworked.
  Feeling of being underpaid.
  Fear of loss of job or loss of authority and position.
- Delaying work with the excuse that the collective decisions of the supervisors are responsible for the delays.
  Lack of information needed to perform their tasks.

These discrepancies can be removed by proper communication and transparency in dealing with the supervisors. Each supervisor must know how the others are performing. Your control points must be in place to enable you to detect even a minor aberration in work in real time as it is happening.

MARKET VACUUM

You create the market through advertising and promotion and building relationships and then if you cannot provide the goods and related services the vacuum gets created and this is the ideal situation for the competition to enter the market and snatch a big chunk of business from you.

Are you looking out for such vacuums created by your competitors?

IS PROFIT A BAD WORD?

Firms agree that the primary reason for their existence is to derive profits from the business. Profits are needed for looking after your stakeholders and for growth. It is profiteering, extracting every single penny from the market possible, which is bad.

Profit comes from the difference between the cost to market the product and the price to the customer.

Price is derived from the cost to manufacture, cost of building the brand image, competition, channel strengths and the market segment you want to cater.

To increase profits you can take the following steps:

- Increase the price – Possible in monopoly or near monopoly situations (the danger lurks as high profits invariably invite new competition). Improve brand equity, acquire market leadership through heavy advertising and promotion.
- Reduce cost by going into economic scales of production, where the fixed costs remain the same and as you increase the production, per unit fixed cost becomes less. You can also reduce the costs through experience curve, where the variable cost gets reduced as your workers gets experienced in production techniques and the wastage gets reduced as also the production time

The extra profit, if the market forces know it, would cause a heavy onrush of competitors, with equal, or better products and maybe, better brand images, larger production bases.

The last five years have seen Indian firms going for downsizing/right sizing approach to cut costs. They should go for the following:

- Cost reduction.
- Improving brand equity.
- Improving distribution for cost reduction.
- Outsourcing non-value adding tasks if it would reduce costs (firms have outsourced finance and accounting operations, manufacture of sub-assemblies, R&D recruiting and dispatch of letters functions).
- Getting foreign participation to improve brand equity.

Most CEOs believe that the cost can be reduced in manufacturing for maximum impact. The following gives on an average the distribution of selling price rupee in percentage.

Selling price	100
Material cost	10
Labour cost	12
Transport cost of raw material upto and within the factory and finished goods movement from factory to retailers	30
Cost of money	18
Overheads	14
Profit margin	16

The cost may vary from unit to unit, but the point to be noted is that there can be savings beyond the cost of manufacturing.

You must have periodic exercise of understanding your product portfolio. Are you carrying some extra baggage as products, are some products ego products for you, "no, whatever happens I will never let go of this product. After all I started with it and made tons of money with it. Soon it should be back with profits" such delusions only harm your organization.

ASSIGNMENT OF WORK TO EMPLOYEES

Several times, if you do not take care, some employee says, "this is not my work". The quantity of work gets reduced due to experience curve and yet you have too many people. Should you plan wages and salaries on the basis of quality and quantity of work output for each worker? This may be the remedy in relatively smaller firms where number of persons is less.

You should plan flexi-tasks, multiple jobs and train the workers accordingly.

All the jobs must be important and the employees must know their importance. This, along with freedom to work to produce timely results in his domain, with status in the society, can be the best motivating factors.

Built-in feedback system is essential for the employees' own sake as then you can correct them from going astray and losing the job at the right time.

The take-home money for the employees should be based on their performance and the results obtained through their efforts.

Most firms look after their line staff people and neglect the staff or support persons. These are at times the brain trusts of the firm, like the Finance Manager and the HR Manager as they research to look after the nerve centre needs of manpower, finance, and technology.

How Good Are You?

Can you make others what you are not? A sluggard, deceitful person can hardly train his team for optimum results. You should have the following qualities in you:

- A good self-image
- Confidence
- True values

Change these if you find them on the low side. Do small tasks well, with dexterity, with good intentions and see these areas improve in you.

Get others to give their view about you secretly from your employees and peers and seniors as well.

To imprint the values and the organization's vision, mission and goals in your team, you must use your skills to have them committed to these values, through good communication. You must understand the team well, relationships, intra and inter team and with you must remain pleasant even in trying circumstances.

Job Satisfaction

In the first half of the twentieth century, the workers were asked to leave their mind at home and bring only their hands and feet, "just do the task as per instructions, do not try to use your brains".

Today, with better-qualified and trained workers with multi-tasking skills, the CEO needs to provide them with the job content to include tasks meant for their special skills, sprinkled with some routine tasks, which need to be performed. This would keep the workers motivated and yet the mundane tasks would be taken care of.

MEASURING WORK LEVELS

Workers should be told about the yardsticks you are going to use in measuring their work. Setting up yardsticks in multifunctional areas like marketing, finance, production, purchasing and HR is never an easy task. CEO would do well in setting the standards of each discipline with the active help of the employees, who can suggest the grading system of the yardstick for each discipline in consonance with each other. You can use the Step Ladder Technique for this purpose.

STEP LADDER TECHNIQUE

In a nutshell, the technique suggests that you ask a few persons, say six for the comments on the solution to the problem, separately. Once you get their replies, make a gist of the replies and then give each person opinion of others. Next, let them sit together in two groups of three and sort out their differences in opinion. Lastly get all six of them to sit together and arrive at a consensus, which then becomes the yardstick.

THINK GOOD FEEL GOOD

A good CEO knows his strengths and weaknesses and builds on his strengths, thus virtually making the weaknesses come to a naught. Next you have to get the right people, train them in their jobs well, motivate them through example, praise and benefits, keep control points and steer them to success without meddling in their day-to-day operations. Classroom training, computer-based learning, workshops, seminars and on-the-job training are useful methods of imparting training and you can choose the best option, one or multiple training schedules.

Refresher Courses, once in two years for your employees would give them the THINK GOOD FEEL GOOD life.

R&D Training–Some R&D engineers feel that since they are creating some new product, they are superior people. You do need to have a particular type of mindset to be a good R&D engineer. However, most R&D is actually development and engineering, with no basic research being conducted. The R&D engineers must fall in line with the rest of the firm, take note of market needs based on marketing research conducted by the firm, regarding product needs, product specifications, competitive products and then give a realistic time table for bringing out the product in the market, with stretch.

No R&D engineer should be allowed to get away by saying, "I cannot tell you how long the product development will take." The industrial development process should be time bound with the engineers accountable for delays.

FAILURE–THE BEST TEACHER

Failure can teach you because of the following reasons:

- It makes you realize the value of success.
- Makes you realize the reasons for the failure so that you can avoid their recurrence.
- Takes away any smugness on your part and makes you alert.

Your failure can make your competitor smug and if you plan well, you can bounce back, taking them unawares.

However, for overcoming failures and converting them into success you need the following:

- Your own positive thoughts
- Positivity of your teammates
- Positive ambience

There is a lot of literature, especially Dr. Norman Vincent Peale, which tells you of how positive attitudes help and work for you even if every thing else is against you. With Positive Approach you can and you will achieve success!

Success is a relative term. How white is whitest. Ask some detergent seller. However, with positive intentions, thoughts and action, you can achieve absolute success, there can never be a doubt about it.

Absolute success unlike nirvana keeps changing, as you keep raising the bar.

FOCUS ON YOURSELF

Management gurus tell you to focus on the customers, build relationships (CRM, Customer Relationship Management has become a subject in several MBA programmes and several books are available on the subject), giving customer not just satisfaction, but delight from the use of your product. You are in your own right a customer too as you buy a lot of products. Do you know your own mind, why do you buy a product, a particular brand? Have you analyzed yourself, do you really know yourself as a buyer? Once you do, you can start unveiling the mystery that is your customer.

If you need a simple, easy solution to your problems, how do you expect your customer to accept complex solutions?

Would a single sales-cum-technical person take care of your complex problem to satisfy you or would you accept a multi-specialty team to work for you? Multitasking or specialty tasking, you have to, as a seller provide the right answers (as if you are the customer.) Would you expect a phone call as sales call or personal visit? Can you even think of shutting down your physical sales office ensuring that your sales team is always spending time with your customers? You can then hope to get reports on purchase orders collected at a much faster pace. Reports on orders lost to competitors are also a must to understand consumer behaviour and competitive strategies.

Thank God for the competitors, it is they who keep you on your toes throughout the year.

From the era of paperless office, with the help of computers, internet, LAN, WAN, which maintain your files and records and lets you retrieve them from anywhere in the world, you can move to officeless office. Cellphones, fax machines are adding to the technological help and in the process you can decongest the roads, allowing better mobility to your customers. Your team spending more time in the field would work wonders – you get more information on consumer behaviour, his likes and dislikes, besides information on competition. Keep your sales team trim, lean and on the GO!

You should think each day in the evening, "did I get any fresh information about the competition?" If you haven't, then you may be missing out on some vital area of business.

You have to ensure that you keep rocking the boat, just do not drown it. Rocking the boat means keep your team on their toes always. Get off their backs, just keep motivating them and seeing the results roll by.

Management is a practical workframe with scientific process and artistic temperament, both embedded in it. Science covers the practical side of the market, the truth of supply and demand and investigations into unknown areas like market demand, and buyer behaviour. Marketing research and study of buyer behaviour form the scientific basis of management. And yet, the variables, which exist for altering the hypotheses, are several. The best decisions, therefore, are based on scientific enquiry and what the collective thinking process evolves.

The management art translates the scientific hypotheses into workable plan. You cannot define the salesman's greeting with a smile in scientific terms. The art of handling people, the customers, suppliers, employees, managers and other stakeholders comes from innate sense of justice, fair play and concern for these people.

As the competition grows from being negligible in the first half of the twentieth century to hyper competition of today, the need for scientific enquiry is acutely felt. Several research models have emerged that systematically analyze the market needs, consumer behaviour and these help in projecting the market dynamics and the role of your firm in the market. Once the framework of the market becomes clear, you start the action plan for achieving your goals. In this area, you need to have the heart of an artist who knows how to touch the heart of others, including your employees, without offending them in any way, in a pleasant manner, letting the employees imagine that it was their own method of action.

Market is what drives you and that is one fact you can never forget. Products, their selling techniques, quality programmes, promotions can be considered manifestations of the market. The market is the most essential part of your business as it contains your customers.

The question therefore arises, as to how you can bring all the manifestations of the market, like the product price promotion and placement (all the 4 Ps), adding value to them for the customers. First of all, you have to understand the market, its absolute truth, its ever changing view.

How can you differentiate between yourself, your product and your customers? The linkages between the three are both concrete on transactional level and abstract on subtler, the competitive level, where the urge to buy mindset is the important criterion to your products. Human needs are changing all the time, according to the lifestyles of people. The market reflects these changes. There are times when the products are so well entrenched in the market that no new innovative product can have any impact on it. The only constant for you should be your need to stay in the market making profits. Your customer is experiencing the usefulness of your product through body, mind's thinking process and the collective usage of the product in the surroundings help.

Market is therefore the ultimate reality of your business life and it is present in different layers and strata of the society. Market needs differ as you delve deep into the layer and therefore marketplace needs to take these differences into account. Market is not there for you. You should be there for the market.

SPHERE OF INFLUENCE

Your firm operates in a geographic area, in a subtler mind plane of the customer. You operate from your hub, where you can exert maximum influence in the market. As the distance increases from your hub, your influence keeps diminishing. The hub is the limiting factor, which get created based on your strengths and resources. The influence of the hub gets reduced as you move sideways in the market. Constructive changes in the hub to make it a bit mobile would help in such conditions.

The market constitutes the customers, yes, but there are several other factors, which affect your business as given below:

- Availability of money – the money supply position in the market (it depends on the government regulations like the CRR, New Public Issues)
- The lending and borrowing interest rates
- The reliability of available infrastructure
- The strengths of the channel members
- Migrating population
- Social/religious ethos
- Cultural impact
- Technology updates
- Strength of the brand
- Commitment to ecology and pollution control

Besides you should be aware of sensitivity of market change, consumer preferences. It is important to have the ability to hire the right people, get finance at the right time and interest rate. Besides you should be aware of competitive forces.

Most CEOs get bogged down by these forces and areas and lose their intrinsic courage due to lack of belief in the firm and in themselves. The only reality the CEO needs to know is that firms may come and go, the market stays, grows, shrinks and yet survives for old and even new products. Market in that sense is eternal. Products change, firms come and go and yet the market remains. And this single truth is the lifeline, the essential constituent and reason for the firm's existence. You are there, because the markets and customers exist. To remain in the market, it is essential for the CEO to keep finetuning the firm to be useful to the market, in a manner the market expects and not in the way the CEO wants.

PLANNING PROCESS

To achieve the fine-tuning of the firm with the market, you have to plan. You must ask yourself, WHAT IS THE BASIS OF THE PLANNING PROCESS? Where should the planning begin? You would say, "with the firm's strengths and weaknesses. May be you are right and yet you could be wrong. Planning process, must be extrovert in nature, looking outside, what is the need, where is it, and how much is it? After this investigation the CEO can look inwards - can you provide for the market needs? Do you need to modify any of your Ps, product, price, promotion and placement? If you make the market the basis of your planning process, market action and service to the customers, you will surely succeed.

You have to be efficient and effective.

Become efficient by doing things rightly and effective by doing the right things.

The quantum of success depends on competitive strengths, as they would be doing the same things that you are planning to do. Success would lie in the quality of your plan and action and the level of your sincerity and honesty.

An alert CEO would be able to understand the competitive plans, their processes by being continuously in touch with the market.

Time spent on getting competitive information is most usefully spent and the CEO must keep aside a weekly hour for this task if not more.

The CEO should obtain the information from his team, especially the sales team, channel members, trade bodies and even competitive salesperson, check and cross-check it with the help of stakeholders, suppliers and financiers.

MARKET PERMANENT AND NOT CHANGING

The customers who form the market are always there, they exist and yet their needs, demands are changing. The change depends on the following:

- New products in the market
- New technology
- Stopping of some activity
- Education and income level changes

The CEO needs to understand the market dynamics and this is possible through research. Both consumer and industrial market reflect the change in buyers' attitude and the CEO must know it like the back of his hand.

CONSUMER MARKET

The demand in the consumer market is a direct demand - it can be extrapolated to a high degree of accuracy by marketing research, by computing the number of buyers in your market segment, the percentage of buyers, competitive brands and their strategies. It also depends on money supply in the market, the hire-purchase options and the interest rates. Purchase of durables is increasing with leasing options and credit buying, with bank loans. You have to exploit this to your advantage. Regarding FMCGs you need to upgrade the product, packaging for the elite market segment, while you may bring an economy pack for the middle-class segment. (Gillette keeps upgrading its products by bringing new products once in six months).

THE ART OF MANAGEMENT

The art signifies grace and skills in performing to please others, in your case the customers. Everyone, including you has the natural ability, the latent potential in this area. You only have to hone your techniques. Consider your product as a service, which you provide to your customers. Each product has an element of service with it as each service has some product with it. It is the service, which makes the difference in today's world of hyper competition and ME TOO products. People provide service down the line in any organization including yours. These service providers have no say in the running of the organization. Don't you think that this situation needs drastic and dramatic change? Can you expect superior service from inferior untrained uncouth people? The answer lies in getting the right workers, training them and then empowering them to take spot decisions while dealing with your customers. Every one has noticed the rude behaviour of guy on the petrol station who fills air in the tyres. Do you want that to happen in your area of operations? The frontline people need the best training, a little pampering at times, a lot of encouragement and motivation to enable them to perform to the required level of service with courtesy and élan in a happy frame of mind. Going an extra mile in the service is what brings in customer loyalty.

The art of management helps you in giving full value to your stakeholders including customers, suppliers, financiers and employees. In this art you learn to value the role of each of your stakeholders, understand their requirements and how best you can fulfil them. You learn to create value rather than divide it. You strengthen your will power through conviction in your firm's bright future. You enrich yourself through the stakeholder's activity streams flowing through the organization and its positive impact, due to your own goodwill, towards the stakeholders. With this power, your intellect becomes strong and profound, sharp and focused and fully alert. Alertness is a prerequisite when you are scanning your business general and competitive environments. You remain proactive towards achievement of your goals.

Business world is ever changing and there is no room for stable thinking and non-changing plans. With your developed psyche, clarity of mind, you can question the status quo in your firm and with concentration, you can develop your plans of action for achieving your goals. You get the uncanny ability to gauge the future, almost like a seer.

Your full work potential will bring several aspects of life fulfilment, like happy family, life in the society and as a citizen of your great nation. Using the full potential helps you in understanding the real issues, the size of problems and competitive plans. Your success does not depend on the business environment. It depends on how you use your full potential and that of your team members in the existing environment. The CEO who fails tends to justify his failure by blaming the business environment and the competition. While you succeed it is the result of your own actions and hence the failure should also be coming out of your own actions. Surely you want to succeed always, so why delay-start working on using your full potential now, today!

Science says every action has an equal and opposite reaction. Art tells that with the help of your full potential you can overcome action against you of any size, dimension or ferocity, because you are surely more alive than anyone can be.

If you like your team members, they will like you. If you respect your seniors and even competitors, they will respect you. If you care for your stakeholders, they will care for you. If you give proper service to your customers they will give you their loyalty. It is a wonderful chain of relationships, which you nurture and it nurtures itself in an ever-expanding spiral form bringing you success you may never have even dreamt about. If you retaliate a wrong done to you the chain is broken. Such negative actions also build a chain, which drowns you in a bottomless ocean of misery. Hence, keep the following with you always:

- A large heart, not bothered by minor problems.
- A sense of justice and fair play.
- Commitment to your vision, mission and goals.
- Work towards using your full potential with the help of relaxation techniques, meditation.

You can thus remove any impure thoughts of retaliation or neglecting your stakeholders, ignoring your competitors easily and it is wise to do it for your ultimate good, which is also the good of your firm, your society and your country.

POSITIVE THOUGHTS FOR SUCCESS

It is the CEO who can make or break an organization. CEO if he leads from the front, can ensure continued success. However, if he takes a back seat and tries remote control leadership management, then in no time one or more of his teammates can cause serious damage to the organization.

CEO's role demands multitasking, he is a planner, a motivator, a role model. At times, he is also a buyer, a seller, a project person seeking finance, a PR person and a coordinator with the trade bodies, the government. He divides his time performing his duties, wears several hats, but as a person he remains the same. Or does he?

Suppose the CEO is seeking finance for the organization's new project. He would get the finance requirements inflated in the hope that even after negotiations he will get what he really needs. Just imagine, if the CEO gets the full amount, what will he do with it? That is where wrong ideas get into the CEO's mind and he wants to derive personal benefit out of the situation, subtly at first and brazenly as he gets accomplices in his team for the purpose. The damage does not stop here. Once the CEO gets into this groove, he will adopt other methods for similar benefits, like interfering in the purchase deals for getting his cut, reducing production costs by lowering product quality, so that he can give bigger commissions to the channel members, ultimately to get his share. The list is almost endless. However, all these are going to be counterproductive, as when you do not get the right quality RM from your suppliers and do not have any control on the organization, you will lose sales due to bad quality of the product, get a bad name, lower brand equity and ultimately lose the job.

While doing several tasks, the CEO should remain the same sincere person in each one of his roles, duty bound and committed to the vision, mission and goals of the organization and his primary task of planning, motivating and being a role model. This way he will ensure that same upright way of functioning is kept in each area of activity. If anything goes amiss he can catch the problem in its infancy and put the organization back on track with his control points without fear or favour. No person can follow separate norms, yardsticks of work for different areas, for different people. Intrinsically, the CEO's honesty of purpose must coexist with transparency in action, in the entire range of activities. You should not take this as a lesson in morality, but practicality as results of good and bad come soon enough.

CREATIVE INTELLIGENCE

CEO's creative intelligence is what makes the organization grow, if it is canalized properly. If the CEO is going astray, he will find it impossible to correct the path taken by his teammates. Therefore, CEO's entire being, body, mind, soul should be in harmony with the organization's vision, mission and goals.

The market reacts to the individual actions of the CEO. For example, if you reduce product price you will gain larger market share at least temporarily, till competition catches up and follows suit. The result could affect your organization adversely in the long run. Hence, your task as the CEO is to ensure that the firm gets a large chunk of market share (Pepsi and Coke fight for even half per cent of market share and no one wants to give up even a fraction of that). Price reduction may not be the right tactic. The CEO has to look for other options like increase in brand equity, increase in geographic coverage, motivated sales team and channel members. The CEO's creativity comes into play in these areas of business. It is in these activities that your ideas and actions in getting your team's commitment in the vision, mission and goals can be most useful. Singularly you cannot achieve the goals, it has to be a team action.

The CEO is all the time influencing his team with his thought word and deed (*man*, *vachan* and *karm*). The team is also influenced by the surroundings, the physical environment. Therefore, it is a primary task of the CEO to provide a congenial ambience, supportive work culture and encouraging place for the team. In such a place the team members, on their free will, on their own steam, will perform and achieve the desired results.

As CEO you need to attract the best talent in your team. For this purpose, you have to exhibit qualities of peace, serenity and a level playing field where people work without fear of prejudice or favour to others. Personally your total personality must reflect the ideals you cherish, as this will have a rub off affect on those coming in contact with you. You are the sum total of the influence you can exert on your teammates in inspiring them, resolving their conflicts and problems and as a role model.

An inspired CEO influences his surroundings without any effort. His thoughts, words and actions create positive vibrations in the atmosphere. The quality of vibrations depends on the quality and the strength of action. The influence is a constant one and hence the CEO must never be caught off guard, indulging in some inane pointless activity, unless it is his leisure time, when the team should never be allowed to be near him. The main outcome of positive or negative influence is that the teammates would be producing and providing similar influences in the organization and this will have a snowballing effect. Positive influence will secure the future of the organization. The outer environment too gets influenced. Environment of business will become friendly to you and your organization. A negative influence will sap the energy of the CEO and the team and harm the organization, including other stakeholders. Therefore, the responsibility of fostering positive influence rests on the CEO. The benchmark of the CEO's action is the effective positive influence he can have on the organization.

The direct and practical way is to do good to all the people all the time, be fair to them with a sense of justice and fair play, have a large heart and a vision for the organization's future.

RESOLUTION OF CONFLICT

The CEO has to decide if the action required to correct a mistake should be strong or mild. A strong action will produce a strong effect and likewise a weak action will produce a weak effect. The CEO has to resolve the conflict between two team members and in such cases a strong action can set the conflict at rest forever. A strong action is needed but with a gentle touch, so that the affected team members know that the action is directed towards the conflict and not towards them. The strength of the action should depend on the following:

- How well you have analyzed the problem?
- How well you know the persons involved?
- How deep is your insight into the real cause of conflict?

Any action based on these facts will have a powerful and binding effect on the team members. The clearer your ideas, better for the team.

Planning needs proper understanding of the business environment coupled with efficient thought process for analyzing the situation. You need to develop the capacity of getting the right, creative, powerful and influencing thoughts, that can solve the problems by permeating into the problem area and the concerned people through your body language only, without the use of words. To gain power in your thoughts you need background knowledge and an analytical mind. You can develop immense capacity of the mind by practising Hath Yog, Raj Yog, Meditation and Pranayam.

POWERFUL SPEECH

Once the CEO has gained experience in getting powerful thoughts, you need to learn the art of articulating your thoughts through powerful speech. Speech should be powerful and yet correct in content, pleasantly given and useful to the listeners so that you gain their full attention. It is not necessary to shout at all! With anger the mind gets clogged and coherent thinking and speech becomes impossible. The mind should be free and coordinated with the speech faculty to be of useful effect. If the thoughts are weak you need more energy in gearing up to the situation for reinforcing weak arguments through speech, which is never effective enough.

You need to coordinate the following:

- Mind with thoughts
- Speech with mind
- Strong supportive nervous system with mind
- Ability to select the right words for the audience
- Ability to avoid emotional outbursts and impulses in your speech
- Control on your anger, as "those who anger you conquer you"

You must practice the skill of making a speech as if you have to deliver an address in many places within and outside your organization. The following areas need special attention in learning the art of public speaking:

- Have a positive attitude towards your audience.
- Prepare your speech and remember the points in the right order.
- Use conversational style, it is quite impressive most of the time.
- Change the decibel voice level to bring home a point.
- Speak from heart, it shows, and it is possible if you truly believe in what you are saying.
- Use the voice coming from your stomach and not just from your throat. You can learn to throw your voice to great distances, practice it or take the help of an expert.
- While speaking, look at some one sitting in the middle of the third row and everyone in the auditorium will think you are looking at him.
- Take care not to use bad words, abusive language as words spoken can never be withdrawn.
- The influence you create on your audience can never be withdrawn either.

You need to be truthful in your speech, pleasant and tactful. Unpleasant words would negate the entire speech. The best way is to practice talking pleasantly in a natural manner, because any attempt to sound pleasant in a deliberate contrived manner will not produce the desired results and acceptance by the audience resulting in strain between you and them.

You know your subject well and can speak pleasantly and yet powerfully. The subject matter must directly relate to the audience and they must find the speech useful. Use of hands while speaking is important as you can become articulate with their help. The more you practice the more confidence you will gain and become less conscious when you face your audience.

PLAN YOUR ACTION

The next step after thoughts and speech is action. The CEO should look after the following while getting into action phase:

- Properly plan your action.
- Act with speed, value your time and that of others.
- Plan the outcome of your action.
- Monitor your action and midpoint results.

- Try not to harm anyone through your action.
- Enjoy your action and try to make action enjoyment a mass movement of your team (if action or work is enjoyable it ceases to be work).

By understanding the art of your thought, word and action you get the most powerful tool for influencing your team members.

THE PLANNING PROCESS

Efficient planning depends on the state of your mind, circumstances, resources and your goals. The other prerequisites of planning process are a positive attitude and an ardent desire for achieving your goals. You should have an idea of how you can obtain additional resources, if needed. With careful planning you can ensure that you have enough resources required for your tasks ahead of time, and the sanctity of your goals helps in this process. If the goals are basically wrong there will always be resource crunch.

The human mind is nature's biggest black box or computer, which when fed with right inputs, achieves automatic planning process. This helps in achieving legitimate and lawful goals.

As is well known, automatic machines produce faultless products, free of imperfections. If the machine is not automatic, the products may not be perfect. If planning is proper and effective, the action will take less time giving maximum output. As you progress, you should arrange for a plan review as the machinery, environment, market and even customer taste may be changing. Some firms make a yearly plan and they review it quarterly, like a rolling plan, which takes care of the abnormalities exterior to the organization.

Speed of operations comes with confidence and firm decisions taken at the right time. If the plan as conceived makes you lose time, you keep trying to improve the results. This undermines your confidence, creating a vicious circle, where more time is lost. Time is a vital factor in business and you can achieve great things if you value time.

ART OF GETTING DESIRED RESULTS

You need the following for obtaining the desired results and achieving your goals:

- Motivation in your team
- Energy of your team
- Skills and ability
- Confidence
- Good working conditions

You need to concentrate on your actions and coordination of your team's efforts. Physical ambience, like cleanliness, serenity, quiet and air-conditioning, if required for the processes add up to good, well-timed, and result-oriented action. In the absence of the ambience the team members are prone to move about aimlessly to find peace without coordinated efforts towards the goals. When you work according to your plan in congenial atmosphere you feel happy, and so would your team. It is therefore important that you leave them to their tasks, which they perform (within the parameters and time frame given by you) in proper workplace. As they are enjoying the work they will not be roaming about aimlessly.

There are the following two ways of keeping your employees tied to the workplace:

1. Tie them up with draconian instructions.
2. Create an ambience in which they would love to work.

Even if you tie them up, metaphorically, they will pull against the chain and run away, defeating the very purpose of the chain. Therefore, the second way is the only way for the purpose.

There are the following two ways of getting work done from your employees:

1. Telling them how to do it.
2. Giving them training, facilities and goals to achieve and letting them perform on their own.

In the first half of the twentieth century, workers were told to do the task as per instructions, as mostly they were uneducated. "Bring in only your hands and feet, leave your brains behind at home".

Today, in the twenty-first century, with educated workers, the best way to motivate them is by empowering them to perform their tasks as they think fit. This is also conducive to the progression of TQM in your organization.

With motivation, the employees are energized. The energy gives power to think positively, creatively and creates a happy mood. It helps in performing the tasks to perfection. With proper ambience, singularity of goal and purpose, dedication to the activities, energy gets stimulated, which further motivates the person. The equation therefore reads as follows:

$$\text{Motivation} \longleftrightarrow \text{Energy}$$

With proper result-oriented action, the employee gains in confidence. Confidence is essential for performing the tasks for effective achievement of goals. Confidence comes from knowledge, skills, experience, encouragement, rewards, motivation and a positive state of mind. It is an important aspect of the CEO's task to keep the employees motivated and confident. With confidence the employees need to acquire single-minded approach to achievement of goals. The single-mindedness and commitment comes from the CEO, who must display the goals' fixation in his thoughts, words and actions, even as you stay in your own role. Employees should look up to the CEO not in fear or awe, but as an elder brother for guidance and sharing of confidence and experiences.

As CEO you need to have multitasking skills, as you have to operate at different levels, as a counsellor, motivator, communicator, PR person and the change in activity should be smooth and natural. The important point is that when you are trying to accomplish task you should give your fullest attention to it. The focus and concentration are a must for the CEO with the task at hand. However, as the CEO you have the integrated responsibility for the organization and you cannot ignore any part of the entire basket of activities.

Purpose— — —Concentration— — —Action— — —Goals

Purposive action with concentration and with the goals in mind is the essential ingredient for success. The wavering mind is distracted, causing loss of concentration, proper and timely action and you lose out on success.

Concentration and ability to perform with speed comes from the basic character of the CEO. The CEO must be clear headed, positive thinker, large hearted, without hatred or malice towards anyone. The success percentage will improve and develop on the percentage of uprightness of the CEO's character. He should never go back on his words, should back his team in distress and have enormous strength of positive thinking to help him in crises and in crossing the myriad temptations along his path.

The magic mantra for maximum success is to bypass the hurdles, negative thoughts, which drag you away from success. You should act with courage and faith till you get the positive results. When there is purity in thoughts, words and actions, you get extra energy and intelligence to counter the hurdles in your path. Any action with extra energy and intelligence becomes enjoyable.

8

CHAPTER

CEO's Behaviour

With your behaviour you can make people happy, better in many ways, taking you and others on a higher plane as human beings.

When you meet others, you give and take. The more you give, the more you gain by way of mental satisfaction. CEO's behaviour should be that of a giver. You can give happy greetings, praise, sympathy, love, and advice for the benefit of the person you are interacting with. You can also give a gift if the occasion demands it or even for no reason. A genuine show of concern and care produces joy at the meetings. Therefore, the first idea in behaviour pattern is to be giving something, at least warmth of your heart.

"What goes around comes around"

CEO–CONTINUOUS EDUCATION AND TRAINING

Education helps you to achieve full potential of body and mind by controlling the mind towards the aim of your life. It helps you develop your personality. As you grow in age and in profession, you get into a groove and start losing some of your expertize, spontaneity. It is therefore important to keep reinventing yourself through continuous education and training, whether through formal programmes or self-learning through books, CDs and the Internet.

Study of humanities, philosophy, literature, and history tell about the values held by people and what should be sacred in different areas of human activity. Understanding of values down the ages helps in understanding your own organization's position in the present business world as you relate those values with your own values. Philosophy aims at the study of the sublime, where at times the logic fails. And yet, the great philosophers of the past have given pearls of wisdom to the mankind.

Economics takes you in the realm of production, distribution and consumption of products to satisfy human needs. Satisfaction is a relative term, which keeps moving in different directions, providing opportunities for new products, innovations.

Political science gives the insight into the past conflicts between people, classes and nations. The cause of the conflict, in most cases is economic disparity. To succeed, the business should attempt to bridge the gap and that is what the CEO should learn to do.

Sociology tells about groups and communities and their common behaviour pattern. It shows the way of improving the human conditions with the help of improved social institutions. You have to learn that when some one suffers from discontent, his behaviour is controlled by his desire to achieve his own peace. This creates artificiality in behaviour and it can corrupt relationships. The harmony of the organization is therefore broken. The CEO should understand and help improve behaviour between unscrupulous and oppressed persons in the organization.

The study of psychology covers the area of human mind and the CEO can appreciate the action and reaction of his team members with indepth insight. A good CEO has to be a good psychologist too!

MAJOR DECISIONS OF THE CEOs

At times when as the CEO you find an offender in your team, you have to take a major decision to either retain him or throw him out. Some persons take short cuts through criminal acts to satisfy their cravings, beyond the legal limits. Many talented persons come in contact with misguided people and they change their path to righteousness. The CEO needs all his correctional and motivational skills, courage and serenity in dealing with such team members. At times the CEO can use fear and at other times just show the right path and related consequences if they continue on the same path. However, the CEO must leave the task of settling the hardcore delinquents and criminals to the law enforcement authorities only.

If you lead your life according to the dictates of your awakened conscience, you tread on the right path only. You should, however, remain alert of the demons, which try to reside in your mind like, lust, greed, avarice and anger.

The CEO who has achieved the highest level of spiritual standard will remain humble of his attainments, as pride of his position will bring him tumbling down the path. Even saints like Vishwamitra could be made to slip badly because of the demon of lust. The best way is to keep a safe distance from all such attractions. The CEO has to aim for continuous struggle for achieving the goals. The struggle is continuous because once you have achieved a goal, it gives rise to new goals. If the struggle is carried out with correct values coupled with the cultural ethos, you will attain the blissful state in your everyday life. However, if your actions are in any way harming innocent persons, the bliss will turn into misery, be sure of it.

PARADOX OF THE TWENTY-FIRST CENTURY

Industrial revolution started in the west in the eighteenth century and has continued ever since. With mass production techniques, the demand supply divide kept on increasing, which calls for the best brains to survive and excel in the growing competitive scene.

Today, at the start of the twenty-first century, the world looks as given below:

- Communism ousted from Europe
- Berlin wall gone, Germany reunited
- Japan loses its sheen as a commercial superpower
- Unipolar world
- IT, Telecom and Space technology are at the forefront

The demise of the NEWMAN of the classless Bolshevik society came about because of the worst mindset it produced, which was full of corruption, greed, lust for power, distrust and cynicism.

Democracy and free markets promise dignity of human beings and a FREEMAN. In 1992, J.K. Gailbraith stated that in the USA 70% of income growth went to 1% population. The talk of merging the social and capital economy has no takers so far.

Peter Drucker, the management guru said in 1993 that in the 21st century poor nations will become developed and fast growing. It has been recognized that education is a prerequisite for economic progress. In India, you can see it happening in Kerala to some extent. The key issue is–can the country give priority to education and human resource development over industrial development.

The business world is likely to be divided into two groups, the Brain Trust people and the users of the Brain Trust results, the employees. With paperless office, even officeless office is possible now as people can operate from homes with internet, fax and computers. With the emergence of robotics, factories may become peopleless, automatic units. As CEO you face the challenges of succeeding in the new paradigm, which negates the earlier opportunities and throws up new ones. Piracy, computer crimes would need a new kind of policing. Laws are being amended worldwide in this direction. The rate of product development brings about product obsolescence faster and the PLCs are getting shorter by the day, providing new challenges to you as CEO.

The new paradigm in business is to arrange synergy in the following directions:

- The CEO is an inspiring person, motivator, role model, a team builder, friend, guide and philosopher, an ideal person with a vision for the organization. These attributes lend charisma to the leader.
- The CEO has to give respect to all kinds of work. No work is small or menial. Respect your employees and they will respect you. (In one firm the clerk receiving and dispatching letters was looked down upon as doing routine clerical work, till it was realized that if even a single letter went missing it could mean a loss of millions of rupees for the firm).
- The CEO has to plan strategies, which will work for the teams' success.

In the world dominated with profit motive only, ethics have been given a go by. As CEO if you are working towards profits only, it is like playing tennis looking at the scoreboard and not on the ball. Unethical tasks discredit the person and the organization and the shortlived gains disappear fast, bringing the organization's downfall.

Management with ethical norms gives power to the CEO for planning for success and hence, it should be taken seriously as a major responsibility by the CEO. Only profit plans tend to get converted into profiteering plans, which take the organization to its ruin. In the last two decades, people have exploited the position in pursuit of their own gains and the society loses out on misplaced ideology. These people want to use their position today, forgetting the future. However, if you as the CEO stick to the vision, the organization, society and the nation will benefit - such is the power of CEO's positive vision.

ZERO DEFECT VS TQM

It has been found that TQM helps in quality management and yet it is a long drawn out process, as the workers' experimentation for process improvement take time. Through new technology organizations can plan zero defect production and gain customer goodwill and improved productivity. These build volumes and related profits. Just-in-Time (JIT) inventory management helps in reducing the current assets burden, but to make it really effective, you should plan for JIT right up to your suppliers - they should also get their raw materials JIT.

THE NEW MANAGEMENT PHILOSOPHY

Sony of Japan has propounded the new management philosophy as follows–"Firms should not be allowed to continue their single-minded pursuit of economic efficiency and success in the market, especially overseas. They should build more humane and fair society by paying higher salaries and ensuring better living conditions to its employees". This came about because the industry leaders had lost faith in the old system and were looking for new directions. The new drive of the organizations is to improve the quality of life for the employees.

The business cycle oscillates, going up and down periodically due to market forces and the CEO has to understand the position of the cycle and plan his strategies accordingly.

Peter Drucker, one of the gurus of modern management says, there are three basic objectives of management as given below:

1. Survival
2. Growth
3. Profits

He is disturbed by the culture of only material success and believes they are part of the moral and spiritual degradation of business leaders.

The modern management can therefore be defined as follows:

"It tries to achieve the ideal through detailing of plans and their execution, it focuses on people, on quality and service, on innovation, while it does not condemn failures. It strives to achieve formal and informal transparent communication, economic growth and profits. The definition should include honesty, integrity, compassion and selfless service to the stakeholders, without expectations of returns".

In 1980s in the USA the management was with very young persons, CEOs of ages between 24 and 32. This was because of their virtues of being blunt, brash and go-getters (dynamic), who did not mind treading on anyone's toes to achieve their goals. With single-minded agenda they created a reign of terror among the teammates – perform or perish became their mantra, without realizing that the same rule will be applied to them. The widespread insecurity led to some great achievements, as also frustrations and desire to make quick money, before getting the sack, make hay while the sun shines approach. Unscrupulous attitude and behaviour of using their power by even cheating on the organization became rampant, which brought the downfall of the organizations (a look at the scams in the USA and court cases arrests would confirm this point), and their own too. The CEO had forgotten the basic theory of ethics, which brings in resilience in the organization. Twenty-first century needs a major shift in the CEOs' mindset to bring ethical norms into their lives.

In capitalistic society consumerism flourishes. Today, the workers of the west are asking about the level of sacrifices they have to make for increasing the profits of which they are promised a bigger share. The workers of the USA are finding it hard to compete with the workers of Japan and India, because they get higher salaries and have more money and time to relax and enjoy, take vacations rendering them not so focused on their work and yet they want more.

The world has been long divided into rich and poor nations. The rich have contrived to become richer, when they look at the poor nations, they want to expand their market as they find the developing nations as the only expanding markets in the world. Paradoxically the poor nations yet do not have enough money to buy. The west has lost its sheen as an economic power due to limited markets owing to saturation and depth of product penetration, which has already taken place. Their population is also static. The west business has been busy in increasing wealth and physical well being and has lost its soul in the process. That is why, today lot of businessmen are looking towards India for finding salvation in yoga and other ancient principles of ethical management. From the practical viewpoint the west wants salvation, which is possible only if it genuinely plans and helps the poor and less privileged nations to come up materially and become its market. India holds centrestage as the new market in the world along with China and that is the reason why several firms like Philips of Holland, Samsung of Korea are making India their production base. Many other firms from the rich nations have already done so and others are going to follow suit.

The invasion of firms from the west, the foreign direct investments and the new technologies have provided both an opportunity and threat to the Indian business. The CEOs would do well to take up the challenge posed by these firms and yet remain rooted to India's cultural ethos, the ingrained moral fibre, which would act as a catalyst and bring India on the top of the industrial world. The key to success in modern management would be ethical and moral values, which are fast disappearing from the Indian scene, while the west is trying to come to India to imbibe these values. The Indian business has to come forward and make its mark in the world and there is no time to lose. An attitude of honesty, care, motivating the employees is the only way to succeed in the market today. Profit should not reflect greed, but confidence of your customers in the organization and its products. At the current rate of obsolescence of not only products but also systems, structures and marketing channels, you and your organization need to be in a continuous learning mode, making your organization a Learning Organization.

FORGET THE NEGATIVES

As CEO you should look at the following closely:

- Your actions, which lead you to retrograde situations
- Negative views expressed by any one from your team member
- Fragmented ideas
- Hit and miss solutions to problems
- Favouring your pet team member without any reason like good work
- Criticizing any team member behind his back

Attitudes and intentions are important aspects of your personality. If you make a mistake, admitting it makes you a valuable asset to the firm. More importantly it makes you human. When your team members know you can make mistakes too, they will be encouraged to experiment for the good of the firm.

Failure in experimentation should not be suicidal for the employee, otherwise Process Improvement would become impossible and the idea of TQM would fail, despite your best intentions.

Process Improvement takes place in the following manner:

- It starts with an idea.
- The idea becomes a theory.
- The theory gets converted into a hypothesis after it is discussed or brainstormed with knowledgeable persons.
- The hypothesis becomes a law or a proven process after experimentation.

Successful experimentation must be used by the firm and acknowledged, applauded, while failed experiments, including yours should be discussed to ensure such failures do not recur.

IDEAL EXPERIMENTATION– THE MIDDLE PATH

Experiments conducted by the small worker levels, while should not be discouraged, being in small operational areas, do not bring significant results, while the experiments done at the top level, if failed can do a lot of harm to the firm.

The experiments done by middle managers are ideally suited, as these do bring sufficiently large results and their failure is not so drastic either.

In corporate world the chairman of the board and the directors have all faced the snakes entering the boardrooms, trying to swallow the entire organization. How they come into the boardrooms, who they are and who is responsible for their entry would not only make interesting reading, but also put the CEOs on guard against the snakes. It should become relatively easy to recognize them, identify them from a host of others interacting with the organization. However, of late, the conmen have taken the guise of respectability!

It is best to start with self-analysis. Are you directly or indirectly creating frictions in your organization, debilitating the same? You need to find a quite corner, away from the noise zone, where you can think with a clear mind, which focuses on itself, renews its energy through meditation and generates an aura, a healthy glow, which permeates around you and can significantly change the negative vibes in your area of influence into positive ones. In this way success can be achieved in the most difficult situations, with venomous snakes surrounding the organization as inside villains and competition.

The uniqueness of the persona of the CEO, who stands heads and shoulders above the rest, is the best generator of brand equity of the firm. His actions, his mere presence can turn the tables on his rivals. We see such personalities in the corporate world only once in a while. However, with practice you can develop yourself to such an extent that you can remain on the frontline always. You need only to liberate yourself from the prison you have created for yourself by remaining in the boundaries of the static thinking. The dynamic nature of corporate existence calls for dynamism of the CEO in his personality. This dynamism comes only from your faith in yourself and centreness of your mindset on your mega goals.

As the CEO, if you have the driving force, you can guide the best of your team members, some of them being even more knowledgeable than yourself. The important point here is that for achieving that level of status, you should remain in midst of genuinely good knowledgeable persons. It would be important that you learn from the best teachers, and confine yourself strictly to the best of behaviour, responsible and dignified. Always!

A good teacher removes the darkness of ignorance, selfishness, nepotism and lethargy from you and takes you onto higher planes of knowledge, selflessness, large heartedness and work. It is only for this reason that the teacher or the guru has been given the position even above the Gods, and knowledge and wisdom the position of greatest wealth on the earth, as can be seen from the shloka given below:

(*Gurur bramh gurur Vishnu gurur devo maheshwra*
gurur sakshat parbramh tasmai sri guruay namah)

It means that the guru is the same as the Holy Trinity of Hindu gods, Bramha Vishnu and Maheshwara and therefore we should offer him our profound obeisance.

Once you lose your selfishness, only pure godliness remains, as in the void nothing can exist except the parity of mind, heart and soul. Tough task it is, yes, but has anyone achieved greatness by easy means? Think about it! (For reference please look at the ancient scripture-Skandopanishad).

SELF-REFLECTIONS

Interactions between people are basically a reflection of oneself only. If you are good then the other person will be good to you. The same theory reflects in the market as well. If you play fair the chances are that your customers will also play a fair deal with you. If you cheat then you should not get baffled if your bottom line starts cheating on you. You must keep a rein on your mind, as it is the mind, which keeps you a prisoner of desires and lust, rendering it incapable of achieving its goals. You must be devoid of ego in totality as it would only fool you into considering yourself as the wisest, creating untold misery and suffering on you, and you would be leading your team as a blind person leads other blind persons. (The word blind is used only allegorically with no offence meant for the visually handicapped persons).

Conversely, those who lead an austere life and are serene by nature, who believe in control over their emotions, who are dedicated to their mission in life, attain their goals without any major problems and delays. Such life unfetters the mind from the chains of ignorance. To be fully successful you need to be devoid of greed and full of energy of a bullet, which will cut across the ignorance in no time. Once you understand yourself, you can reach above the normal; the only thing which will push you back is the return of your ego. It is, therefore, important to understand this vital truth, which is the sole remover of confusion, doubt and frustration.

Material success in today's world tends to manifest itself with the usual contraptions of success like a BMW car, a penthouse and other luxuries. These are all to the good, as long as you are using them without any attachments with them, as when you lose anyone of them it causes a lot of sadness and frustration. Swami Vivekanand has rightly given the permission to live in luxury as long as you can distance yourself from them at will. Firms are offering big cars, huge villas as corporate perks. These signify your position and go with it. They come and go with it. It is best not to have any emotional bondage with them.

Once you have understood your own position on the firmament of the business world, you realize your insignificance as compared to the market forces. Market is the only truth, unchanging, eternal as it is there forever; only its desires, needs may change. The rest is untrue. Even the demand for products is ephemeral, as you have known through the product life cycle. If you focus on today's success only, catastrophe awaits you round the corner.

With clarity of mind, knowing the market and its trends becomes easy. Through research and analysis, you can achieve your desired objectives and can attain the market position as per your plan. By continuing research you can get the glories and can stay tuned to the success as long as you do not get a swollen head as a consequence of success. A positive decision towards success ensures that you become success personified till your next fall on account of your bloated ego. You get away from the failure syndrome, away from the knots of negative passion and start an unending journey on the road towards salvation, both personal and that of your firm.

Personal Compulsions

For a person seeking permanent success, you have to look at your inner self as without knowing it you cannot know anything else. You understand yourself as self and also as a buyer in the marketplace and you understand the product you want and your compulsions for buying it and you would have attained the marketing nirvana. This process is the same as repeated by all your buyers all the time. In your customers lies your success. It is hidden till you unveil it for the benefit of your firm. You need an overpowering force to carry you through the changing markets, competition and new product launches. That force comes to you from within yourself through the process of meditation. A wise man keeps his composure, his morality, his equanimity and his faith in human goodness, as these are the essential ingredients for everlasting success. You create an aura around you without even realizing it, which helps in transforming your team member into success promoters.

> Do not play God! Try to be God-like! A person's entire life remains a battleground for the war between his inner God and the demon-fighting goes on! Can a person even think of having his God lose? And yet, that is what is happening all over the world.

It is best to select a role model for yourself. The person becomes your guru and you should accept him as the epitome of goodness. He is standing tall amidst dwarfs of the corporate world and he can lead you to unfathomable success just by being with you as a source of inspiration.

Without even carrying an arm, Lord Krishna won the battle of Mahabharata by inspiring Arjun on the battlefield with his Gitopadesh.

Hence, you should have feelings of devotion and adoration towards your guru and he will endow you with the arts and craft of success in the corporate world through indications and subtle hints only. As you know your guru you start understanding your market, your customers as you start operating on a higher level of efficiency. After the first initiation, the market itself becomes your guru and you have to pay heed to it all the time. By constantly understanding your master, the market, you start valuing it even more for what it is giving you and what it is teaching you. You develop the faculty of sifting the important from the mundane and get the needed keenness for activating your decision-making powers almost as a psychic and you become a true leader of your team.

You rise to the top position as you acquire the skills of multitasking. However, why do so many of the leaders fail to deliver, once they reach the leadership positions. The reason is quite simple: because they do not let go of the multifarious tasks they keep doing and keep for themselves, as their work portfolio.

If you know the tasks well, it is better you delegate the same to your team members, as you can then supervise them as also monitor their actions. The rule to follow is, never oversell yourself by taking on too many tasks on yourself. At that level, even small errors can be devastating. With work overload, you are more than likely to miss out on a few important areas and also make mistakes along the line. Finding the right people, training them to do their jobs well and then delegating authority and responsibility to them is the ideal way of getting things done. It helps to have monitoring and control points to keep your team members in line with their job and task objectives.

Even when the leader is physically weak, he can lead the firm, because of his strength of character. He can lead with his skills, knowledge and motivating abilities. He need not be a wrestler to be the leader. The path of righteousness is the only one for the leader. Knowing the customer, the mark dynamics help, as without their knowledge, the firm cannot even survive. When you worship work, the tasks you delegate never reduce in value and you fulfil your objectives fully. You have to keep motivating the workers to do the task, by telling them the importance of the task being done by them.

Knowledge is power, hence give voice to the power within you, delegate it, let others feel the power and then perform. Power is a highly motivating factor. Use it with genuine delegation and control and see the firm going beyond all stretches of success.

Only the knowledgeable person succeeds in his tasks. Therefore, it is necessary to encourage your team members to remain knowledge hungry. Only a seeker of knowledge can develop into a successful leader. Your success as a leader depends on your quest for knowledge. A leader should be in a learning mode always. Mind's focus can, at times, becomes slippery. However, if you can put on bifocal glasses you are, at once, connected to your own tasks as well as on the tasks of your team members. Today's competitive world does not tolerate delays of any form in a firm.

Besides the market dynamics, you should thoroughly know your firm's strengths and weaknesses. Without this knowledge, there cannot be any improvement in your firm's status. All good planning and action goes waste without this knowledge. Armed with the firm's knowledge, you go into details about product knowledge, its PLC, brand positioning in the appropriate segments, and master the art of managing the markets. You are now ready for planning for the firm's success!

The formula for sweet success, therefore, emerges as, " remain a seeker of knowledge always" the Sanskrit word Jigyasa means urge for knowledge and you have to become a Jigyasu, a seeker of knowledge all your life to remain on the path of promotion, liberation and success. With knowledge comes the power to achieve, you get elevated with this power, which in turn frees you from restrictive bondages of stereotyped thinking and planning process. Market is, after all an illusive phenomenon and yet it is your saviour too! As the mysteries of the market are unveiled before you, you become wiser to handle its idiosyncrasies too.

The Learning Curve

Several entrepreneurs believe that they are fully knowledgeable about the market. Unfortunately, what they know is not the market or its dynamics, but some fragments in that area. Market can never be far from the firm for it to even survive. Those who believe the firm to be a totally different entity than the market, they lose control over both the firm and the market. Remember that the firm, market, its relevant segments and your products are fully intertwined and integrating them would be to your advantage.

Market Focus

The changing market size, its needs require continuous efforts for understanding them. Minor efforts, sporadic surveys are not effective at all, as they disappear as a drop of water disappears in the ocean. BCG Matrix and methods of market segmentation along with product positioning should be used for remaining focused on the market. Pre-empting the market needs, remaining proactive would let you lead from the front. Otherwise, all the technical knowledge, financial expertise and human resource management would come to a naught.

When you are having a meeting with your customer, you should divorce yourself away from all other problems, worries and concentrate on the meeting. Such meetings produce extraordinary results if they are managed properly. For instance, never go into a meeting without getting the answers for all the questions which the customer had raised in the earlier meeting. As you try to convince the customer about your product, never for once, question his basic intelligence. You can only subtly suggest that there may be more to the product and your plan than meets the eye. The ideal way is to let the customer think that your idea is actually his brilliant thought. Once the customer reaches that blissful state, he is not easily rattled by competitive efforts. Such loyal customers remain loyal only on a temporary basis and you have to continuously sell them your idea–"as their own idea". The semi-permanence comes from the fact that you have been truthful in your sales story, which is verifiable and that you have not oversold yourself, or the firm and its products. The very nature of our universe, including the market is temporary and hence there is no point in looking for permanence in terms of customer loyalty.

You should never forget that even a single unhappy customer could be the cause of total collapse of the firm. After all, it was only a missing screw, which leads to the drowning of a ship.

As you satisfy your customer needs, even delight him with your product; you cannot just afford to forget your responsibilities towards him as a citizen of the country, your copatriot. He is a stakeholder too in your venture, and it is essential that you keep the planet for him and others like him in better shape and remain environment-friendly, stop all pollution from the factories. Otherwise, the generations to come will never forgive you for your misdeeds.

Delight your customers by all means and keep the welfare of the communities at heart if you want to achieve positive results and success on a long-term basis.

Your acts for the welfare of the communities will be remembered for a longer period than the delight from your products. Therefore, right from your planning stage, pay attention to the urgent and pressing question of keeping the environment clean and remaining eco-friendly, always. Your customers may not directly realize the contribution of your action in their healthy living and yet such deeds have two major advantages to you, one, sooner or later people get to know about them and secondly, intrinsically these are highly self satisfying by themselves too. Those marketers, who forget or ignore the environment, are surely going to face to ruin sooner than anyone can even imagine! Naturally staying in the marketplace as a healthy player is just out of the question.

Business Ethics

There are a lot of pseudo intellectuals in the corporate world, who are ever ready to show off their wisdom. They believe that by taking their skewed path, they will appear to be different and hence better. They use their cunning for personal betterment to the detriment of the firm. Such persons remain ingrained in their unethical ways, their mind is never concentrating on their goals and therefore they can never even think of achieving success for the firm. Their yardstick of success is different as it is meant only for their personal goals. The CEO is the charioteer of the firm; the firm is the chariot while his morality is the road for success. The CEO must keep a firm control on his emotions, and keep a healthy distance from his so-called friends who advocate deviations in his work for personal gains. The body senses should be made to look inwards, to enable the person to look for his own faults, as also he can totally avoid looking at the glamour of the sin, which is the sure means of personal ruin. Such a person remains undefeated and calm even in the most trying circumstances.

And such a CEO is ready to climb the rope to reach his destination, while the snake will swallow the other.

Here, even at the cost of repetition it must be stated that the CEO with his ego will vitiate all his chances of success.

The best method is to listen to the advice of sane persons, to watch only the ethical performances, today as well as tomorrow; such eternal truths do not change with time at all.

The Syndrome of Duality

The CEO's daily prayer should include that he gets the power of combining his thoughts, speech and actions in line with the firm's goals. Usually, his mind resides in the learning mode, while speech reflects his views on a subject and actions are driven by the imminence of the situational need.

The CEO should learn to keep his knowledge and wisdom at the back of his mind while speaking to his team and his actions should conform to his speech. As a role model the CEO has the task of remaining true to his words in his actions. He should never forget his skills, wisdom and knowledge. In fact, he should keep himself continuously updated in his sphere of activities by reading books and magazines and interacting with the wise, knowledgeable persons.

The CEO should never waste even a moment of his precious time. He should learn to speak in a controlled yet unaffected voice, which is pleasant and strong and direct to the point. His speech should be totally devoid of falsehood, clichés, ambiguity and platitudes. He should shun abusive language, because even annoyance can be shown in not too harsh words. He should cut out words, which cheat or give wrong impressions to the listeners. He should try to be a giver, a giver of solicited or at times even unsolicited advice, suggestions, words of encouragement and even reprimands, if the situation warrants it. The reprimands should be more in the nature of guidance unless the nature of problem is too serious. The reprimand should always be given in camera and not before an audience, to be of any effect at all. When a person hears reprimand before others, he starts justifying his wrong acts for face saving and will never learn how to correct himself.

The CEO should be a caring person, who looks after the interest of his team members, besides those of his stakeholders. The caring nature starts covering the interests of his customers, suppliers and financiers, the more notables among the stakeholders. Needless to state, this caring nature ensures the goodwill of the stakeholders, making the life of the CEO easy and interesting. He also becomes the central figure in the firm and ceases to be a figurehead only.

The Force Within

Most persons use only ten to fifteen per cent of their faculties, especially the mental ones throughout their lives and when they do not get the success they had aspired for, they blame fate or karma of previous births for their failures. Needless to add, they can grow their psyche to such a level that they can use their intellect upto seventy to eighty per cent. The wealth of wisdom, unused lies right within them only. The unfortunate thing is that they are not even aware of their wealth. Once the era of wisdom knowledge dawns on them, it brings unfathomable powers, mingled with a sense of satisfaction, serenity to them. These qualities have a snowballing effect on them and then their success knows no boundaries at all. Most persons look for incremental successes in their work life. With meditation and thought control process the powers they get are supremely more effective than whatever they have achieved otherwise. With the superconscious state you can achieve a stage of paradigm shift in your mindset, provided the success it gives does not get into your head because of your ego. When you achieve oneness with your own self, you are at peace within and with the world. You must shed all your facade of being a highly effective person, as it will never be necessary anymore. What you discover about yourself does not need any definition as it is the productivity spiral, which you generate, is what really matters. Measuring success at that point of time becomes meaningless as it is extremely difficult to define your position when you are running a race towards infinity; how near you are or how far from infinity is impossible to measure. It is like understanding infinity, and then you realize that the power for grasping the infinity was within you all the time. Your superconscious state is the best way to define infinity.

Many spiritualists define infinity as the supreme power, the God Almighty. Unfortunately, it is the talking about God, which has caused most frictions on the planet. There are Gods and Gods; several denominations of hundreds of religions have almost made a mockery of the Supreme Power. The wise thing to do is to keep religion and the Gods as personal theories, where each person can draw his own definitions and equations with his God. The religious wars started from the beginning of time and the result is a divided world in terms of religions, sub-religions, sects and untold denominations with unnecessary fighting for supremacy between them.

Coming back to the theory of the powers within, you can understand that a religious person gets solace and strength from trying to be with the Gods. If you can discover the Gods within how much better it would make your life that you can get the same solace and strengths right within you. Ancient scriptures, sages of the yore tell us that your conscience, your inner voice or your *antaraatma* tells you the right from wrong. What else you expect your God to do for you? Surely He cannot live your life for you. The evildoers have killed their conscience and joined the devils' brigade. Do you think they can achieve anything worthwhile? Maybe they get rich, even famous (notorious), but they do not contribute at all towards the welfare of the firm, the society, the community and the country. Such heroes remain unsung except in their nefarious coterie of likeminded scoundrels. However, you should never forget that the greatest obstacle on your path towards salvation is your giant sized ego, which gets bigger and bigger as you climb the scales of success. Unfortunately, the ego becomes the catalyst of you steep fall from the august heights you may have achieved. With humility and egoless personality, you keep climbing the success ladders with no fear of tumbling down from it. It makes you so strong that even if the ladder is in fact a snake (a barrier for your success), you are totally unmindful of the fact as you attain your goals, despite the hurdles in your path (the snake). A few of the examples given in the book would help you in understanding and accepting this theory.

It is essential that you condition your mind well in advance. A farmer prepares his field, much before he puts the seeds in it. Later on he puts fertilizers, pesticides, irrigates it and then only he can be sure of a good crop. Similarly, the mind needs to be prepared before you can cultivate it for becoming a super achiever. This conditioning of mind can be done in the manner given below:

- Shun the company of negative people.
- Stay close to the positive thinkers, God-fearing persons.
- Sweep away all negative thoughts from your mind, once and for all.
- Read books which inspire you to have good thoughts, words and deeds only (*man, vachan* and *karma*).
- Seek no deviation, assiduously avoid all distractions and delusions in your path.

As you plan to climb the snake you must fortify yourself with strength, courage and a positive mindset, which transports you into the domain of real brave people. In such an event you get the will power far beyond your own expectations for surmounting even the most difficult hurdles. How to achieve that state of righteous attitude and become a winner every time is the question which baffles the CEOs of today. You can look for the most workable answers in the following passages:

- Know yourself is the first mantra, which requires a close introspection of yourself. You do a SWOT analysis of self, your personal and business life. You will soon get to know your real self, as most of the time you have been play acting in the business arena, saying and doing the right things expected of you. At times you could be even lying to yourself in order to salvage respect or even face in times of crises. If you have been projecting yourself as a self-respecting, correct individual and then you get exposed for a misdemeanour you would either run miles away from or start a damage control exercise by telling lies. How much better would it be if you had refrained from the dubious action altogether? There is, however, no point in crying after the event and that is where you need to lead a life of precarious existence, where you remain upright without succumbing to temptations. It is like tight rope walking except when you align yourself with the spiritual lines of forces, keeping a strong faith in the God Almighty.

- With a resolute mind and with strong commitment to the achievement of your goals you become immune to the temptations and still you should never underestimate the power of the devil that is always ready to pounce upon you as you show even a slight weakness. The ideal situation is when you do not tempt fate and stay as far as possible from the temptations as no one in this world is totally immune to the influence of the allurements around him or her.
- If you keep purposefully busy and do not leave any time for the devil's traps, you may find yourself free of the temptations. Even then, if you develop an ego about your power over the devil, you are likely to lose the power, as ego is part of the devil's own manifestation. If you believe that you can avoid the lure even as you face it, then you are surely the next victim of the devil. For sure success, there is only one way, that of avoiding temptation by running miles in the opposite direction when you see it coming your way.
- Introspection is the main point for gaining the priceless gift of wisdom and intuition. You get away from the present state of confusion and attain perfect balance between self and its goal. As you study psychology you get a practical guide for insight into the mind and success. Lasting success come from peaceful adventure into the mind's domain and not from continuous firefighting operations.

The Snakes Within

If you want to remain in the success zone always you need to understand the need for meditation on a continuous basis. If you miss out sometimes, do not be dejected and you should restart at the first opportune moment. If you miss out on success, you should not get discouraged as it will dissolve your faith and you would like to give up to the situation altogether. Good healthy food – the saatwik food is best for attaining self-realization, as it keeps your body, mind and soul strong and healthy. With practice of meditation, yoga and pranayam, you come closest to perfection, the Godhood. A healthy mind helps you keep a cheerful atmosphere at the workplace and at your home.

As you go to sleep, it rejuvenates your body and mind. However, over indulgence in sleep is like taking drugs and it becomes counterproductive. As you meditate regularly, your sleep needs come down. Lack of proper sleep causes tiredness and then the mind cannot function to its designated capacity, enhanced through yoga and meditation. If you sleep less than required by your body, you may fall asleep during meditation.

Lack of sleep has a vicious circle effect as it causes lethargy and depression. Poor eating, physical illness, bad company can cause lethargy and depression, which in turn causes sleep. Lethargy can come from an unbalanced life, where youth's enthusiasm remains without a proper direction. Even as the CEO the unbalance can enter your life if you neglect to prioritize your assignments. You should start by disciplining your life by adhering to a dynamic timetable, which covers all your activities and yet has the flexibility for change in emergency situations.

As the CEO you should be ready to operate in unfavourable environments, uncongenial atmosphere and these should only spur you to develop powers, which would help you in achieving your goals. You should build strengths in discrimination of right from wrong, empathy with the victim and will to succeed in difficult situations.

The old saying, "a person is known by the company he keeps" is still valid as bad company does affect you, whether you accept it or not. Most persons think that they are immune to the effects of company, which is a totally wrong assumption. The religions also preach that you should shun the company of those persons who distract you towards the wrong path, even if they happen to be very close to you. You should have a list of undesirable company, including books, songs; movies lead your mind astray from your main goals. Even as you think that the distraction is only temporary, please believe that once you succumb to the temptations, you become addicted and bound to it by strong chains of your baser instincts. The only way of avoiding the chains is total abstinence of the temporary pleasures right through your life. The temporary pleasures are tantalizing as they keep pressurizing your psyche in order to tie you down permanently.

People surround you, not only from your firm, but also from other areas like your stakeholders. These people could be inducting greed, hypocrisy, flattery, lies and selfishness into your firm and even as they come as your friends, in fact they are your worst enemies. These so-called friends surround you when the going is good and abandon your ship, when they think it might just sink. Such fair weather friends distance you from your goals, give unsolicited advice meant to derail you and waste your time in idle talk. The façade such friends create like an aura around themselves is so deceptive that you need to be extra clever and careful to be able to isolate them after understanding their real motives of entering the firm. The selfless nature of their initial advice is meant only as a trap in which they believe you will soon fall. You should permanently cut off all your connections from such people without loss of anytime.

The world is full of hypocrisy, flattery, and it is not easy to keep away from them. As the CEO you have to decide what is good for you and take difficult decisions, which would transport you to the success area.

If you have friends who are more of gossips, they are taking you away from your destination, your goal. When you get into discussions even with your friends, if you win the debate you are likely to lose your friend. If you lose the debate you lose face. Idle talk can result in heated debates, enmity and exhaustion. If you give up on the debate, become silent and instead of finding faults with others, do some introspection you can plan to improve your own decision making power as then self improvement becomes your focus. You can go beyond the limits of your work area if you give into criticizing others and getting into their affairs. You should start looking for the plus points of others and your own shortcomings if you want to really improve. Most of the people keep rationalizing their mistakes as they shift the blame on others, other persons who are not part of the present company in any meeting.

The major problem in the area of personal improvement is the non-acceptance by the person that there is a problem with him. Ego takes control of the person, which keeps justifying the mistakes with all possible lies. This way the person is closing the door of his improvement totally. However, if the mistakes are admitted quickly, improvement comes faster than you can even imagine.

As you plan meditation, you must do inner search for problems within, as that is the only route to salvation. You need to correct the following areas if you are looking for personal and organizational salvation:

- Your personality to become inline with your mindset.
- Lifestyle takes the route of selflessness, caring and goodwill for even the unknown.
- Values to be the guiding factors in the decision-making process always.
- Focus should be correcting the errant behaviour of certain individuals.
- Correction of emotional instability would also remove the weaknesses within you.
- Development of your strength through the value system would ensure you never get into energy sapping situations. Changing habits is not easy and as you practice meditation and indulge in selfless service, you gain immense power within you.

Ego Busters

People wear the ego as a mask, which hides the true person; as the ego gives vent to thoughts articulated by the persons are mostly for an effect, they never truly represent the innerself of the person. The person becomes a slave of the ego, which invariably lowers the standards of behaviour of the person in the society. Therefore, unless you lose the ego, the façade will continue and your real progress towards gaining strength for fighting the serpent would vanish. After a time you become habituated to the ego behaviour and yet, if you decide with firm determination, you can shed the ego to take you place in the path to progress for defeating the snake.

You need to work towards ego busting with the help of yoga, meditation, pranayam and the total relaxation technique. You need to keep company of like-minded good people who have shaken off the demon of ego and who can help you do the same. As you want to come close to your goals, you must get rid of the ego without any delay. The main thing to remember is that any success or other positives with you are part of the God Almighty's handiwork and you should not take any credit for it. If you do not want to become undisciplined, rude, selfish, arrogant and impertinent, you must endeavour to shake off the ego.

Ego, when it surfaces, reduces you into a hypocrite, secretive person, incapable of imbibing the success coming through your legitimate work ethos. For maintaining your ego, you will resort to playing games, lying as you can manage to serve your own interest only. The best part is that as soon as you realize that you have a giant-sized ego, you can act to correct the situation and can do it in no time. Knowing the problem is half the battle won.

Power, fame, name, success stories and awards are ego boosters and once you know the triviality of these ego fixations, you can easily give them or at least remove them from your portfolio.

In the open market situation, where individuality is respected and acclaimed, ego busting is a difficult problem. That is where the Indian ethos come into picture as they let the person feel liked and loved without him having to develop a giant-sized ego.

The Emotional Barriers

When you do not achieve your objectives you get angry and anger is a devastating emotion, which lends itself as a tool for confusing the person; you lose your main tasks, your memory becomes short, irretrievable and you cease to be responsible for your outbursts and actions under anger. Anger kills your thought process, saps your energy. If you like, however, you can sublimate your anger for a highly energizing thought process. You only need to submit to meditation as the anger burst tries to envelope you. In this process, your guru or your guide will help you into submitting your SELF to the Almighty!

Anger has a snowballing effect as a little anger leads to bigger anger till you reach the position where you become blind to the realities of now, the present and your own limitations in the vastness of the universal canvas of activities.

Fear is another of the emotional traps, which take you away from the situation of today. You will find that in all cases your fear is unfounded unless you get into bad company and indulge in unlawful or unethical activities. Shyness and timidity are both manifestations of fear and you need to work fearlessly. With fear you lose 40 per cent of your mental capacity.

Fear, ego and anger need to be nipped in the bud, before they have the devastating effect on you and your business.

Most persons fear death, disease, loss of job, fear of non-acceptance in society and once you analyze the fears you find that they are either totally unfounded or at best, their basis is flimsy, with no strength at all.

Diffidence

When a person lacks self-confidence, worries about his own capacity to perform and succeed, it recoils on him with loss of courage to perform. He gets ready to give up his efforts or at least make the efforts in a half-hearted manner. This can become a big problem for you, if you get into such a rut. At such times you must remember the successful periods in your life in order to dispel the doubts totally. In such an event, you must redouble your interactions with the positive people; take more time out for introspection and meditation. It is therefore important to get a good guru, who is there for you through your good and bad times. As good times do not last, similarly even bad times do not stay with your for long. You can make the best use of this period in communicating with your guru and in planning your strategies for action.

Your goals for self as well as for your team should be realistic, achievable but with a stretch. Goals, which are achieved easily, are not satisfying should be sub delegated to others for whom they would be not so easy to reach. The saying is, "Rome was not built in a day" helps you understand that while urgency should be the byword in business, haste should be avoided as it "makes waste". When you are planning innovations in your work, chances of failure are there and if you fear failure then never even attempt experimentation. However, on the flip side of the coin, without any experimentation there cannot be any genuine progress or improvement in your working systems. You must experiment and encourage your team members to take up experimentation. The successful experiments should be rewarded and their results used in the work, while failures should not be cause for an employee's ouster from the firm. You should discuss failures, including your own, only to see that such errors do not recur. During innovations, strange thoughts come and some of them are used during experiments and when the results fall short of expectations, there is chaos, as every one is shifting blame on others. The chaos can be set aside by you if you keep your activities transparent and the team with you knows the parameters in which they do the experimentations. During failures self-destructive doubts can cause immense damage and it is important that you prevent it from happening by proper planning and control systems. Therefore, you must kill the doubts instantly before they take roots in the firm, eroding its very structure. However, once you have developed a culture of experimentation and that of acceptance of their failures you can eliminate the doubts altogether.

Energy Levels

The firms depend for success on the motivation and energy levels of its workers. As the CEO you would do well in keeping a Motivation-Energy Level matrix for your key players, who have a great impact on the firm's results, as given below:

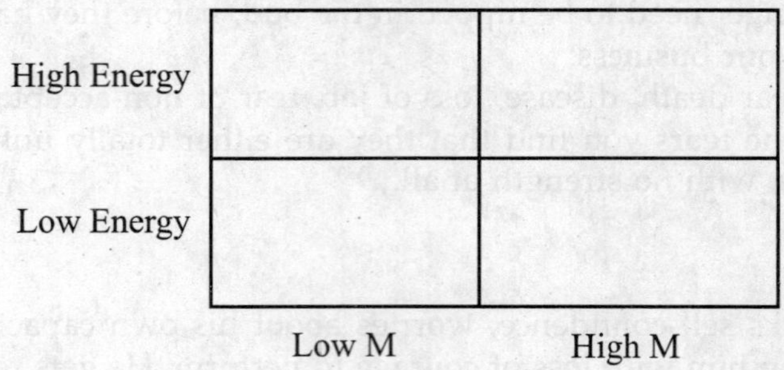

You can place people in the right place in the segment they deserve and as the energy and motivation increases or fluctuates you can keep the position shifting accordingly.

The best way to improve the energy and motivation levels of your own and that of your team is to keep tuned to the vision, mission and goals of the firm firmly entrenched in the psyche. When you are focused on the tasks at hand, nothing else distracts you and you become totally charged up, energized and motivated. Can you keep up to the higher planes of energy and motivation all the time? The answer would be an emphatic yes, if you have been meditating regularly.

The Mind

As you must be aware the human mind is the fastest moving thing on the planet. Even then you are supposed to use it for achieving the planned results. Concentration is the vital ingredient in your menu for the success of the firm. With myriads of temptations, distractions around you it could be almost an impossible task. For exactly such situations only, the ancient scriptures have given, by now, the world famous recipe of yoga, meditation and pranayam. With their help you can become totally focused on the tasks at hand with temptations and distractions receding in oblivion. It is best to learn these three; yoga, meditation and pranayam from a learned guru, otherwise, not only the benefits of these are lost, you could get into problems as well. The three combine to gradually but surely remove the negatives in your life, bit by bit and you can perceive the difference yourself in a short time.

Negative thoughts create a negative force field around you and as you interact with your team members, they too get negatively charged. And when failure comes knocking at your door you appear surprised. How can you expect apples from the tree you have yourself sown with the babul seed? The team itself causes most of the destruction unconsciously with the negative attitude.

When your mind is in an easy and relaxed mood, you have no regular timetable for the period; the devil takes control of the mind. As the saying goes, "An empty mind is the devil's workshop". Now comes the difficult part when you have to instruct the mind to keep off the devil's path. If you have been praying and meditating, you will find a number of ways of removing the temptations from your path altogether.

When your mind starts hating someone it can become the most severe restraining factor in the path of your progress. When anyone gets into its clutches, hatred makes him its slave. It becomes almost impossible to shed hatred, as like lust, greed and envy it never dies out completely, unless the concerned person makes special efforts. Hatred has been known to have spreading quality and it is almost contagious. There are a number of examples where family hatred is carried on for generations. Hatred saps your energy, reducing your capacity to take important decisions. At times hatred, like contempt & prejudice is for a trivial reason and it is best to analyze the same and get out of it at the earliest. Hatred, on account of religious differences, is much too common and it is leading the planet on the brink of disaster.

Nepotism, infatuation and other relationships disturb the mental balance, as the CEO stops thinking straight. These give you a sense of belonging to each other. In return you become a slave of these emotions and you become weak in a great measure.

Those who live in the past glory will find the power to succeed receding from their hands. All successes of yesterdays, yesteryears are of no consequence today and the sooner you forget about them the better. The pride of success removes you away from your team members, as you feel superior to others. This leads to an unspoken contempt for lesser achievers. You should never get into the ego syndrome, as it is likely to bring you in their category.

Success may take the person away from his team and in isolation he cannot achieve his goals at all. The person has to stand the trial of his strengths and courage of conviction. He must stand by his commitment to his goals as he removes thoughts of likely failure from his mind. With practice of meditation he will find himself endowed with special psychic powers and can perform business miracles by succeeding even in the most hostile business environment. However, if he starts to use the powers for his personal gains, they will disappear in the shortest possible time.

REWIND NETWORK MODIFY AGENDA

The question you face is, "Am I good enough for the salvation I am seeking and what should I do to prepare myself for the same?"

If you know yourself, it should not be difficult to do so. Here is the road map if you want to change your perspective, you should use it:

- Understand thoroughly your present mindset. Are you distracted by the demons of lust, anger, greed and/or nepotism? If yes, then you must plan self-purification through meditation with the help of a good guru. If you are stressed out due to work pressure, take timeout to relax as stress saps your energy and your ability to think in a rational manner.
- Next, discuss with your guru the final position you want for your mindset, where you want to reach? The road to salvation is rough and steep and you need to go step-by-step, putting your feet firmly in each step, otherwise there is a grave danger of slipping back as the temptations and distractions are around you all the time.
- Once you have decided the destination, you have to work out a travel plan. This again requires a guru, who has practical and theoretical knowledge of having traversed the path. The route you take will be full of travails and if anyone tries to give you a quick-fix technique he is, most likely a hoax. You should be careful and cautious in finding your path as it will lead you to salvation or it could take you to a pseudo land where the temptations come camouflaged as mantras.
- You can use your own success stories for reinforcing your faith in your own abilities. Past success can be used to build confidence level. As you improve your confidence, the negatives from your mindset would start disappearing fast.
- As you plan to make major changes, you need to give yourself time. You should have perseverance, patience and a strong desire and you will surely succeed in your endeavour.
- Once you attain the desired levels of mental attitudes, you must never become complacent as it would only lead you to decay as you lose the benefits acquired with great efforts. You must have an internal feedback plan, which tells you when you have slipped down the levels you have set for yourself.

If you follow the directions in the correct manner, you not only attain the spiritual platform you need, but you also stay there. The only snake, which is likely to swallow you, is the ego, your inflated esteem of self.

SUPERIOR BEINGS

Six Russian soldiers were asked by their commander to play the Russian roulette, as there was no war and nothing else to be done. The commander used his prerogative as the senior to stand at the end of the line. As the soldiers were to pull the trigger, the last person had the best chance of survival, because if the revolver with only one bullet passes without killing anyone till the five shots, he could again use his seniority for not pulling the sixth time, as the country needs him, more than it needs the other soldiers. However, one person was waiting near the gate and when asked, "What are you waiting for?" he replied, "for the seventh person to join the club, when I will stand as I am standing, the last one in the line".

9
CHAPTER

Soft Skills Essential for Leaders

LEADERSHIP SOFT SKILLS AND VALUE SYSTEMS

Leadership in corporate world starts with the CEO or the MD and group leadership at the Board of Directors level. The CEO, the leader needs the soft skills to steer the company to success as he creates a cohesive team out of a group of people. The CEO must gain respect and confidence of the team members by his actions, behaviour patterns that will enable the CEO to instil the company's vision, mission and goals in the mindset of his team members. Only then can the CEO be sure of leading the company to its corporate goals.

These CEO skills include political sensitivity, business and commercial acumen, strategic policy making and understanding funding mechanisms. On the next level, the CEO must be able to manage and sift the plethora of information available to the CEO. Besides, the CEO's approach regarding interpersonal relations is important.

The following areas need the CEO's focus:

- Organizational control points
- Team building
- Communication and persuasion
- Networking and Public Relations
- How to Lead through organizational changes

The CEO's working life consists of nearly 10 hours a day seven days a week. Their office becomes their virtual home. Time is used for problem solving that cannot be deferred and mostly belong to the team members' highhandedness and infighting. At times the reason of aberrant behaviour of the colleague is not clear and requires CEO's concerted efforts, positive attitude that builds goodwill among the team members. For influencing the team members the CEO must have their respect that can never be taken for granted but it has to be earned through his actions.

Some of the common difficult behaviours of team members are given below:

The team members form formal or even informal groups. At times these groups are meant for show of strength against the CEO. Team members feel secure belonging to a group, as the group can have a forceful voice that can be used for fighting legitimate and even unreasonable demands of the team members. Even if there are no issues the group membership ensures enthusiasm in going to the workplace and performing to their ability. The group has a positive role to play for the company too, that of dissemination of company policy, rules and systems that can be informally brought to their notice in casual meetings and then allowed to spread through the grapevine.

The negative value of groups is the deliberate remarks made to vilify the company, its CEO and its policies. The remarks, especially the caustic ones, come from unprofessional group members who can create mental torture resulting in communication road blocks. Such innuendoes can cause negativism that could affect team members' performance or even increase the rate of company's attrition.

LUNCH ROOM CHAT

The annoying thing at the workplace can be groups of men/women chatting about maid servants, clothes, cosmetics and jewellery, or even cricket scores, films and the like. Some of them can be even seen selling some items at work. It is really unprofessional and causes irritation to those around. However, a thin line exists between annoying diatribe and some small talk and the CEO must be able to identify them for what they are worth.

Flattery

This is widely accepted as omnipresent and is universally detested.

Sweet behaviour in front of persons and backstabbing comments behind their back are known to prevail in virtually every kind of human interaction. The natural fallout of such hypocrisy at the workplace is failure of trust, which affects work relationships and productivity. The CEO therefore must never agree to be a party to either flattery or listening to backbiting.

Individual Bias

When angry with something the boss does, people tend to control emotions and behave in a subdued manner. However, if a lower ranked person goofs up even slightly, most don't think twice before berating at him. Can this be justified in any manner? Dignity of labour and respect for all kinds of work is a prerequisite for a healthy work environment. It must be appreciated that people at all levels provide value with whatever work they do. It can be downright discouraging if they are not treated with dignity, considering they work to the best of their ability, given individual constraints. In case mentoring is needed for a wrong doer, it is best done on one-to-one basis when no other person is present. Praise of good deeds must be done in the company of peers and others concerned.

Office Neighbours

There are certain annoying habits like keeping your workplace dusty and dirty that can really upset people. Eating at the workstation and dropping titbits of food, or having heaps of papers and files that spill over to neighbours' desks can be bothersome. A lot of people are fussy about cleanliness and are used to a certain standard of hygiene around them. If those standards are not met at the workplace, it can be demotivating.

Nosey Colleagues

It is common for colleagues to become friends over a period of time, certain level of formality is expected at work. When the formality is breached, not everyone takes it well.

When colleagues are unduly concerned about where someone went the previous evening, with whom, why, one really feels like telling them it is none of their business. If one would wish to share personal thoughts with someone at the workplace, one needs to be comfortable with that person. It has to be voluntary. The concept of personal space and privacy is rather alien to a few corporate cultures. CEO needs to create cultural ambience suited to this common principle.

I did it

It is natural that people want to be appreciated for the work they do. However, since most of the work they do in an organization is team effort, it is important that credit too is shared.

The seniors often give pep talks on how teamwork is important. However, when the results come in, individuals and departments want the credit. In most organizations, the marketing and sales people take the appreciation. The back-end operations group is forgotten, even though they contribute significantly to the success, rendering them frustrated and disheartened.

Limelighting

Some persons have resonant voices, good for recording purposes and they use their voices talking loudly, disturbing the neighbourhood peace. One would wish such people had attenuators fitted to them. At work, formal, subdued behaviour is called for. Etiquette demands that one would keep voice low so others are not disturbed. The most annoying bit is when people excitedly almost yell over their phones for no reason. It must be equally annoying for the person at the other end of the line. Talking loudly is often associated with rustic behaviour that lacks sophistication. It is advisable to keep your tone and pitch low when colleagues are in hearing range.

LEADERS' ROLE

It is indeed difficult to keep cool and focus on productivity when behavioural factors affect performance at work. It is necessary to be assertive to solve the problem. Assertiveness is different from being accusatory. Assertiveness is all about talking in a factual manner without being judgmental. It involves conveying facts and their possible repercussions without getting emotional, or rude, in the process. It is easier said than done; professionalism really needs that one remains objective and calm while dealing with such situations. At the organizational level, the entire HR department, including managers and supervisors, need to have a keen eye for observing team dynamics. Active intervention and counselling go a long way in smoothing frayed tempers. The best course is to avoid irritating behaviour by proactive actions, such as:

Avoid Listening to Backbiting

While at the workplace, one should never discuss a person in his/ her absence. This simple rule goes a long way in maintaining a healthy environment. If the CEO thinks a colleague has been shying away from him/her for a while, the CEO should casually enquire to find out if the CEO's behaviour has upset him/ her. If that is the case, one should patiently listen to the colleague's feelings without getting defensive. Once the person has opened up, it is easier to resolve the issue.

Give and Gain Respect

Suppose in a hotel the entire housekeeping team goes on strike. One often takes a lot of people for granted simply because they may not demand attention. But that does not mean their work is any less important. A lot of colleagues may become friends over time. However, work ethics dictate one to remain sensitive to the feelings of everyone at the workplace and over-friendly behaviour ought to be avoided.

Soft Skills Training

The training methods are far removed from conventional methods of training where lot of interactive activities are conducted related to behaviour. The training helps in bringing out behavioural changes among the individuals. During this training, real life environment is created and participants are trained in a simulated environment through several role plays, activities, exercises and participation.

Aims/Objectives

Soft Skills Training helps people develop competencies and capabilities. It develops and strengthens several work related skills making them competent and confident in handling tasks effectively and efficiently. It brings out behavioural changes among the trainees so that they develop interpersonal communication, team building skills and leadership skills. It helps them in enhancing productivity and performance at the workplace. In case of students, the training helps them to acquire employability skills so that they can get employment easily.

How-to-Do?

The process of training programme involves role plays, case studies, group activities, exercises, management techniques and feedback and evaluation for takeaways, through well-crafted feedback forms. The process depends on the profile and the requirement of audiences. It is essential to bring the participants out of their comfort zones through effective interaction and participation. The practical interaction helps the participants in re-energising and reactivating themselves.

The training gets people involved, gives them new abilities and capabilities and enhances their awareness and worth by discovering and developing their psychic powers. The trainers should develop their own psychic powers and tried and tested tools and techniques drawn from their industry or corporate experience. The training methodology should be based on experiential learning where a facilitating learning environment should be created for better takeaways.

The training methodology must include interactive sessions, role-plays, games, practical exercises, questionnaires and feedback should form an integrated part of learning process to enable the faculty to keep updating the programme. In addition, the training sessions must include psychometric tests that give insights and ideas to the leaders on the areas to be developed.

An ideal soft skills workshop should contain the following topics:

- What are soft skills and their importance?
- Understanding communication
- Body language
- Active listening
- Socializing interaction
- Hidden data of communication
- Team building skills and stages in formation of teams
- Role plays and activities for team building
- Group discussions
- Interview skills
- Decision-making
- Presentation skills with exercises
- Corporate etiquettes
- Business ethics
- Mentoring, coaching and counselling
- Benefits/Takeaways

An ideal soft skills workshop should have training in the following areas:

- Communications Skills
- Assertive Skills
- Behaviour Management or Interpersonal Skills
- Emotional Intelligence
- Personality Development
- Managerial Skills

- Time Management
- Stress Management
- Business Etiquettes
- Team Building
- Leadership
- Mentoring
- Managerial/Supervisory Skills
- Conflict Management
- E-mail/Telephone Etiquette
- Negotiating Skills
- Creative Thinking
- Networking Skills
- Business Communication
- Entrepreneurial Skills
- Feedback and Takeaways

The above content is only tentative and it depends on the level of management and also the experience of the CEOs. In fact, any training programme needs to be tailored and customized as per the needs and profile of audiences.

TRAINERS

The trainers should have skills in assessing training needs, designing, developing, delivering, administering and even evaluating training solutions. It is essential to blend technology with traditional methods, problem-solving tools and techniques, communication skills, promotional skills through practical training.

The essential characteristics to become trainers are:

- Communication skills
- Domain knowledge
- Handling the questions
- Ability to align the answers of the participants in tune with the standard responses.
- Confidence
- Facing huge crowds
- Presence of mind
- Tact
- Pleasing personality
- High energy levels
- Industry experience
- Cheerfulness
- Analytical, incisive, logical, and sound observation
- Jack-of-all-trades and master of a particular domain
- Passion and ability to share experience and expertise with others

The trainers should be able to observe and correctly interpret what is happening before, during and after the training. They should be imaginative and must surely possess the ability to think on the feet and tackle situations. They must have the ability to encourage others to go beyond their current level of performance. To achieve this, the trainers should be willing to share experiences and expertize and invest time for the sake of others and the organization. They must strongly believe that people are capable of higher performance. They should enjoy working with people rather than expecting to take credit for improvements in others.

VALUE-BASED MANAGEMENT

For the CEOs it is better that he/she should never think about size, revenues and profits of the organization. The dream, right from day one, should be to build a company that was having high brand equity/image. Brand image is a reflection of the values that drive the company. Market share and brand equity are arguably the most important assets of any company. It is rightly said that a company is known by the men it keeps, their value systems and the support of their stakeholders.

The CEO must have strong commitment for value-based management. Company's interest should be paramount for the CEO and personal interests should always be subservient to company' interest. It should be remembered that no person is indispensable, not even the CEO. It is important that one gives challenging assignments to deserving people, whether they are young or new in the organization, after they have been tested for their loyalty. Youth and empowerment are important to value scalability and longevity. The trust of employees is an important ingredient for successful leadership. To gain the trust of people, there is no more powerful leadership style than leadership by example. The leader must be the role model for the followers and that is possible only through proper and correct actions. The world respects performance and action, not rhetoric.

It must be understood that if you want to look smart, you must surround yourself with people smarter than you, or at least as smart as you. Everybody needs incentives to perform. Money is not the only motivator; respect, dignity, fairness and inclusiveness are essential to get the best out of employees.

The leaders must have sense of justice and fair-play. They must be broad minded. In their leadership every employee must feel happy, even excited when talking about the company. Each member of the company must behave like its Public Relations Manager; from the CEO right to the down peon.

A company's value system is its main strength. A value system is a set of behaviour in a company that enhances the trust, confidence, commitment, energy and enthusiasm of the members of the community. Leaders need to practice the value system they want to propagate as this is the best method of inducing values in the team. They must be clear in their approach, when they interact with the team to enunciate the company's code of conduct, its value system. Otherwise, there are chances of the entire company sinking into the numerous pitfalls in the marketplace. Such deliberate fixation with values has to start with the company's induction process when the newcomers get full impact of the same and easily assimilate it as they are still new to the company. Companies have to initiate their value-based management to the new entrants. For the newcomers the value coordinates must become the guiding principles. Each person must shoulder the responsibility of his/her ethics.

A leader is an agent of change, and progress is about change. In the words of Robert F Kennedy, 'Progress is a nice word; but change is its motivator.' Leadership is about raising the aspirations of followers and enthusing people with a desire to reach for the stars. For instance, Mahatma Gandhi created a vision for independence in India and raised the aspirations of our people. Leadership is about making people say, 'I will walk on water for you.' It is about creating a worthy dream and helping people achieve it.

Robert Kennedy summed up leadership best when he said, 'Others see things as they are and wonder why; I see them as they are not and say why not?'

PROBLEM TIMES

A leader has to raise the confidence of followers. He should make them understand that tough times are part of life and that they will come out better at the end of it. He has to sustain their hope, and their motivation and energy levels to handle the difficult days.

There is no better example of this than Winston Churchill. His courageous leadership as prime minister of Great Britain successfully led the British people from the brink of defeat during World War II. He raised his people's hopes with the words, 'These are not dark days; these are great days — the greatest days our country has ever lived.'

Strong leadership is most needed at times of crisis. In the words of Seneca, the Greek philosopher, 'Fire is the test of gold; adversity, of strong men.'

DESTINATION VALUE

The leader has to create hope. He has to create believable stories about better future for the organization: everyone should be able to see the rainbow and become a part of it.

This requires promoting trust in people. And for trust, the leader has to create a value system: a catch phrase for behaviour that enhances the confidence, commitment, motivation and enthusiasm of the people.

A value system creates the environment for people to have high aspirations, self-esteem, and belief in fundamental values, confidence in the future and the enthusiasm necessary to undertake even apparently difficult tasks. Leaders have to walk the talk and demonstrate their commitment to their value system.

Mahatma Gandhi said, 'We must become the change we want to see in the world.' Leaders have to prove their belief in personal sacrifice and hard work. Such behaviour will motivate the employees to make even bigger sacrifices. It will help win the team's confidence, help leaders become credible, and help create trust in their ideas. Chrysler's Lee Iacocca took over its reins when the company was in doldrums. He accepted a salary of $1 per year till the company was back on its feet. His followers immediately accepted salary reductions that helped the company recover fast.

ENHANCING TRUST

Trust and confidence can coexist where there is transparency. The leader has to create an environment where each person feels secure enough to be able to disclose his or her mistakes, and resolve to improve.

Investors respect such organizations as they understand that the business will have good times and bad times. What they want the companies to do is to be on the level with them at all times. They want companies to disclose bad news on a proactive basis. In one of the top Indian companies, Infosys, the philosophy has always been, 'When in doubt, disclose.'

LEADERSHIP GOVERNANCE CHARTER

Good corporate governance is about maximizing shareholder value on a sustainable basis while ensuring fairness to all stakeholders: customers, vendor-partners, investors, employees, government and society.

A successful organization overcomes downturns. The best index of success is its longevity. This is predicated on adhering to the finest levels of corporate governance, business ethics and code of conduct. Infosys has consistently adopted transparency and disclosure standards even before law mandated it. In 1995, Infosys suffered losses in the secondary market. Under Indian GAAP (generally accepted accounting principles), it was not required to make this information public. Nevertheless, the company, true to its credo published this information in their annual report.

CREATING AND SUSTAINING AN ENVIRONMENT OF SUCCESS

Transparency about the organization's operations should be accompanied by an open environment inside the organization. The leaders have to create such an ambience where any employee can disagree with you without fear of reprisal. In such a case, everyone makes suggestions for the common good. In the end everyone will be better off. The employees need to know that not all their suggestions need be accepted and not always the leader would give the reason thereof. At times there could be policy matters yet in the melting pot, and therefore confidential. The leaders should understand that whenever any member of the team is not transparent enough, and shows his indispensability, he or she is not right for the company. Like at Enron, the CFO was running an empire where people were afraid to speak. In some other cases, the whistle blowers have been harassed and thrown out of the company, while they should be protected. In any case in a smooth running company where the leader has chosen and nurtured his team well, the leader should not listen to backbiting ever.

MANAGERIAL REMUNERATION

Companies have gone towards excessive salaries and options for senior management staff. At one company, the CEO's employment contract not only set out the model of the Mercedes the company would buy him, but also promised a monthly first-class air ticket for his mother, along with a cash bonus of $10 million and other benefits.

Not surprisingly, this company had to file for bankruptcy.

Managerial remuneration should be based on three principles:

- On a structured base with fairness with respect to the compensation of other employees.
- Transparency with respect to shareholders and employees, with no hidden perks.
- Accountability with respect to linking compensation with corporate performance, although subjective assessment can be a tricky proposition.

Several companies therefore are planning the compensation with a fixed and a variable component. The variable component should be linked to achieving long-term objectives of the firm. Senior management should swim or sink with the fortunes of the company. And the leader's association with the company should be strong enough where they do not desert the sinking ship. Leaders need to keep trying to salvage the company in the best possible manner. The decision to divest should be based on solid reasoning, taking the interest of stakeholders at heart.

Senior management compensation should be reviewed by the compensation committee of the board, which should consist only of independent directors. Further, this should be approved by the shareholders.

It is often asked how senior management compensation has a ceiling when the company is making millions. However, the millions represent the dividend portion for the stockholders and compensation for the promoters, risk takers along with the capital market.

The leader should have full consideration for the entrepreneurs and the compensation for senior manager. They need to keep the difference between the top and bottom salaries and the disparity should be manageable that does not create rancour in any group.

FAITH IN LEADERSHIP

Leadership helps win the trust of the stakeholders, making it more likely that they will stand by them in their hour of need. As leaders who dream of growth and progress, integrity is the most wanted attribute. This should remain true even in adverse situations.

Leaders need to lead teams to fight for the truth and never compromise on values. The corporate leaders, through honest and correct behaviour, will reap long-term benefits. For their stakeholders a leader is an agent of change, and progress is about change. In the words of Robert F. Kennedy, 'Progress is a nice word; but change is its motivator.' Leaders motivate followers and inculcate the desire to excel.

Leadership is about making people say, 'I am ready to do even the most difficult tasks for you my leader". It is about creating a worthy dream for the followers and helping them achieve it. Robert Kennedy summed up leadership best when he said, 'Others see things as they are and wonder why; I see them as they are not and say why not?'. This becomes definitely possible when the leader shows unbiased equanimity in dealing with the team members. THIS HAPPENS WHEN THE LEADER HAS BUILT TRUST AMONGST HIS TEAMMATES.

DIFFICULT TIMES

Followers need confidence, especially in difficult times, and the leaders must have the acumen of building confidence in their team. The followers would understand that difficult times are part of company's life and they should steel the company and not demoralize the followers. Followers must remain energized and motivated during the crises periods. Winston Churchill showed his courageous leadership as prime minister of Great Britain by successfully leading the British people from the brink of defeat during World War II. He raised his people's hopes with the words, "These are not dark days; these are great days – the greatest days our country has ever lived".

LEADERS' VALUE SYSTEM

Leader has to create hope through a plausible story about a better future for the organization; by creating trust in people everyone should be able to see the silver lining. And to create trust, the leader has to profess to a value system; a behaviour that enhances the confidence, motivation level, energy, commitment and enthusiasm of the people.

Adherence to a value system creates the environment for people to have high aspirations, self-esteem and belief in basic values, confidence in the future and the enthusiasm necessary to take up apparently difficult tasks. Leaders have to "do and show" and prove their commitment to a value system. Mahatma Gandhi said, 'We must become the change we want to see in the world.' Leaders have to prove their belief in sacrifice and hard work. Such behaviour will motivate the employees to make sacrifices. It will help win the team's confidence, help leaders become credible, and help create trust in their ideas.

Trust and confidence can only exist where there is a premium on transparency. The leader has to create an environment where each person feels secure enough to be able to disclose his or her mistakes, and resolves to improve.

Investors respect such organizations. Investors understand that the business will have good times and bad times. What they want you to do is to level with them at all times. They want the leaders to disclose bad news on a proactive basis. At Infosys philosophy has always been, 'When in doubt, disclose.'

GOVERNANCE

Good corporate governance is about maximizing shareholder value on a sustainable basis while ensuring fairness to all stakeholders: customers, vendor-partners, investors, employees, government and society.

A successful organization tides over many downturns. The best index of success is its longevity. This is predicated on adhering to the finest levels of corporate governance. The leaders need to have transparency and disclosure standards.

TENSION-FREE ENVIRONMENT

Transparency about the organization's operations should be accompanied by an open environment inside the organization. You have to create an environment where any employee can disagree with you without fear of reprisal. In such a case, everyone makes suggestions for the common good. In the end everyone will be better off. On the other hand, at Enron, the CFO was running an empire where people were afraid to speak. In some other cases, the whistle blowers have been harassed and thrown out of the company.

MANAGERIAL REMUNERATION

We have gone towards excessive salaries and options for senior management staff. At one company, the CEO's employment contract not only set out the model of the Mercedes the company would buy him, but also promised a monthly first-class air ticket for his mother, along with a cash bonus of $10 million and other benefits. Not surprisingly, this company has already filed for bankruptcy.

Managerial remuneration should be based on the following three principles:

- Fairness with respect to the compensation of other employees.
- Transparency with respect to shareholders and employees.
- Accountability with respect to linking compensation with corporate performance.

Thus, the compensation should have a fixed component and a variable component. The variable component should be linked to achieving long-term objectives of the firm. Senior management should swim or sink with the fortunes of the company.

Leaders and senior management compensation should be reviewed by the compensation committee of the board, which should consist only of independent directors. Further, this should be approved by the shareholders for bringing in total transparency in the organization.

The leadership problem comes when it has to cope with the accusation that while the company is minting money how the senior managers remuneration can be restricted. The balance has to be made with respect to the profit margins to the promoters, the risk takers and the stockholders with compensation, remuneration to the senior managers and the leaders.

The leadership must understand these two distinct systems, otherwise entrepreneurship will be curbed, and new companies will not come up, no industry business will get stifled. The compensation must be fair and the difference between maximum and minimum salary-wage structure should be minimum.

VISION AND INTEGRITY

Strong leadership in trying times helps win the trust of the stakeholders, making it more likely that they will stand by the leaders in hour of need. For leaders who dream of growth and progress, integrity is the most wanted attribute. Leaders need to lead the teams to fight for the truth and never compromise on values. With confidence corporate leaders, through honest and desirable behaviour, will reap long-term benefits for their stakeholders.

ADVERSITY

A leader has to raise the confidence of followers. He should make them understand that tough times are a part of life and that they will come out better at the end of it. He has to sustain their hope, and their energy levels to handle the difficult days. Winston Churchill's courageous leadership as prime minister of Great Britain successfully led the British people from the brink of defeat during World War II. He raised his people's hopes with the words, "These are not dark days; these are great days – the greatest days our country has ever lived."

VALUES

The leaders create hope for their followers. They have to create a plausible story about a better future for the organization: everyone should be able to see the silver lining in the dark clouds and catch a part of it. This requires creating trust in people. And to create trust, the leader has to subscribe to a value system: a protocol for behaviour that enhances the confidence, commitment and enthusiasm of the people. Compliance to a value system creates the environment for people to have high aspirations, self-esteem, and belief in fundamental values, confidence in the future and the enthusiasm necessary to take up apparently difficult tasks. Leaders have to walk the talk and demonstrate their commitment to a value system. As Mahatma Gandhi said, 'We must become the change we want to see in the world.' Leaders have to prove their belief in sacrifice and hard work. Such behaviour will enthuse the employees to make bigger sacrifices. It will help win the team's confidence, help leaders become credible, and help create trust in their ideas.

INTEGRITY

Strong leadership in adverse times helps win the trust of the stakeholders, making it more likely that they will stand by you in your hour of need. As leaders who dream of growth and progress, integrity is the most wanted attribute.

Lead the teams to fight for the truth and never compromise on your values. Corporate leaders, through honest and desirable behaviour, can reap long-term benefits for their stakeholders.

LEADERSHIP DEVELOPMENT

In the knowledge era, leadership often comes as a result of a single, powerful idea. In the years to come, the best ideas will triumph, irrespective of what nation or culture they come from. Organizations are performance systems that process great ideas into frames of action. Organizational leadership in the knowledge era will come from imagination, speed and quality of execution of ideas. Leadership is an idea whose time has come.

Human values are assimilated ideas that have stood the test of time. Values provide the knowledge framework for powerful and positive action. Values also provide leverage points for sustainability of any human enterprise. A values system provides a clear reference point for mobilizing the right idea at the right time. Leadership is nothing but an expression of deeply held human values.

Leaders transform information into insight – the source of innovation and change – through which an organization is propelled from the gravitational pull of the past to the grand vista of the emerging future, setting into motion a cycle of vision, integration, action and transformation.

The Tata group believes in creating a corporate leadership based on human values. Identifying, incubating and developing leaders is the group's prime HR strategy for the knowledge era. Leadership courses are among its most important, capped by executive development progress.

HUMAN RESOURCES

The companies need to have a clear notion of what they require to be capable of achieving their goals and business success. They need to have a process and logic in place by which they can identify what those capabilities are across different businesses. They must make sure that their HR systems, processes and procedures are aligned in a manner that helps bring those capabilities into operation. HR managers need to learn the process of creating a clear linkage between HR practices and the organization's business strategy. They need to evolve their company's desired HR practices working backwards from its strategy. More important, they need to find ways to transition from current practices to the desired ones. How does HR strategy link to business strategy? Each of the major subsystems of HR can be assessed for an organization through process and outcome metrics, using qualitative and quantitative data. Given the right tools, the major HR activities of an organization can be audited, provided there is a clear understanding of the intervention nature of the audit and of the sensitivities around audits. Audit outcomes can then be translated into appropriate action plans.

BUSINESS STRATEGY

It is not enough to develop a dynamic and creative corporate strategy. Key personnel at all levels in the organization need to develop a clear understanding of the strategy that the company is trying to execute. More important, that strategy must be translated into a definition of the capabilities that the company needs to succeed. The sum total of these events is successful corporate planning.

Leaders need to train senior managers in the design of organizations to support business strategies. It has programmes in creating strategic alliances, strategies in creating competitive advantage, managing and measuring business performance.

FINANCE

Finance is one of the critical corporate functions, even more so in a rapidly changing business environment. Where is the company headed? How will it get capital? How will that capital be deployed? How can the cost of capital be minimized? How can capital utilization be optimized? In the modern corporation, dynamic finance management can be a prime tool in maximizing return on investment and enhanced profitability.

CUSTOMER ORIENTATION

Competence needs to be built in formulating and implementing market-oriented strategies. Plans and programmes in a dynamic environment are essential for successful companies. This requires an in-depth understanding of the concepts underlying strategy formulation, for the development of capabilities to make pragmatic conjectures / assumptions about competitive actions and reactions that have strategic implications. To ensure that the sales force delivers in line with the brand and marketing objectives of the organization, it is critical to align the selling strategies with the marketing strategies of the company. This includes relationship marketing and leverages the emerging role of IT in the area of sales and marketing.

Leader needs to understand the situation and propagate his thoughts to his team members, work out the possibilities to foster the "success dreams".

10
CHAPTER

Solving Ethical Problems

Several times ethical problems are such that there cannot be a yes or no answer. These problems need focused study of the problems and locating alternate solutions. Suppose the CEO wants to sack an employee who has been the blue-eyed boy so far and is in fact taking a larger hose in the hope of a big rise soon. Should the CEO inform him before he buys the house or leave it as a personal matter of the employee? Suppose there is competition between you and your best friend and colleague and you have come to know about one of his personal faults, should you tell the boss about it to get a leverage over him. Should you decry your competitor's unprofessional behaviour before a customer who could prefer the competitor to you?

The best way would be to carefully and clearly delineate the issue involved along with the people involved in it. Next, decide who is going into the details before finding out the alternative solutions to the issue. Getting the relevant details would bring the exact problem into focus leaving out the unnecessary padding, which people place in order to mitigate the problem.

It is also important to understand the size of the problem. It should not become a case where in order to collect an outstanding due of ten rupees the firm spends a hundred rupees. For minor aberrations it may be sufficient to warn the erring person, while for major irregularities, more severe action could be called for.

It is best to look for both viewpoints, the pros and cons, playing even the devil's advocate. It is better to consult your legal advisor, if you doubt the legality of the problem. The gravity of the problem would be the guiding factor in meting out the justice, where intentions of the wrong doer, his past records, his standing in the firm due to his stay for a long period could become the mitigating factors. If the error has been made inadvertently then clearly a warning would suffice, while in case of intentional blunder, even termination could be justified. People have at times gone to the extent of making public announcements through the newspaper regarding the dismissal of an employee, giving graphic descriptions for the reason of the dismissal. Some others have even written to the next employer of the dismissed employee about the error made by the person. This type of victimization is like capital punishment, which could result in the person remaining unemployed for long periods and his family is the one, which will suffer the most. It is better not to play God in such circumstances.

A storekeeper was given the sack when he was found cheating the firm. However, when on the next Sunday, the sacked person came to the CEO's house with his wife for seeking a job as secretary for his wife, the CEO graciously recommended her name and ensured that she got a job in one of his friend's firm. "the quality of mercy"

To sum up, the best way is to decide if the issue or the problem is really an ethical one or if it is just an administrative issue. You can then look only at the ethical issues involved in the problem, to understand if the issue is people based or is it a moral issue. At this stage it is better to consult like-minded moral people. Could the problem be of an individual, or has it come up because of some firm's regulation or is an industry based problem. Oil companies were caught unaware when most found that a low cost white oil meant for dry-cleaning purposes was being mixed with the high cost petrol. They later on discovered that large-scale proliferation of the contamination could not have become possible without the connivance of the firm's own people.

The CEO must try to locate all possible solutions to the problem, and then decide about the best option. He must keep a feedback loop in place to know the result of his decision. The impact of the decisions is often far reaching, both within and outside the organization. Hence, utmost care should be taken while taking the decisions weighing the possible plus and minus points of the decision. Ultimately the decisions on ethical issues cannot be taken by a thumb rule, as each situation needs special treatment and decision. The CEO has to consider what is right from the firm's viewpoint as also from the society's.

The ethical solutions, regarding reward and punishment must be found with a sense of justice and fair play. Recruitment nepotism, gender bias in wages, promotions and even retrenchments are totally taboo. The CEO has to develop high moral standards to make him independent of outside advice and influence, otherwise his peer group and precedents would cloud his judgment. While the CEO has to give equal opportunity to others to air their views, with his high degree of morality he is sure to make the right decisions in ethical issues. The CEO has to ensure that the organizational culture is built on solid foundation of moral and ethical behaviour. Reward and punishment are the pillars on which the foundation of morality of the firm can be built. In such a culture even the employees who are prone to unethical behaviour would find it difficult to go astray, as they would be forced to stay within the limits of ethics and morality.

In a firm, each person including the CEO, has his own code of ethics. Organizations too develop a code of ethics, which needs to be meticulously followed by the employees. Each industry operates in its business environment and hence, the industry's cultural climate affects the working of firms to a certain degree.

A majority of cases pertaining to ethical issues in a firm emanate from its human resources, in hiring, sacking, promotions, increments, and from interpersonal relationships as there are usually clashes of interest between people, the most common being playing favourite between two or more employees. Such behaviour of the seniors brings heartburns and frustrates the employees.

The next level of ethical issues pertain to the external stakeholders like the suppliers, buyers, financiers. Suppliers can be coerced to supply substandard product at a consideration. Buyers can be short changed by supplying inferior products, which may just meet the specifications but would not stand the test of time. Financier can be drawn in the web of the scamsters who promise high rate of interest, only to run away with the cash.

The other areas where the clash of interest comes from are what the boss wants the employee to do by acting unethically for the firm and his own belief in not doing what is wrong according to the dictates of his own conscience. Each employee with a developed conscience would like to follow strictly the company's rules, regulations, plans and policies, which would be written down with ethics and morality in mind, as no firm can write down its policy as working unethically in business.

The CEO has to ensure that the tasks given to employees are well defined without any ambiguity and with no room for manoeuvrability in the realm of unethical behaviour. He must allot the tasks to the employees depending on their individual traits of character, skills, and the requirement for the job. This way he would be able to minimize the risk of unethical behaviour in the firm.

The CEO has to set an example as a role model by the following means:

- Not using the PC for personal work.
- Not using the firm's phone for making personal calls unless there is an emergency.
- Not using office stationery for personal use.
- Not avoiding going to work even when healthy and reporting sick.
- Not faking expense statements by adding items purchased for personal use.

Otherwise he would not be able to admonish the employees caught doing these acts. The CEO has to decide the punishment to be meted out in such cases, if his employees indulge in them.

The CEO must be above board all the time and he should also be known as a person of impeccable integrity. He should shun anything illegal or amoral totally. He should have a sense of justice and fair play, so that the employees know that they will always be treated as per their work only and not as per any personal likes and dislikes. He should praise his employees for good work before the team and yet admonish them for bad work only in private with no one else present. In this way, the employees will understand and consider the CEO's actions and the stand he takes on ethical issues justified. This type of firm's internal environment is conducive to bringing about loyalty among the employees, as the CEO is not just preaching but is also practicing what he is preaching.

CEO'S BALANCE SHEET

The CEO should keep doing introspection to remain on the side of ethical behaviour in the following manner:

He should define the reasoning for his actions to locate any deviations from the firm's policies and its code of ethics. He should take decisions for the common good of the larger number of persons by remaining just and promoting fair play. He should be comfortable with his decisions even when the whole world comes to know about them. He should not have any reason to feel ashamed of his decisions. The CEO's every action should be above board and should be known to everyone concerned that they are so. He should strongly believe in his decisions and then only he will be able to convince others about them. The CEO should make promises with great care and should never make any promises, which he knows he cannot keep. If the CEO is committed to his decision then the employees too will abide by them. Any dithering by the CEO would result in others not accepting the decisions at all. The most difficult task of a CEO, perhaps is saying no to someone or for something. He must learn the art of saying no, firmly and yet politely. This way he will save a lot of his time as also of others as they would not only try to discuss the matter any further once the CEO has said no.

Firms worldwide are looking for managers, including CEOs, who can be trusted beyond any doubt. Honesty in financial terms, honesty of spoken words, like making promises, honesty in actions are the most sought after traits of character for managers. Some persons have it and yet others put sham acting during job interviews, trying to prove that they are honest, therefore, firms have, of late started making random checks of the background of their prospective managers even before they are called them for interviews.

The CEO has to be like the Caesar's wife, always above board. He must, therefore, keep practicing honesty on a day-to-day basis as there is never any room for complacency. Honesty and integrity are the mush maligned buzzwords and yet the persons who have these do not flaunt them, like medals on the coat lapels. In any case integrity and honesty become apparent when they show up as conspicuous in an otherwise totally dishonest world. However, if the CEO wants to rise in his profession, he has no choice but to remain honest and possess integrity always. CEO's integrity becomes visible in his honest and just actions devoid of nepotism, favouritism and personal benefit agenda.

PSEUDO HONESTY

As the country is full of pseudo intellectuals, sadhus and miracle men, in business world too there are a lot of persons, who are experts in conning the gullible managers into accepting their credentials as honest workers, soon to realize their true nature and personal agenda. Unless the CEO keeps his personal antenna up in the sky and his information system in place such charlatans can take the firm for a ride.

There are mostly borderline persons who would normally behave rationally, in an upright honest manner. However, in certain circumstances they too are forced to deviate from the straight path. At times they have to meet certain targets, deadlines, which are tough and a little bending the rules could solve the problem. A little adjustment in product specification could be used to approve substandard product in the hope that the customer would not be able to detect the same, or at worst it would come back for rectification, which would be easy to carry out, because by then, the right component would become available. In the meanwhile the firm would have met the month's target. Such attitude can backfire badly on the firm, as most experienced managers would vouch for. Not only the customer would detect the flaw, through word of mouth bad publicity the firm could lose huge orders too.

> In 1993, Fiat of Italy ran into serious problem when several of its managers were caught indulging in unethical acts. The company had to initiate a code of ethics to be followed by its members.

There have been rampant unethical activities in the professional cadre like doctors and lawyers. Illegal removal of kidneys and other vital organs from gullible patients who may have come for some minor ailment has been occurring in most parts of the world. Lawyers collude with the lawyers of the opposite party to prolong the cases for personal benefit. In business since huge moneys are involved, even slight deviation from the rules can bring in large sums of money to the unscrupulous persons. The thin line of crossing over from the rigid and right path and the erring route is easy to manage as the error can always be considered a calculated risk taken by the manager, while in fact it could be a deliberate ploy to amass personal wealth. Corrupt people are usually very clever, as they take extra precautions to avoid getting caught.

The manager is at times a pawn in the hands of the CEO, who could be suggesting devious ways for attaining quick success. There are pressures for meeting the targets of sales, purchase and for the rest of the business areas, which could force the manager to take the unethical route in order to achieve the targets. In this regard it should be the job of the CEO, to make the managers understand the firm's code of ethics and place it in line with the firm's code of ethics. The managers must be able to discern right from wrong, ethical from unethical, legal from illegal, upto what extent they can go to meet their targets, satisfy customers, and beyond which the managers would find themselves totally isolated. The CEO has to invest time and money in planning the culture of ethical behaviour in the organization. He should be a role model of ethical and moral behaviour par excellence. The culture of ethics should be all pervading in every area of business activity of the firm. The code of ethics must have total support of the top management and the Board of Directors. Vigilance has become the keyword in most firms, because of the unchecked recruitment of people, some of whom cannot pass the ethics muster.

In view of the large-scale induction of people in firms, the relevance and importance of the HRD has increased several folds in recent years. Once a person has been inducted in to the firm the HRD has to introduce the person to the value-based culture of the firm. This becomes difficult when the owners or the CEO keeps indulging in unethical acts, while believing that their transgressions would remain confidential, and expecting the managers to strictly follow the ethics code.

THE CODE OF ETHICS

The code of ethics must become a written down statement in a firm, which gets superimposed on the firm's vision, mission and goals. It must describe the parameters of the behaviour pattern of the employees while interacting with the firm's external stakeholders, the suppliers, bankers, financiers, the government, the community at large and the buyers. It must state the penalties the employees will be given in case of violation of the code. The code must get full support from the Board of Directors and the person enforcing it must be given full authority for implementing the code in an equitable and just manner, without fear or favour, without malice or greed. If the implementation of the code becomes biased then it ceases to have any value or impact on the employees.

The starting point therefore is the time when a new employee is inducted in the organization. He should be made aware of the code of ethics, with practical examples, about what the firm will accept as ethical behaviour and what it would not. He should also be given an idea of the organizational culture as far as possible. He should be told about the applicability of the code, its jurisdiction and how it would be used against the errant workers. He should know the value of ethical behaviour in the firm and its importance in the employee's annual appraisals, which form the basis of increments, promotions and even the continuance of the employee in the firm. Most good firms give even more importance to the integrity and the moral content in a person's life in the firm than his technical expertize.

BUILDING THE MORAL CONTENT

The morality and ethical behaviour in a firm depends on the guidance shown by the firm's CEO. He has to operate in a transparent manner where the employees know his actions, plans and policies. This would help them relate to the CEO and through him to the firm in a positive manner. The employees should be allowed to talk on controversial subjects as well by playing the devil's advocate. This way the CEO would know their true feelings and also lateral views on any topic and it could unfold new opportunities and hidden threats for the firm.

The CEO has to take the recruitment process of the firm into account to ensure that persons selected to join are having an awakened conscience, the persons who keep doing the soul search exercise to alert their brains, their psyche, body functions and their behaviour in line with the code of ethics of the firm. Such introspection must be carried out on daily basis to be of any use to the employee as also to the firm. The introspection would modulate the working of a person's heart, mind, body and soul. Most of the time even the people doing the introspection do it with half-baked knowledge, when they are fully liable to be carried away by any smart operator who can sway them with his rhetoric. It is therefore important to totally surround the person's psyche with ethical sermons. The best teaching would come only through setting of example by the CEO. Such teachings help the pious thoughts to permeate in to the mindset of the employees and reside there permanently. Instead of making the employees lethargic, they bring immense calm and peace of mind, placing the mind in the most possible efficiency mode.

The best of the firms can have some employees who are not totally satisfied by the way the firm functions and more especially, treats them. Therefore, continuous interactive sessions with the employees who are allowed to air their grievances and the problems they face in the firm is the best way for understanding the employees. The grievance redressal needs speed, care and justice with fair play.

The employees should be fully known of the firm's commitment towards the welfare of its stakeholders. They should be allowed to voice their opinion on the subject and their constructive suggestions should be made part of the firm's mission towards its stakeholders.

The employees should be made aware that the firm accepts the high moral code they possess. Any employee showing the courage of his conviction as he follows the dictates of his own conscience must be applauded, as others should be told to emulate him. The employee who informs the real misdeeds of another employee, even of his senior, should be complimented and not victimized as the latter type of treatment would take the enthusiasm from the employee and encourage the wrong doers in keep on doing the evil acts. However, if someone is just blowing his top with the evil intentions of wilfully harming an innocent person then he should be punished severely.

When any employee is working in a sensitive area with lot of opportunities of going astray, he should be given counselling before and during his tenure there to keep him on track.

Case Study – Cold Annealing of Steel

Work on bridge construction was going on over the river Ganga. The contractor who had been awarded the contract had quoted lowest rates on the condition that the Executive Engineer would allow him to use hot annealing of steel, where he would save nearly 200,000 rupees per tonne. The bridge required fifty thousand tonnes and the contractor was to save ten crores of rupees, if the engineer overlooked the provision of cold annealing. The contractor was ready to share half of the extra profit with the engineers. The executive engineer in charge had agreed to the stipulation. He knew that a layperson would never be able to decipher the difference between cold and hot annealing of steel. Usually, the auditing and costing people belonged to that category and the executive engineer was sure that he would be able to keep the audit team happy by looking after them by giving expensive gifts.

The executive engineer had not considered the possibility of a new young assistant engineer joining his team for the bridge project. On his first inspection tour the engineer stopped the work on the bridge site after finding out that hot annealing was being carried out. When the contractor told him that before stopping the work he should consult his boss the executive engineer, who had in fact authorized the hot annealing by explaining that the hot annealing would take care of the bridge for at least the next ten years and by that time he would have retired from service. The engineer remained adamant on his decision and decided to report the matter to the executive engineer.

Assistant Engineer, "you may not be aware that on the bridge site the contractor is cheating the government by using hot annealed steel, thereby risking the safety of the bridge. I have stopped the work, although the contractor was justifying hot annealing as you had approved it. Of course, he could not show any written approval given by you".

Executive Engineer, "I believe what you did was the right decision from a youngster like you. You have no experience of building bridges, while I am a veteran in this game. I can recount at least ten bridges which I got constructed and all of them have stood the test of the time, by being in use for ten years or more".

Assistant Engineer had read the reports of the collapse of the Mandovi river bridge in Goa, which was constructed by the executive engineer, but he kept quiet about it. The executive engineer said, "you have had a tiring day. Go home and relax. You will find your wife in quite a good mood tonight".

The Assistant Engineer found a new thirty-inch TV had been installed in his house courtesy the contractor.

Questions for the students:

1. Accept the gift and fall in line with the executive engineer.
2. Politely return the TV and yet keep protesting with the boss about the unethical practice of the contractor.
3. Report the matter to the Chief Engineer, even though he has a sneaking suspicion that perhaps even he was involved in the racket.
4. Report the matter to the minister and the police.

It is the job of the CEO to organize training programmes in ethical business to the new entrants in the organization and also keep having refresher courses for the existing employees. Such training programmes need the total support and the approval of the Board of Directors. The training should be done by using real life case studies, where free and frank views need to be expressed by the participants, without any fear of persecution at a late date. The HR Department should ensure that no training programme is organized without an element of training on ethics. The employees must be encouraged to report on unethical behaviour of any employee (at whatever level he works in the organization) found guilty. For this purpose, the CEO has to build the organizational culture, which is conducive to ethical behaviour and of non-tolerance of unethical behaviour. Each member of the firm, new and old, must be given a copy of the code of conduct for the employees, with continuous updates on it as and when made. The CEO plays an integral role in the conduct of business of the organization and in today's competitive world he can survive in the marketplace only by conducting himself ethically and creating the organizational culture, which fosters such behaviour among other employees.

MORALITY AND ETHICS

When the CEO shows the way of moral operations, others take notice and try to emulate the CEO. Once the system of ethical operations is put in place it acts as a morale booster and motivator for the employees. CEO as the leader has to show through his work, personality and demeanour his expertize in the area of the firm's operations, besides his commitment to the welfare of the firm's stakeholders. With a CEO who is liked and respected by the employees, the task of training the employees in ethical operations becomes easy. The task is most important in the changing times of the firm, as the CEO has the duty of restructuring the firm for optimizing the results. In this task he needs total cooperation, commitment and hard work from the employees, which is ethically and morally correct. During change phase the temptation of going astray is large, as the employees know that everyone is busy doing his bit and no one is on the lookout for deviant behaviour.

The CEO therefore has to put in place a continuous monitoring system, which would be manned by scrupulously honest and trusted persons, who would mercilessly report the ethical deviations and moral turpitudes. Once the ethics have been ingrained in the work ethos of the firm, the errant employees would automatically surface as the peer group would force them in either following the norms of code of ethics or quitting the firm on their own volition.

As the ethical organization takes shape, it would promote decentralization of decision-making process, hasten the decisions as a result thereof, add to the competitive advantage of the firm. Firms need to look for long-term benefits from the code of ethics, rather than short-term gains. "Let us do it just this once, after all every one, including our major competitors are doing it and gaining ground over us in the marketplace. Once the balance is struck, we will stop such activities at once." This has been the theme song for most of the CEOs and it drags them into a vicious circle from where it becomes impossible to come out. The so-called one time deviation is the quagmire of unethical, immoral conduct. It is best to stay clear from such short-term gains, which are counterproductive always.

Ethics is, however, not a static entity and needs to be updated periodically as the CEO finds out new areas, which could be totally black or even grey, where he and his team has to do the tightrope walking, without upsetting the legitimate operations. The CEO should set up the Ethics Code Regulatory Authority, which would scan the areas of operation in the firm prone to unethical behaviour. Once the code of ethics has been formulated and circulated among the employees, it should lead to character building, integrity in operations and self-respect.

The firm's vision, mission and goals must reflect its abiding faith in ethical and moral operations only. This would become the guiding light for the employees and they would be able to get out of any dilemma they may face on what is the right action and what is not. The HRD has to start the work right from the time when they are in the process of selection of employees. Besides the technical qualifications and experience it is important to know if the applicant would fit in the ethical and cultural stream of the firm. The task of the CEO in keeping the employees on the right side becomes easy with the right selection of employees.

The CEO of the firm has to lead from the front by example, being a role model himself, who behaves strictly as per the code of ethics of the firm. He must stick to his given word and accept its consequences if his decision is found to be wrong. He must not change his statements while talking to different set of people. If at any time he is not in a position to meet his commitment, he must advise the concerned person well in advance, with reasons of his failure, if possible. Clearly annunciated policies and plans help build ethical culture in the firm.

The CEO should organize training programmes, refresher courses for the employees to help them remain committed to the code of ethics of the firm. Accountability in ethical issues should be that of the individual employee, while, the teams should be required to keep monitoring the ethical functioning of the individuals. Employees should have recourse to advice on ethical dilemmas they face at different levels, so that they do not have to approach the CEO all the time. Such counselling would foster loyalty amongst the employees. There should be a just and equitable punishment to the erring employees. There should be an audit on ethical operations of the individuals and teams and such audit should promote accountability and responsibility of the employees.

ORGANIZATIONAL CULTURE

Organizational culture can be defined as a set of values, with which the firm assures of its operations being within the norms of good business practices. It also assures that beliefs and shared values of its employees are based on sound ethical principles.

ETHICS IN MARKETING AND ADVERTISING

Buying behaviour results from ethics in marketing as well marketers, which give value for money to the customers. Non-standard products, defective goods, prices that give wrong impression to the buyers (hidden charges like transport, taxes, duties not mentioned in the beginning) short packing are some areas of unethical practices. Such deals can give only short-term small benefits and in the long run even if the law does not catch up, the customers eschew purchasing such goods and dealing with such marketers. In the bargain even good products of the marketer are discarded. A few examples will make the subject better understood by the students:

- Food items mixed with unhygienic wrong products like wrong non-food grade preservatives.
- Fake branded products.
- Products like video and audio tapes which are pirated.
- Quoting different prices to customers for standard products, unless quantity discounts are being offered.
- Advertising five star hotel when it does not have even three star facilities
- Advertising contraband goods like liquor, drugs, etc.
- Cheating in annual sales where the prices are jacked up from original; then the discounted price still remains almost as original.

Incorrect or misleading advertising should be firmly avoided. It can cause untold harm including legal action, which has become one of the deterrents of such advertisements today.

There are always some get rich quick sellers, who dupe the customers and disappear before the law catches up with them.

Case Study – Dilemma of a Purchase Manager

Madan had joined Pax International as their Purchase Manager, and he had to report to Mr. Gupta who was the General Manage Purchase in the firm. One week after his joining he found a small parcel on his table, which his secretary informed him had been left there by the firm's biggest supplier Sethi. On opening the packet Madan found the expensive Rolex ladies watch worth ten thousand rupees, with a note that it is a gift for Madan's wife. Madan became angry as he had been scrupulously honest so far and had warded off all temptations. He wanted to ring up Sethi to ask him to take the gift back.

At that time, Gupta entered the office chamber and the following conversation ensued:

Gupta, "I see you are worried about the gift for your wife Sethi has left on your table. What do you want to do with it?"

Madan replied," I have no intention of keeping the gift. In fact, I was going to call Sethi just now for this purpose".

Gupta, "Think about the joy you will give your wife when you present the watch to her".

Madan, "Please believe me, my wife too has the same opinion about taking or refusing gifts and she too wants me to remain honest. I know you are just testing me on the subject".

Gupta, "No I am not testing you. Please accept the gift. Sethi has left an even more expensive watch for my wife and I have decided to keep it and give it to my wife today".

Madan, "Sir, do you not believe that taking the gift will compromise our bargaining power with Sethi and the firm will lose in the bargain".

Gupta, "On that account you just do not worry. We will not place any additional orders on Sethi because of the gift".

Madan is facing great stress and he is unable to take a rational decision. If he accepts the gift, he is compromising on his principles, however, he would be satisfying his boss. If he rejects the gift, the boss will get annoyed and he could terminate his short stay in the firm.

Task before the Students

Give your recommendations regarding the way Madan should conduct himself in the situation and what action he should plan.

SUPERORDINATE GOALS

Each corporate house must star with having superordinate goals, which are the higher order objectives going beyond profits, return on investment, growth and similar economic or financial measures. They are certain guiding principles and concepts, a set of values and aspirations, often unwritten that go beyond the conventional formal statements of quantifiable corporate goals and objectives.

Superordinate goals are similar to the organizational vision and mission statements, which are usually altruistic in nature, which signify what good the entrepreneur is planning for the population he wants to serve. These goals are meant to be spread in the entire organization and they become useful once the employees accept them and work towards their achievement.

From these goals the CEO should derive the firm's value base and its culture. A firm with rich cultural heritage would be a storehouse of anecdotes, which confirm its culture. Culture can be defined as "how we do our work here" and as the firms have value-based work ethos, the employees will also get into the spirit of the culture and take pride in being part of the organization. Those who do not subscribe to the culture will automatically be thrown out. The culture should focus on the quality of not only the firm's products but also its operations; its employee-centric philosophies, customer relationship management and it works best when the entire set of employees becomes committed to it. Firms enjoy using metaphors in describing their culture, "we move speedily as the panther" or, "our customer care can be matched only by the ideals of Florence Nightingale". Such metaphors come handy when an employee faces an ethical dilemma as these metaphors remind him of the right path he has to take without exception, discussion or debate. These form the design of employees' conscience and subconscious thought process.

DESIGNING ORGANIZATIONAL CULTURE

The CEO has the basic responsibility towards the firm as he has to ensure profitable growth of the firm. He has to look after the firm's bottom line, besides taking care of the interests of the firm's stakeholders. The CEO, therefore, has to perform the following roles in the firm:

- Role model – The CEO must always behave in an impeccable manner within the cultural values of the firm.
- CEO's actions should be based on justice, far-sightedness and should be influenced by his large heart as he should avoid taking petty decisions, like blaming juniors for his own faults. He should totally eschew nepotism and never play favourites from among his employees. He should be magnanimous enough to forgive the really penitent erring employee. He should be forward looking, planning for the firm's growth as he leaves the running operations to his team members by delegating authority and responsibility onto them, keeping control points to ensure they do not go astray.
- The CEO should be a good communicator, as he has to project the firm's plans and policies, its strategies and what he expects of his employees. This would encourage a sense of belonging among the employees. Communication from the CEO brings in transparency in the working of the firm, and it motivates the employees to give their best to the firm. It also reinforces the employees' commitment to the values and ethics on which the firm's culture is based.
- The CEO must interpret the organizational culture to the employees and in case of any dispute between employees regarding who is on the right and who is not, the CEO has to present an unbiased face as he handles the disturbance.
- The CEO has to explain the cultural and ethical values dear to the organization to the employees, especially the new entrants. He has to organize refresher courses for

the existing employees as the subject matter of organizational culture is such that it keeps taking a beating from the outside influence and employees become easy prey to the smooth talkers who are present in each firm "you do not know, even our CEO takes money for giving orders for purchase. Have you not seen his new bungalow? Do you think it can be bought on his salary? Everyone is becoming rich and enjoying life with the exception of you and me. I have decided that on encountering next opportunity I will make sure that my family also lives well". The CEO must consider the role of advisor to the employees on matters related to ethical values and the firm's culture as the most important role.

Once the cultural ambience of the firm takes shape through the CEO's initiatives, his colleagues put the erring employees on the right track. The culture is built or even altered with the help of success stories, which are circulated through the ubiquitous grapevine of the organization. The symbols of the firm should represent its cultural ethos.

A TRULY PROFESSIONAL MANAGER/LEADER

Professional management has been often equated with non-family based management. However, in today's context, when you hear of so many scams in practically all types of organizations, private sector, public sector and the banking sector, the new definition of truly professional person should read as given below:

The person who keeps his personal interest subservient to the interest of the firm, his own goals in line with the firm's goals, would do everything possible to achieve the firm's goals without ever worrying about his personal goal. Once the firm's goals are achieved his own goals would automatically be achieved.

And this is the important task of the CEO to ensure that the team gets what is due in shortest possible time. The CEO can thus expect total loyalty from his team; this however requires integrated responsibility from the CEO.

This theory emanates from the Karmic theory of the GITA, in which Lord Krishna exhorts Arjuna to fulfil his tasks, howsoever unpleasant they may be without worrying about the consequences and rewards for him. These rewards ensue without your asking for them once you have performed the tasks to the best of your ability.

Krishna says,"Karmanye vadhikaraste ma phaleshu kadaachan!"

ONLY WAY TO SUCCESS

If you look at the history of the big firms of today, one thing common would be found and that is the founding fathers of these firms dreamt and thought BIG. Small minds can achieve small successes, never the big ones. For the CEO the success mantra goes as given below:

- Dream big
- Take integrated responsibility
- Give the credit of the success to the team
- Take the blame for any failure

In this manner you will certainly gain the full confidence of your team, which would never disappoint you:

> The Marketing Manager of a reputed firm was called by the MD of the firm regarding a major mistake committed by one of his deputies.
>
> MD, "Are you aware of the mistake which has caused the firm huge losses?"
>
> MM, "Yes sir, I know it fully and since this has happened only yesterday evening I was to report it to you today".
>
> MD, "Tell me, which of your deputies has done this task and I am personally going to punish him".
>
> MM, "Sir if you want to punish then the culprit is sitting right before you. As the head of the department I take full responsibility for the mistake".
>
> After this dialogue, the MD kept on pressurizing the MM and the MM continued to take the blame. Ultimately, the MD told the MM, that he should take care that such mistakes do not recur.
>
> The MD's secretary reported this conversation to the concerned culprit. Naturally the person concerned became truly loyal to the MM.
>
> The aftermath of the story is that on motivation received from the MM the person worked hard and effectively to reduce the losses and in fact gained some profit from the deal. This success story was given to the MD by the MM in a meeting with the entire team along with the name of the successful person.

The best motivation comes when for mistakes the person is counselled with no third person present and for jobs done well, he is acclaimed in presence of the entire team and possibly the top management/the leaders. This looks like common enough theory but in practice it is seldom found to be true. You are exhorted to try it out and you can see the positive results coming your way. Your entire team will willingly sacrifice a lot to meet the goals you plan for their activities.

EGO HURTS

- Ego makes you believe that you know everything needed to perform your job, blocking any further knowledge.
- Ego makes you smug and satisfied and you can get distracted from your goal.

You try to avoid the uncharted route as you fear the extra toil, the pain may not be of any use. You may be going away from the new realities, the new horizons.

Ego is also a manifestation of low self-esteem, a brave front you try to put, as you fear losing all you possess and this could be the biggest road block in your path to progress.

What you had sown yesterday you reap today and what you sow today you will reap tomorrow. Never cloud your mind with past success stories as the euphoria they generate restricts the good you can do today for success tomorrow.

You need to treat the team members without any discrimination, as it would cause fear among the team members, loss due to conflicts among the members.

You should learn from the mistakes others make as also from your own mistakes.

PERSONAL BEHAVIOUR

As the CEO your behaviour needs to be exemplary, a role model, goal driven and time prone. The importance of time as an asset is seldom realized in most firms. You should maintain self-restrain and the best behaviour patterns. You should have clarity of mind, physical fitness, proper time management and should remove your weaknesses as given below:

1.Weaknesses of mind, body and senses
2.Tensions
3.Cluttered thoughts
4.Lacking the extra sensory perceptions – the ESP.

IMPROVING ESP

We all have felt the availability of a sixth sense with which we get to know future events as they unfold themselves before us. This intuition is God given. You can develop your sixth sense or ESP in the following manner:

- You need ESP in crises times when you have to make split second decisions.
- Your past experiences form part of your ESP faculty.
- The present situation adds to your insight as you try to locate a similar experience of the past, match it with the present situation and then use the success formula of the past experience.
- Have belief in yourself that you can and will solve the problem.
- You should have faith in the Almighty who will surely help you in making correct decision. Even for a non-believer, if he can do tightrope walking of being good and doing good to others he will get help from some superior source, like his guru.
- Think positive.
- Use the Total Relaxation Technique (of digital work rotation with relaxation). (TRT–Two hours work with ten minutes relaxation/meditation period)

You can develop ESP by sticking to your goals, staying away from evil thoughts admitting your shortcomings, reacting to unexpected and complicated situations with zeal, by remaining creative and full of imagination; by sticking to your ideals always and not getting bogged down by numerous temptations surrounding you.

With uplinking ESP, you are ever ready for challenges and risks of change. The negative emotions of jealousy, hatred, lust and anger disturb and distract your sensibility. Lethargy causes laziness and unwanted sleep.

If you remain alert even unfavourable environment, uncongenial atmosphere, hostile competition can be overcome and these would not lead you to defeat. Efforts would, in fact, take you to progress. For remaining on the cutting edge of activity, you should avoid undesirable company, people with negative ideas, indulging in idle gossip, people full of greed, backbiters, hypocrites, flatterers, liars, double-dealers and selfish. These are not your friends but your enemies.

Several persons remain on faultfinding mission. They either justify their acts or shift blame from themselves and if probed plan for retaliation.

Emotions are inevitable for human beings and yet as CEO you must have a control on them, as anger, hatred, sorrow and even happiness sap your energy. Even when you discourage team members and other stakeholders, you are wasting your energy.

Ideally, you should remain modest, down-to-earth, never bragging as PRIDE always has a fall! Take success and failure in your stride; analyze to repeat success formula and drop the failed ones. This way you can acquire only a good healthy self-image.

Remain creative by doing something new and creative. Creativity has the power to keep you organized in the face of environmental changes as you remain with your values and orderliness.

CEO's AUTO-SUGGESTIONS

CEO keeps getting ideas of his own. These can be divided into two parts as given below:

1. Own thoughts
2. Subliminal state

Negative autosuggestions, like, am I good enough? should be removed from the mind immediately. Positive autosuggestions like, yes I can do it, should be nurtured and kept in the subconscious mind. In the cruel and harsh world, even temporary negative thoughts can derail the entire planning process.

Positive thoughts should be made a part of self-analysis, attitude and mindset. Personal goals, which are not in line with organizational goals, should be eschewed. You become a truly professional manager when you submerge your goals with the organizational goals.

When the CEO focuses his mind on the organizational goals without wavering and with full concentration, the CEO gets the power to achieve the goals.

The CEO should know what should be the level of his involvement in the operations and when he should detach himself to concentrate on his basic tasks of planning and motivation.

Changing roles – the CEO needs to have control points built-in process, to enable you to redefine team members' roles and the emphasis and priority on the assigned tasks in case you find that things are going astray.

ORGANIZATIONAL AND PERSONAL GOALS

Each individual member of the organization would have his personal goals as they have different needs. Can the organization meet their needs? If not, it is the CEO's task to say no politely. CEO should be people's manager to activate and motivate the team to get committed to organizational goals. He should not breathe down their necks. Most CEOs will deny doing it and are still guilty of doing just that.

VALUE SYSTEM DEFINES THE ORGANIZATION

It has been proven beyond even an iota of doubt that only organizations with high value system survive in the long run. You have to look at the Harshad Mehtas and Desais to get the full impact of the value system. Yes, any fly by night operator can just force his way in the marketplace and make his packet before either being caught or running away from the scene. The number of persons being prosecuted in scams leaves little to think about the graciousness of the value-based business. It comes from the following areas:

1. Consistent vision, mission and goals intrinsically and with each other.
2. Coordinated efforts using brain trust of the team members.
3. Simple unambiguous statement, why you do what you do.
4. As values are a reflection of the entire organization they should be positive and inspiring.
5. Use of clichés should be totally avoided in value statements.
6. Value statement should be broad enough to cover the entire gamut of firm's activities.
7. Employees' contribution and acceptance will help in getting their commitment to the vision and values of the firm.

Vision and value statements can be translated into making of the public image of the organization, if these are advertised properly, in the right media.

THE LEADERSHIP QUALITIES

The leaders must be confident, self-starting, no nonsense accepting individuals with the following traits of character:

1. Far-sightedness towards organization's future
2. Sense of justice and fair play
3. Large heart

In 2012, the leader should be planning for the organization, as it would exist in 2022. He should use the same yardstick for his entire team, while giving rewards and punishments. He should not be bothered about minor problems, which can be taken care by any of his teammates to whom the task has been delegated.

ORGANIZATIONAL HIERARCHY PROBLEMS

As you motivate your team, there is danger when you find some supervisors getting too big for their boots, with the newfound authority. The smugness or rebellion could be caused by any of the following causes:

- Feeling of being overworked
- Feeling of being underpaid
- Fear of loss of job or loss of authority and position
- Delaying work with the excuse that the collective decisions of the supervisors are responsible for the delays
- Lack of information needed to perform their tasks

These discrepancies can be removed by proper communication and transparency in dealing with the supervisors. Each supervisor must know how the others are performing. Your control points must be in place to enable you to detect even a minor aberration in work in real time as it is happening.

FAILURE–THE BEST TEACHER

Failure can teach you because of the following reasons:

- It makes you realize the value of success.
- Makes you realize the reasons for failure so that you can avoid their recurrence.
- Takes away any smugness on your part and makes you alert.
- Your failure can make your competitor smug and if you plan well, you can bounce back, taking them unawares.

However, for overcoming failures and converting them into success you need the following:

- Your own positive thoughts
- Positivism of your teammates
- Positive ambience

There is a lot of literature, especially of Dr. Norman Vincent Peale, which tells you of how positive attitudes help and work for you even if everything else is against you. With Positive Approach you can and will achieve success!

Success is a relative term. How white is whitest. Ask some detergent seller. However, with positive intentions, thoughts and action, you can achieve absolute success, there can never be a doubt about it.

Absolute Success unlike NIRVANA keeps changing, as you keep raising the bar.

FOCUS ON YOURSELF

Management gurus tell you to focus on the customers, build relationships (CRM, Customer Relationship Management has become a subject in several MBA programmes and several books are available on the subject), give customers not just satisfaction, but delight from the use of your product. You are in your own right a customer too as you buy a lot of products. Do you know your own mind, why do you buy a product, a particular brand? Have you analyzed yourself; do you really know yourself as a buyer? Once you do, you can start unveiling the mystery that is your customer.

If you need a simple, easy solution to your problems, how do you expect your customer to accept complex solutions?

Would a single sales-cum-technical person taking care of your complex problem satisfy you or would you accept a multi-specialty team to work for you? Multi-tasking or specialty tasking, you have to, as a seller provides the right answers (as if you are the customer). Would you expect a phone call as sales call or personal visit? Can you even think of shutting down your physical sales office ensuring the your sales team is always spending time with your customers? You can then hope to get reports on purchase orders collected at a much faster pace. Reports on orders lost to competitors are also a must to understand consumer behaviour and competitive strategies.

Thank God for the competitors, it is they who keep you on your toes throughout the year.

From the era of paperless office, with the help of computers, internet, LAN, WAN, which maintain your files and records and let you retrieve them from anywhere in the world, you can move to officeless office. Cellphones, fax machines are adding to the technological help and in the process you can decongest the roads, allowing better mobility to your customers. Your team spending more time in the field would work wonders – you get more information on consumer behaviour, their likes and dislikes, besides information on competition. Keep your sales team trim, lean and on the GO!

VALUE-BASED MANAGEMENT

As the CEO sets about designing the culture of the organization he has to ensure that the entire lot of the employees is not only aware of what is sacred and sacrosanct in the firm but also he must get their total commitment to the values. This can happen only when the CEO is able to communicate the values to the employees. It can be done in the following manner:

- Official circulars
- One-to-one notes
- Grapevine coverage

The following written or even unwritten statements cover the values and the expected ethical behaviour by the employees:

- Organizational vision
- Mission
- Goals
- Strategies
- Code of ethical behaviour

> Vision of a firm is the all-encompassing intent, which outlines the areas of common good the firm wants to cover. These are altruistic in nature.
>
> Mission statements are vision concretized, which give the firm its character, its boundaries of ethical behaviour and it helps in building the firm's strategies.
>
> Goals are the operational task-oriented statements, which talk of both financial and non-financial issues, they are reachable but with a stretch, they talk of multiple time zones and they cover the entire organization.
>
> Strategies are the plans and policies according to which actions take place in the firm.
>
> *Code of ethical behaviour describes in detail the outer limits of ethical behaviour, which should never be crossed by employees under any circumstances.*

The firms, which have taken the above stated route, have reported less number of moral and ethical transgressions than others.

Firms have been making unrealistic goals in the past, which often led the employees to bewilderment when they got perplexed about the route they should take to achieve the goals. The goals should be achievable even with a stretch. However, goals, which remain in the realm of inapproachability, which are almost impossible to achieve, lead to frustration and at times unethical behaviour by the employees. They believe that perhaps the almost impossible goals have been set to allow unethical practices without officially sanctioning them. The unrealistic goals also help the firms in throwing out the unwanted employees, without assigning any apparent reason for it. Such goal setting amounts to unethical practices and the firm should never resort to them. For example, if the employees were given the impossible task of a major cost reduction they would be tempted to reduce the quality by unethical means.

THE WORST OFFENDERS

Among the offenders of unethical crimes the following is an example of the worst ones:

- Sellers of impure foodstuff – every one has heard of the persons who sell condiments and spices, which are mixed with cheap inedible stuff, which resembles the main product. The buyers buy these in good faith and when they fall ill as a consequence of eating the stuff, they cannot decipher the exact nature of the problem. The food control administration has stringent laws to control such adulteration and yet only a handful of the offenders are ever caught. One TV channel had shown how even milk, which is the life giving food for children and the infirm was being adulterated by mixing fertilizers in it. Any sane person would recommend severe punishment for these criminals, who are like murderers only.
- Sellers of cooked food items use substandard or even rejected materials. This happens at wayside railway stations, bus and trucking stations, as the passengers are in transit only, not likely to come back to complain. In one such place a person selling tea is known to be lacing the tea with opium, which has created a niche' market for those living nearby or even frequent travellers passing through the place, as a large number of vehicles pass through it en route to a hill station in north India. The offenders must get the most severe punishment, as they are no less than killers. In fact, they are mass killers.
- The unscrupulous people do not spare even medicines and life saving drugs. At times people keep taking the medicines with no effect. Only a chemical analysis can determine the cause of failure of the medicines. Even the innocuous looking homoeopathic medicines can be laced with drugs or cortisone, which may give temporary relief, but in the long run would have adverse effect on the patient.
- Mechanical, electrical and electronic gadgets are made by offenders by using substandard materials, which can cause even death to the users. The product does not look any different than others and yet the moment they are put to use they fall apart or at least cause problems to the users.
- Construction firms use substandard cement concrete, which may cause the building, the bridge or a dam to break apart causing loss of innumerable lives, property, and livestock.

- Exporters, who show samples of good acceptable product and, on receipt of the order, supply substandard products. These people bring bad name not only to their own organization, but also to the entire country. Once the country's brand equity goes down it takes a long time to build it again.
- Power supply and other service industries give enough leverage to its employees to enable them to extract money for providing the services to their clients. This has been happening in the past due to the monopoly enjoyed by the service sector.
- Law enforcement agencies, the police and others are notorious for setting free the real culprits, while harassing the good law abiding citizens.
- Makers of spurious liquor, who are interested in making a quick buck only and have no qualms about destroying the health of their customers. Several persons lose their lives each year on this account.

India has been rated as the seventh most corrupt country in the world. It should be no consolation to Indians that there are six countries even more corrupt than India. India has been a spiritual country, which has given the world the philosophy of "Simple living high thinking". The saints of the past, the ancient Vedic literature are there to show us the path; we only have to follow it to achieve salvation. In the business world, ethical decisions make prudent choices, as they lead the firm to long lasting path of success, while unethical operations can bring quick results and soon enough bring the firm to disrepute.

Looking after the universal ecological balance, the firm follows the natural laws. Nature is mostly benevolent as can be seen from the bounties given by the nature in terms of agro-products, minerals and animals. When trees are cut, the ecological balance is disturbed affecting the cycle of seasons. In India, tree cutting has brought in devastating floods, draughts and in their wake, hunger, death and misery. People blame the weather Gods, or their luck, little realizing that all the misery is of their own making. It is, therefore, imperative that all the members of a firm and not just the CEO should be consciously involved in the eco concerns.

National boundaries are manmade and yet negligence of nature by one country could adversely affect the ecobalance of another country. That is where the Indian thought of the world being a universal village (Vasudaiv kutumbhkam) becomes even more relevant now than ever before. The world, especially the western hemisphere is realizing the importance of Indian philosophical thought as they are increasingly turning towards India for guidance and leadership.

11

CHAPTER

Leaders Enhance Brand Equity

ITC started in the British days as Imperial Tobacco Company. After India's independence it became India Tobacco Company, dealing in cigarettes and other tobacco based products. Late in the last century the company diversified into other areas like hotels, food, FMCG. That is when it changed its name to ITC and that became a brand name as also a logo for the company.

In recent years, ITC has diversified further into sports wear and even formal dresses. The company is using Wills as its brand for readymade garments. Wills is also a brand of ITC cigarettes. Wills has started signifying excellence in readymade garments for stylish men and women and for sports persons.

ITC believes that Wills garments give the wearer a lifestyle, the Wills Lifestyle. The Wills brand has been successfully extended from cigarettes to garments. It indirectly helps in promoting Wills cigarettes too as the name rubs off on the smokers' psyche too as a reminder of what is good, good not only for garments but also for cigarettes. The Government of India is not allowing direct advertisement of tobacco products, liquor and companies marketing these products have to resort to surrogate advertising by using product bonding or brand extension techniques to promote prohibited products. Companies use different advertising media for the purpose including press, audio-visual advertising and through sponsoring sports and cultural events.

To add further to Wills garments' upmarket status, the company has opened a nationwide chain of exclusive high fashion stores, the "Wills Lifestyle" stores.

The Wills Lifestyle brand showcases a complete wardrobe that is trendy, taking the fashion capitals of the world by storm. The brand offers a guaranty, a truly international shopping experience. It is, in the process, winning awards including the coveted award as the "Most admired exclusive brand retail chain of the year". The garments make an elegant statement at work as well with Wills classic, the new age formal.

ITC believes in creating brands for enriching the quality of life for every Indian because they and the country deserve the best with enduring value.

USE OF BRAND BUILDERS BY LEADERS

Over the years certain celebrities like Amitabh Bachchan, Shahrukh Khan, Sachin Tendulkar have themselves become big brands. They are like the king Midas, who had the power of converting all he touched into gold. Companies vie with one another for signing the celebrities for endorsing their brands. Some celebrities even let their names be used as brands. Perfumes have been named after Elizabeth Taylor, Zeenat Aman, both actresses, one from Hollywood and the other from India. Recently Sanjeev Kapoor, the famous chef has given his name as brand to an oven.

RICHARD BRANSON

Richard Branson of Virgin Group of companies has been hailed as one of the greatest brand ambassadors for his companies. He is known to have the skills and abilities like his uncanny ability to close onto growth opportunities with speed. He builds small management teams and gives them the authority to run the company. He creates successful joint venture companies. He knows how to motivate his teams.

Branson believes that one way of leveraging his brand Virgin is to place it in direct competition with the big players, big brands. He believes that the big brands become fat and lazy and to compete you need to give better value for money. He has the bravado and guts to take the big names on and he does it with impunity.

Branson knows that the lesser brands too have a chance to come up against the big names. Being small, he feels he can give better value for money to his customers. He dares his competition through his audacity and that leads them into making mistakes because Branson annoys them. However, he takes calculated risks only. Branson companies being small have nuisance value to the big companies and the irritation can cause them to make blunders. Branson strikes the competition in their most vulnerable spots. He is a crusader with his mission, as he lets his companies play underdogs and then makes his competitors complacent. He then hits them where it hurts most.

Branson's success is because of his motto of putting the people on the top, his staff and his customers. He loves his staff and therefore they are ready to work for less than the going rate. In the long-term career plan he surpasses every one of his competitors. He believes in an informal lifestyle, no jacket or ties for him.

Branson believes in working hard and playing hard too. On weekends, the entire Branson team parties, enjoys and no business talk is allowed. Branson wins through his gift of the gab and he is a great negotiator. He is friendly, listens and speaks only when necessary. He walks away if he cannot win a point. He is street smart.

With his approach Branson has remained a leader for three decades of one of the better-known companies in the world. He has taken his brand market share from some of the aggressive companies of the world. He is guided by a coterie of business associates whom he has kept for this purpose.

Branson's style of working is that work should be enjoyable to himself and to his team members. Branson believes there is no limit to what a brand can do, only if it is used properly. Stretching brand can dilute it if it goes to a wide range of products. However, Branson is sure that brand's integrity should be kept infinitely elastic and sacrosanct.

Virgin brand is an asset for the financial services, airlines, and railways, for the entertainment business, megastores, soft drinks, and clothes. Brand is recognized instantly as for good quality, low cost prices and trendy products. Branson asserts that brand value built on product quality builds brand reputation and brand equity. He wants best quality in his product with innovation, value for money to challenge competition, as the products become user friendly and fun to use. Branson has become an equally effective brand like the brand Virgin.

BRAND MICROSOFT AND BILL GATES

Microsoft has invaded the world like no other brand has, in the last twenty years. Bill Gates, arguably the richest person on the planet, has masterminded the success story of Microsoft. In building of brand he has used highly skilled and knowledgeable workers, technical expertize, innovation as its mortar and bricks.

Bill Gates foresaw the emergence of PCs as all-pervading equipment that would change everything; offices, industry, business and even homes. Microsoft embarked on a unique journey of developing and launching in the market software needed for the PC revolution. With his band of experts that he selects with care, he is assured of staying on at the top of his competitors. With continuous experimentation and innovation, Microsoft makes lesser mistakes and learns from the mistakes made by his competitors.

Microsoft has had a number of bitter competitors, but it has stayed on top, always. This has happened because of the seer like quality of its owner Bill Gates, who has the uncanny ability of visualizing the future needs and technological possibilities.

Microsoft brand has a relentless approach to innovation in its products and services that remains unmatched despite serious competitive action.

Task for the Students

Discuss the ways Bill Gates is protecting his brand against severe competition.

Case Studies

1
CASE STUDY

Organizational Behaviour

R.P. Verma established Verma Garments – VG – twenty years ago in Delhi, to manufacture and market readymade garments for men, ladies and children. As its Managing Director, Verma has brought the firm from a small one with a turnover of Rs. 30 lakhs to one having a turnover of Rs. 200 crore in just two decades. Till the last four years they were making a net profit of 11%. However, in the last four years competition from both Indian and foreign firms has increased substantially, depleting the profits of the firm. In fact, several small firms have closed down because of the severe competition. VG has, however, now a net profit of only 4%.

VG has the following organizational structure:

MD

CEO

VP-PROD VP-MARKET VP-FINANCE- VP-HRD

Chander, 50, is the VP Marketing. He has been with the firm for the last ten years. He has a good grip on the market. His market intelligence is becoming weak as he lost a big overseas order to Indian competitor through lack of knowledge. He has built his team strictly by discipline and has few friends there.

Rajan, VP Finance is 45, has been with VG for over 3 years. He has been blamed for poor cash flow although he blames it on marketing. He knows his job well tends to inflate expenses to show lower profits. His MD knows that he is doing it on his bidding.

Vyas is 47 and has been VP Production for the last 5 years. Last year there were some quality problems which he had solved in three months' time, but marketing had put the blame of lower sales and profits squarely on him. Chander even claimed that due to quality problems they lost the overseas order. Vyas is not much for product innovations and wants status quo to prevail. He has been MD's pet so far.

Kumar is 60 and has been VP HR for the last twenty years. He was the first employee to join Verma. He has been training Verma's son Som to take over from him in the next 5 years when he is supposed to retire.

Three months back, Verma inducted Kamal as the CEO of the firm, ignoring the claims of the VPs. Kamal 35, is an MBA with ten years experience in garment trade. He has a good track record of achieving success in short time.

In the last three months Kamal has taken the following steps, which he feels will benefit the firm:

- Purchased an expensive software worth Rs. one crore for modernizing the operations, but no one knows how to use it so far.
- Reduced the staff by 30% as cost cutting exercise.
- Appointed second advertising agency against the wishes of VP Marketing.
- Is dealing with juniors directly ignoring the VPs?
- Planning farming out production to outside parties.
- Has instructed VP Finance to get low cost money?
- Has started some schemes for staff welfare?

Now the three VPs have joined hands against the CEO. They are also questioning the MD for ignoring the claim of the three VPs for the CEO's position. They have called a meeting with the MD where the CEO will also be present.

Task for the Class Teams

Arrange a mock meeting with role plays of MD, CEO and VPs.

2
CASE STUDY

Microsoft Inc. USA

Microsoft genesis begins with a 14 years old Bill Gates getting a computer as present from his mother. He along with his three friends started a club for development of computer software as computer hackers. In 1973, Gates went to Howard to look for business opportunities. A little later Microsoft was found as a partnership firm. In 1980, IBM came to Microsoft with an opportunity unparalleled in the short history of Microsoft. Later on when UNIX System came and Microsoft software was not so popular, its relations with IBM became strained. In 1991, it also got into problems with the US Government's Federal Trade Commission, which felt that Microsoft is going to monopolize the PC Software, through Windows.

Start any computer around the world and more than ninety per cent would be running on Microsoft windows operating system. The firm is as controversial as it is successful and influential. It touches the lives of billions of people and it has changed the way people manage and work in offices, homes, factories and how they correspond with others.

It is a firm, which evokes intense feelings of love or hatred. It is Microsoft! Its founder, Bill Gates is already a cult figure, worshipped and idolized by millions of young and old in the world. From a middle-class family, he inherited his acumen from his mother and shrewdness from his father. In just twenty years he is the richest man on the planet.

Where do they go from here?

Microsoft strives to produce innovative products to meet the evolving needs of the knowledgeable customers.

Mission – Microsoft started in 1975, with a **mission** to create software for the personal computer that empowers and enriches people at home and at their workplace, at schools and in the laboratories.

Vision – Its early **vision** was to see a computer on every desk, every home and it is now coupled with a strong commitment to internet technologies expanding the reach and power of PC users.

Values – Microsoft's values are enshrined in the following tenets:

- Customers – Helping them achieve their goals by listening to them and quickly delivering new innovative products; building relationships based on trust, respect and understanding and service support.
- Innovation – Moving with the speed of light for bringing new products in the market to remain competitive with reduced costs as well.
- Partners – Helping them grow in their business.
- Integrity – Acting with utmost integrity, Microsoft's team is guided by what is right for their customers.
- People – The team must have an exciting and challenging career with growth opportunity and well balanced home and work life.
- Entrepreneurial culture – The team must remain passionate about the work, contributing to evolution of technology to remain competitive.
- Diversity – The team is encouraged for diverse activities, with equal chance of promotion and increments for the members.
- Community – Microsoft feels responsible to the community in which they operate and wants to make a meaningful difference in its life.

Finance as on June 1999
Net revenue – $ 19.75 billion
Net income – $ 7.79 billion

Microsoft headcount and revenue growth is given below:

Year	Head count	Revenue $B	%Growth	Income $ M	%Growth
1990	5635	1.18	47	279	63
1991	8226	1.85	56	463	66
1992	11542	2.78	50	708	53
1993	14430	3.79	36	953	35
1994	15017	4.71	25	1150	20
1995	17801	6.08	29	1450	27
1996	20561	9.05	49	2200	51
1997	22232	11.94	32	3450	57
1998	27055	15.26	28	4490	30
1999	31575	19.75	29	7790	79

The headcount is in the vicinity of 40,000.

Microsoft has been living in the shadow of its illustrious founder. While Bill Gates has many friends, his opponents believe he is shrewd and manipulative and wants to dominate the world. Microsoft needs to improve its image to come out of the predicament it faces today.

In 1995, the firm almost lost the battle of internet to Netscape and Sun Microsystems and Microsoft was caught napping. Microsoft needs feedback from marketing to do their R&D to meet the latest customer needs. Microsoft must make more friends than foes. It should not consider that it is a **Know All** firm. It could consider splitting into several small firms with independent decision-making under one overall umbrella.

IBM is reeling under competitive pressure and does not know what hit them. Microsoft must not fall in the same trap. If they do not learn from history, then history is likely to repeat itself.

Task for the Students

Discuss the strengths and weaknesses of Microsoft and recommend a marketing strategy which would help them in retaining their leadership position.

3
CASE STUDY

Asian Paints Ltd.

Mr. Choksey of Andhra Pradesh belonged to the laidback business community of India. Yet his vision was to "See Indian homes painted in a variety of colours from a truly Indian company".

His mission statement read as 'To provide paints as per market demand ensuring desired level and quality of customer (dealer) service, continued availability of right product mix of right quality at right time.'

With near servile attitude, Macs took pride in serving metros and large cities through dealers who also supplied the products to semi-urban markets. They were however concentrating on metros and found the rural market non-existing. Business environment was hostile to the Indian Paint Industry and more so to a new entrant.

Suppliers were favouring MNCs with their money power. MNCs kept the metros satisfied with their service. Goal of Asian paints was "Setting up manufacturing facility for Paints in a large variety".

Strategy was to build paint company as a role model of outstanding performance.

Competitive Environment : Market for paints was at dead end. It was totally dominated by MNCs and Indian companies were looked down upon. MNCs had a cartel approach and had dealers with long-standing relationship in an Oligopoly Market. Entry barriers were not there as paints were low tech and low capital projects. Brand loyalty was remnant of Raj days. Alternate products were lime based and low cost used by most people in poverty-ridden India. In rich homes and offices wood panelling was being used increasingly. Market was largely controlled by MNCs.

Mr. Choksey found that to fight MNCs he had to look at the market segment so far neglected by them. He surveyed the market and found that near vacuum exists in semi-urban and rural market. They, however, had special needs. "Low cost paint in small containers." The segment needed a new distribution system as well.

Asian Paints' value for the customers was to build an innovative package (size), distribution and communication. In 1970s, they decided to computerize and network their 30 depots round the country to provide proper feedback of market needs resulting in quick response to meet the needs.

They planned new distribution structure, smaller packages and computerized communication network.

Mr. Choksey did not have any animosity towards MNCs who had shown hostility and created entry barriers for him. Asian Paints' differentiation strategy starts from market segment, distribution and packaging. With increasing volumes in chosen segments, Asian Paints achieved economies of scale for cost leadership. With a dominant position, they diversified in product range as also market and geographic segments. Asian Paints' strategy of quick response translates into having 95% orders' supply in 48 hours and is a positive competitive advantage. Their R&D has developed new products to cater to the industrial and scientific segments. Paint industry is in the growth stage in India as construction activity has a high priority.

In order to maintain market leadership (with 27% market share they enjoy double the market share than their nearest competitor), they have drawn up the following strategy:

1. Backward vertical integration by going into manufacture of raw materials for paints.
2. Product diversification into industrial paints. Now with large market share, they have strong distribution network even in metros.

Mr. Choksey's style of functioning was informal as he kept friendly relations with depot staff, sales team and he could be seen having tea in some rural dealers' shops. He started the overseas operation to expand his horizons further.

With liberalized economy, international brands are likely to enter the market as entry barriers are low in the paint industry.

To keep their dominant position, Asian Paints showed vigorous R&D for innovative products, increasing the number of depots for covering the entire country, advertising separately for each market segment and arranging continuous market research to their competitive advantage.

Index